An Introduction to Wesleyan Theology

Christian Heritage Rediscovered

The Series, as the name suggests, is meant to focus on Christian Faith & Living vis-à-vis topics like Literature & Poetry, Indigenous Philosophizing, Ethical response towards Agriculture, Health & Healing, Science & Technology, Eco-feminist Theology, Sociological approach towards Human Rights, Law & Politics, Arts, History of Ideas, Ancient Civilizations, Cultural Contiguity, Religious Cosmologies & Mysticism, Footsteps of famous Theologians, World Peace & Harmony, Global Capitalism, Network Marketing, Cybertheology, Population & Demographics, Epigraphic Studies, Contextualized Education, and many others. We welcome a Mss. on any topic/s mentioned, whether they are original works, scholarly monographs, collections of conference papers, revised dissertations, or translations of historical documents. Through the Series we, the Publishers, are striving to put forward published works that may help Institutions, Academic Bodies, Researchers, Scholars and the World at large in furthering their respective knowledge and understanding on the concerned subject. We welcome your comments on our efforts and further suggestions on how we can foster the upcoming thought provoking theologically grounded books.

Foreword

"After that whole generation had been gathered to their ancestors, another generation grew up who knew neither the Lord nor what he had done for Israel" (Judges 2:10).

What a tragic, sad commentary involving drift. A whole generation moved away from the faith of their parents. Drifting from God and his ways, from the spiritual heritage of previous generations. Drifting into moral danger, even into dishonoring and neglecting God. The consequences in ancient Israel were catastrophic.

Critical to the avoidance of drift is one generation stewarding and living out well God's truth, effectively passing it along to the next generation. Apart from this, drift is inevitable. By nature people tend to move away from the moral and spiritual moorings of their parents and other key influencers in their early upbringing. This often begins with small compromises here and there, followed by increasingly larger ones. This has happened repeatedly throughout history with devastatingly painful consequences.

To preclude the repetition of this cycle, champions are needed, people who take what they've learned, practice it well, and teach it through word and example to others. Dr. Amit Thomas is this kind of champion.

Taking John Wesley as a vibrant example of biblical faith from a previous generation, Dr. Thomas compellingly lays out the truth Wesley so warmly embraced and heralded to others. Insights from Scripture, history, and the dramatic impact God made through Wesley are intricately intertwined in Dr. Thomas' writing. He moves from the story of God's work in and through Wesley, and the preaching about holy living Wesley so passionately communicated to his generation, to how this impacted future generations.

Reviewing the lives of several spiritual giants who were deeply influenced by the teaching and preaching of Wesley, Dr. Thomas challenges his readers to learn from their examples.These were people who "caught and taught" Wesleyan theology. God used them to have impact in the lives of countless people around the world.

If our generation is not vigilant and careful, this sad story of drift will become our story. The truths from Scripture espoused by Wesley will gradually fade into obscurity. And the world which Wesley described as his parish will be spiritually poorer, not richer.

Standing against the tendency to drift, Dr. Thomas wants our world to be richer in the knowledge of our loving, infinitely holy, redeeming God. May readers experience him in all of his fullness and then share him with others! May we become increasingly like Christ. And may our hearts become more like the warm, passionate heart for which Wesley was known, a heart resembling the heart of our precious Lord!

Rev. Dr. Bob Fetherlin(President)
One Mission Society
Greenwood, Indiana

Christian Heritage Rediscovered - 54

An Introduction to Wesleyan Theology

Amit Thomas

CWI
Christian World Imprints™

First Published in 2017 by

Christian World Imprints™
Christian Publishing & Books from India
H-12 Bali Nagar, **New Delhi-110015**
info@christianworldimprints.com
www.ChristianWorldImprints.com
Phone: +91 11 25465925

ISBN: 978-93-5148-217-8 (HB) ISBN: 978-93-5148-218-5 (PB)

Cataloging in Publication Data--DK
Courtesy: D.K. Agencies (P) Ltd. <docinfo@dkagencies.com>

Thomas, Amit, 1975- **author.**
An introduction to Wesleyan theology / Amit Thomas.
pages cm. -- (Christian heritage rediscovered ; 54)
ISBN 9789351482178 (HB)
ISBN 9789351482185 (PB)

1. Theology, Doctrinal. 2. Methodist Church--Doctrines.
I. Title. II. Series: Christian heritage rediscovered ; 54.

BX8331.3.T46 2017 DDC 230.7 23

Printed in India

Contents

Acknowledgments

At the very outset, I want to thank the almighty God for his ever present help without which it would have not been possible to do this work. God's grace has enabled me to take up this and encouraged me to write on constructing Wesleyan Theology.With immense joy and deep gratitude, I humbly acknowledge the valuable role of many people who have helped me in this area. I want to really thank all my students who have really helped to see the need and bring this work.

I would like to express my heartfelt thanks to my wife Ashita and children Anant and Arman without their support, I would have not been able to take this work and set apart time to do this work. I am also grateful to all my teachers for their positive impact on me which has really envisioned and encouraged me to carry on with this Wesleyan theology thinking. I would want to express my gratitude to Rev. Dr. Bob Fetherlin, Rev. Dr. Bill Vermillion, Rev. Dr. William T. Purinton, Rev. Dr. Leroy E. Lindsey, Rev. Dr. Myoungsoo Park, Rev. Dr. Changhoon Park, and Rev. J. Sundara Raj for their endless support and encouragement to me. I am grateful to Dr. Nomita Eusebius and Mrs. Ashita Thomas who helped me in editing and in proof reading of the book.

I am immensely grateful to Christian World Imprints and its editorial staff for their support and help and their undiminished commitment for letting the book to be published. God bless you all!

Rev. Amit Thomas
Allahabad Bible Seminary
Allahabad - Uttar Pradesh
India

Introduction

The study of Wesleyan theology is an Endeavour to systematically analyze the origin and development of Wesleyan thinking as an important area of Christian theological understanding.The study of Wesleyan theology enables to see many facts and discussion which down through the church history had become important thinking in Christian church. Wesleyan holiness had impacted the church greatly and led people to commitment to Christ.

In this book, the attempt has been made to construct Wesleyan theology in the contemporary world.This book begins with the discussion on 17th and 18th century background of John Wesley's time which surveys the socio-political, economical and cultural background and tries to deal with historical development of Wesleyan theology. The Book also deals with the life of John Wesley focusing on the major influencing factors which helped for the development of Wesleyan thought in general.

There has been strong focus on the theological thinking of John Wesley where different major themes are dealt such as understanding of Scripture, Human Being, Justification, Christian Perfection and Sanctification, Church, Sacrament, Salvation, Atonement, Moral Ethics and Eschatology. In the later part, the construction of Wesleyan theology in 19th and 20th century is discussed mainly focusing on the prominent Wesleyan thinkers such as Francis Asbury, William Carey, Nathan Bangs, Phoebe Worrall Palmer, Daneil Steele, Charles Elmer Cowman, Ernest A. Kilbourne, Wesley L. Duewel, and Billy Graham. This book also deals with the origin and development of Evangelical Church of India and its contribution towards the development of society. These developments show that Wesleyan theology challenges for Holy living which helps in shaping of theological perception of the people in any given context. Wesleyan holiness thinking needs to be inculcated among the people of all faiths.

Chapter 1

Constructing Wesleyan Theology

Introduction

In using the designation "Wesleyanism" is to make things clear only for identification of a certain way of thinking connected with common interest. The interest is developed in Wesley's thinking primarily because of his catholic spirit, his tolerance with those who belong to other people. This was to focus on people of all segments of life.[1] Wesleyan Approach (holiness theology) is not a different kind of Christian thinking but is more obliged to recognize the personal dimension of Christian experience other than any emphasis. It is precisely the personal dimension that differentiates holiness from the abstract nature of theology. In simpler words it is to keep theology viable. John Wesley's major contribution to Christian thinking could be seen in the concept and experience of the personal involvement in grace which the Reformation theology seemed to have lost. He would have for sure rejected the contemporary thought that men/women are saved in principle not in fact.

John Wesley became a "folk-theologian" by his own design. He had all the academic credentials to be a "theologian's theologian," but he preferred to preach to and write for "the people." Wesley chose the working classes and the poor as his "parish," although he still had connections with the middle and upper classes. Wesley remained an evangelist who had a passion for preaching the gospel: a call to repentance, faith, justification, regeneration, and "holy living."[2] His task was to close the gap between theology in its philosophical form and religion as

[1] Mildred Bangs Wynkoop, *A Theology of Love: The Dynamism of Wesleyanism* (Missouri: Kansas Hill Press, 1972), 54.

[2] Albert C. Outler, "John Wesley: Folk-Theologian," *Theology Today* 34/2 (July, 1977): 150-160.

a practical experience. What we could understand, as that Wesley understood religion as a personal involvement in God's grace. In order to understand John Wesley's thought more noticeably it would be good enough to understand the background of John Wesley's 'time first'.

1.1 Religious and Moral Life of Church in 17th & 18th Century

It is interesting to see how much religious and moral life of John Wesley's period influenced ongoing work. By the beginning of the Eighteenth Century, the appeal of faith was abandoned completely. **Deism** exalted reason above everything, even at the cost of supernatural aspects.[3] Richard P. Heitzenrater viewed that, "*the emergence of Deism, which portrayed a view of God and creation based on reason, was carried by the rise of modern scientific fields... which saw a decline on the traditional moral values in society.*"[4] It was a period of shallow and confident Deism, which had influenced both literature and the general thinking of that time. Deism was a subtle form of atheism which on one hand did not deny the existence of God but on the other hand it rejected God as a force to be reckoned with human life. People who were influenced by Deism had no respect for the Bible. Revelation had no real value for them and they saw it as an imagination. Thus, for them God was ambiguous who was not related with creation.[5] In other words God was seen as non involving entity or not concerned with human affairs of life. So, the religious life of this time opted for rationalism rather than revelation.

The Eighteenth Century England was characterized by a decay of religious licentiousness of moral, public corruption and profaneness of language.[6] In other words corrupt behaviors in public life and foul language seemed common in Wesley's days. Loose living, rioting and lawlessness were normal/ common sight during this time. Christianity had no bearing for the people.[7] John Wesley in his appeal to Men of Reason and Religion dealt with issues of ignorance, immorality, and irreligion of all classes. He viewed that at least during the first half of the century these issues were not seriously challenged by the church. He said, '*our nation stands on the very brink of destruction, and why we are thus, but because the cry of our wickedness is gone up to heaven? Because we have so exceedingly, abundantly,*

---

[3] Joseph Basappa Suray, *Towards a Theology of Universality: John Wesley's Socio-Economic, Political & Moral Insights on British Class & Indian Caste Distinctions* (New Delhi: Christian World Imprints, 2015), 52.

[4] Richard P. Heitzenrater, *Wesley & the People Called Methodists* (USA: Abingdon Press, 1995), 19.

[5] Joseph Basappa Suray, *Towards a Theology of Universality: John Wesley's Socio-Economic, Political & Moral Insights on British Class & Indian Caste Distinctions*, 53.

[6] H. G. Mithra, *Wesley's Philosophy of Education for Socio-Spiritual Change* (New Delhi: Christian World Imprints, 2016), 22.

[7] H. G. Mithra.

beyond measure, corrupted our ways before the Lord.'[8] The religious literature of Wesley's time shows that the lives of ministers and their understanding of God were very ambiguous and hopeless. People were expected to live better life without having exemplary life from clergies. The political division and worldly influence was affecting the church very much. It was also seen that the religious life of the church was exploited for political gains. Henry Rack says that, "the church was systematically exploited for political advantages."[9]

The Church of England (the Anglican Church) had become very lax, complacent and conservative. It was an integral part of the Establishment. Both Church and parliament were dominated by the same socio-economic class: the landed gentry and aristocracy. The monarch was (and still is) the Head of the Anglican Church. Defense of the status quo was prevalent and the ruling classes did not contemplate reform in any shape or form. Religion was comfortable and respectable. The Anglican Church ministered to the gentry in a form of what might be called 'snob Christianity.' Most people's interest in religion was generally academic and pragmatic. 'Enthusiasm' was considered to be dangerous - a left-over from the English Civil War (1642-9) and the Wars of Religion in Europe in the Seventeenth Century. A general rule of thumb is to see the Church of England as a political institution. Bishops were appointed for their political leanings rather than for their spirituality, and could (and did) make or break legislation. Many religious leaders were diverted from their primary task of ministry of the Word of God during the Eighteenth Century. They were more involved in national politics than in building the Church the body of Christ. Since they were dull they were not able to nourish their sheep well which lead for a spiritual dryness over the years. It is said that it was a time when the spiritual life of England was dwindling.

People see clearly that the Church of that age was, in many respects, in an undoubtedly unsatisfactory condition, sleepy and full of abuses, and are sometimes apt to think that the Evangelical revival (the expression being used in its widest sense) was the one redeeming feature of it. The Evangelical revival, both that which is chiefly connected with the name of the Wesleys and of Whitefield, and that which was carried on more exclusively within the Church of England, closely corresponded in many of its details to what had often occurred before in the history of the Christian Church. Throughout the whole of the eighteenth century, almost all the writers who had occasion to speak of the general condition of society joined in one wail of lament over the irreligion and immorality that they saw around them. This complaint was far too universal to mean little more than a general and somewhat conventional tirade upon the widespread corruption

[8] George Eayrs, *John Wesley: Christian Philosopher and Church Founder* (London: The Epworth Press, 1926), 21. Cf. also Robert G. Tuttle, *John Wesley His Life and Theology* (Michigan: Francis Asbury Press, 1978), 35.

[9] Henry Rack, *Reasonable Enthusiast* (London: Epworth Press, 1989), 8.

of human nature. The French political philosopher Montesquieu opined that among the English society he visited, "If one speaks of religion, everyone begins to laugh."[10] Situation was such that anyone who spoke of religion was considered a person who was out of his/her mind. In that context Christianity for people had become meaningless. John Wesley himself had commented that nine-tenths of the English people had no more religion than horse.[11]

No age since the founding and forming of the Christian Church, was ever like, in open acknowledged atheism, blasphemies, and heresies, to the age we now live in. The simple view is that nobody bothered about religion and acted upon it. Everywhere those who should have known better entirely discarded it.[12] By and large an impoverished church was incapable against the onslaught of secular philosophy. Few clergy men cared to discourse on the subject but they also went back looking into the results. The established churches were highly political in nature. Queen Anne (1702-1714), the younger daughter of James II, took a High Church line which stressed the importance of connection between Church and State more and more. Dissenters were persecuted. The stage was almost set for the revival within the Church of England.[13] At that time most of the clergymen with real integrity were *'non-Jurors'* (those who refused to take oath to William III because he was not considered to have succeeded legally to his office) but there were few exceptions also.[14]

In general the public life during the eighteenth century was corrupt where many clergy were forced to compromise. This brought the sense that church was inactive in relation to the spiritual affairs of the people and its theology had hardly an impact on the people. This was the context of Wesley's time which was looking for a spiritual revolution to bring back people to God. According to W. H. Fitchett, "Wesley was seen as God's chosen man to respond to the historical context and social situation of his time."[15] Dogmatic teaching from the Bible was almost absent from the pulpit. This was the situation where church had forgotten or failed to recognize the practical implication of the Christian faith. It was very difficult to find people who really obeyed the Lord and walked on his teaching. When people did not practice religious teachings, they also refused to take their

---

[10] John Wilkins Sigsworth, *World Changer: Karl Marx and John Wesley* (Canada::Easingwold Publications, 1982), 40.

[11] John Wilkins Sigsworth.

[12] Robert G. Tuttle, *John Wesley His Life and Theology*, 35.

[13] Robert G. Tuttle, 36.

[14] Robert G. Tuttle, *John Wesley His life and Theology*, 36

[15] Joseph Basappa Suray, *Towards a Theology of Universality: John Wesley's Socio-Economic, Political & Moral Insights on British Class & Indian Caste Distinctions*, 54. Cf. also W. H. Fitchett, *Wesley and his Century* (London: Balloutne Press, 1906), 148.

moral life seriously. In England the first half of the Eighteenth Century was a period of Moral disorder."[16]

The causes which elevate or depress the general tone of society have a corresponding influence, in kind if not in degree, upon the whole body of the clergy. Church history, throughout its whole course, shows very clearly that although the average level of their spiritual and moral life has always been, except, possibly, in certain very exceptional times, higher in some degree than that of the people over which they are set as pastors, yet that this level ordinarily rises or sinks with the general condition of Christianity in the Church and country at large. If, for instance, a corrupt state of politics have lowered the standard of public virtue, and have widely introduced into society the unblushing acknowledgment of self-seeking motives, which in better times would be everywhere reprobated, the edge of principle is likely to become somewhat dull even where it might be least expected. The early 18th century was noted for its lack of religious enthusiasm and the churches in England lacked vigor. However, in the mid-18th century things began to change. In 1739, the great evangelists George Whitefield (1714-1770) and John Wesley (1703-1791) began preaching. John Wesley eventually created a new religious movement called the Methodists. His brother Charles Wesley (1707-1788) was a famous hymn writer.

1.2 Social, Political and Philosophical Background

1.2.1 Socio-Cultural Scene of Wesley Days

Wesley period was the climax of social discrimination and moral disintegration. It is also observed that notorious indulgences such as gambling and drinking were openly associated with each other. The plight of this social discrimination had left no chance for them to improve their moral standards. Wesley played a practical role in improving the moral life of the lower class.[17] During the 17th century the population of England and Wales grew steadily. It was about 4 million in 1600 and it grew to about 5 1/2 million by 1700. During the 17th century England became steadily richer. Trade and commerce grew and grew. By the late 17th century trade was an increasingly important part of the English economy. This time is mostly referred as dim ideals and expiring hopes. Streets were littered and piled up with the horses' manure, which polluted the residential areas. Diseases like typhoid, small pox, dysentery, and cholera had been common in the cities. One fourth of the baby died in the very early age after birth.[18]

---

[16] Joseph Basappa Suray, *Towards a Theology of Universality: John Wesley's Socio-Economic, Political & Moral Insights on British Class & Indian Caste Distinctions*, 55. CF. also A. Skevington Wood, *The Burning Heart* (USA: Bethany Publication House, 1978), 9.

[17] Joseph Basappa Suray, *Towards a Theology of Universality: John Wesley's Socio-Economic, Political & Moral Insights on British Class & Indian Caste Distinctions*, 56.

[18] H.G. Mithra, *Wesley's Philosophy of Education for Socio-Spiritual Change*, 18.

In the late 18th century the **industrial revolution** began to transform life in Britain. Until then most people lived in the countryside and made their living from farming. Meanwhile industries such as glass, brick making, iron and coal mining expanded rapidly. England was in the grip of industrial revolution.[19] In the late 18th century everyday life in Britain was transformed by the industrial revolution. Towns, industry and trade had been growing for centuries, but about 1780, economic growth took off. Economic growth was helped by vast improvements in transport. In the early and mid 18th century many turnpike roads were built. Local turnpike trusts were formed. They maintained a road and charged people to travel on it. In the late 18th century a network of canals was built. One of the first canals was built for the Duke of Bridgewater by James Brindley. But the industrial revolution brought changes in society where people were caught up with disease, death, crime and malnutrition.[20] From 1712, a man named Thomas Newcomen (1663-1729) made primitive steam engines for pumping water from mines. In 1769 James Watt (1736-1819) patented a more efficient steam engine. In 1785, his engine was adapted to driving machinery in a cotton factory. The use of steam engines to drive machines slowly transformed industry. By the mid 19th century most people in Britain lived in towns and made their living from mining or manufacturing industries.

In the eighteenth century Britain, most people earned their living by cultivating the land Farming. Conditions of life and labour varied with each small difference of configuration, sub-soil and climate.[21] Farming techniques were improving but the industrial methods were extremely primitive where life had become very cheap.[22] In the 18th century there was an agricultural revolution in England. It began with Jethro Tull. In the 17th century seed was sown by hand. The sower simply scattered seed on the ground. However, in 1701 Tull (1674-1741) invented the seed drill. This machine dropped seeds at a controllable rate in the straight lines. Tull also invented a horse drawn hoe, which killed weeds between rows of seeds. This was, obviously, wasteful, as one third of the land was not used each year. In the 18th century, these new methods became common in England. A man named Charles 'Turnip' Townshend (1674-1738) did much to popularize growing turnips. Turnips had another advantage. They provided winter feed for cattle. Previously most cattle were slaughtered at the beginning of winter because there was not enough food to keep them through the season. Now fresh milk and butter became available all year round. Moreover, in the early 18th century farmers began to improve their livestock by selective breeding. One of the most famous pioneers of selective breeding was Robert Bakewell (1725-1795).

---

[19] Wesley Tracy, "Christian Education in the Wesleyan Mode" in *Wesleyan Theological Journal* 17/1 (March, 1982): 31.

[20] Wesley Tracy, 32.

[21] T. S. Ashton, *The Industrial Revolution, 1760-183*0 (New York: A Galaxy Book, 1964), 18.

[22] Robert G. Tuttle, *John Wesley His Life and Theology*, 32.

Owning land was the main form of wealth in the 18th century. Political power and influence was in the hands of rich landowners. At the top were the nobility. Below them were classes of nearly rich landowners called the gentry. In the early 18th century there was another class of landowners called yeomen which was between the rich and the poor. However, during the century this class became less and less numerous. However, other middle class people such as merchants and professional men became richer and more numerous, especially in the towns. Below them were the great mass of the population, craftsmen and laborers. In the 18th century probably half the population lived as subsistence or bare survival level.

In the early 18th century England suffered from gin **drinking.** It was cheap and it was sold everywhere as one did not need a license to sell it. Many people ruined their health by drinking gin. Yet for many poor people drinking gin was their only comfort.[23] Wesley regarded it as destructive for both body and soul. He incorporated into Methodist general rule a clause against buying or selling of such liquors. His effort at some point of time contributed to the reduction of consumption of liquor. J. H. Plumb had opined that, "in the midst of death people sought palliative and found them in drink, gambling and violence."[24] Thus, drinking had become a part of life irrespective of Class and status, people were in the bondage of drinking. The most effected people of this situation were the poor class. When the inferior gin was introduced it became the staple drink of the poor class which harmed them much and in a quicker way. Violence was adopted by the lower classes as the means of fulfilling their desires. There were incidents when streets were full of demonstrations of mob burning, looting and vandalism. This disturbed the peace of the society.[25] Alan Lloyd described the moral life at this time as a combination of violence and drinking. He further stated that, "violence abounded in the Capital. Riots and disorders were commonplace and drinking and rioting almost went hand in hand. Crime in London as elsewhere flourished openly."[26]

Economically people were poor which resulted in greater debts. This further led for the development of low moral standards. Law and order failed to gain co-operation of the public. Along with drinking, **gambling** also was very strong which had become a universal passion. E. H. Carter says that, "gambling was a universal passion where thousands of pounds changed hands every night and estates

---

[23] Tim Lambert, "Daily Life in 18th Century Britain," http://www.localhistories.org/18thcent.html, 05/07/16.

[24] J. H. Plumb, *England in the Eighteenth Century (1714-1815)* (United Kingdom: Penguins Books Ltd., 1966), 13.

[25] Joseph Basappa Suray, *Towards a Theology of Universality: John Wesley's Socio-Economic, Political & Moral Insights on British Class & Indian Caste Distinctions*, 57.

[26] Alan Lloyd, *The Wickedest Age: The Life and Times of George III* (United Kingdom: Brydone, 1971), 4-6.

were thrown away at the card table."[27] The given situation had really challenged Wesley to practice holiness in the midst of immorality and human suffering. Both drinking and gambling was responsible in reducing the moral standards of the class. Gambling attracted people from every occupation to earn more money, to improve their life style.[28] These led to increase in crimes in most of the places bringing disorder in the society. Highway robbery had become common because of which many travelers were afraid to travel after dark. Gambling had almost become a national disease and gin drinking had become a national pastime. It is said that one child in every 25 attended the school of any kind. Into this context John Wesley came and tried to change the social set up by revolutionizing it.[29] As the minister of the church, and one who was concerned about the people and intent on their reform, he tried to change the continent and spread scriptural holiness over these lands. He was against the political bribery, smuggling and collection of extra taxes. Gin and rum were the most probable smuggled goods long with tea also.

He also raised his voice against **slavery**. For John Wesley the greatest evil of all was slavery and the trade that went with it. He had called it as that terrible sum of all villainies. He had written a booklet named *Thoughts Upon Slavery* in 1774 which was against the whole system of slavery. Captains, merchants and buyers were called on to give up their business. He was a frequent visitor to the prisoners and many prisoners received the message of God and found peace. It is said that Wesley's thoughts on slavery was most effective treaties ever written to expose many myths. Wesley believed that the nation's spiritual and moral integrity was more important than wealth and prosperity. Slaves by thousands were brought to England and sold by auction to work in estates there. This whole system was even approved by the Bishop.[30]

Child labour had become rampant in those days. Increase in population meant that there is increase in children. The children of the poor had always worked as soon as they began to walk but by this time they were more used by factory owners. Children were easy to handle as well as easily brought to discipline. They were cheap and full of energy to be used by the owners. Most of the factories and mines got them to work. One of the most visible and appalling exploitation of child labor in the eighteenth century was the chimney sweep. The children of the poor were used as laborers in industries and other sectors. The living conditions for them was poor and almost the houses were overcrowded where life had become bitter experience. Most of the cellars which had been there accommodated both poor workers as well as their cattle pigs. In brief it could be

---

[27] E. H. Carter and R. A. F Mears, *A History of Britain* (Oxford: Clarendon Press, 1957), 648.

[28] A. Skevington Wood, *The Burning Heart: John Wesley* (USA: Bethany Publishing House, 1978), 11.

[29] H. G. Mithra, *Wesley's Philosophy of Education for Socio-Spiritual Change*, 18.

[30] H. G. Mithra, 21.

said that it was an inhuman condition for poor people who worked as slaves and their kids being child labours to the masters. They worked for sixteen to seventeen hours per day.[31] Kids of seven year were almost working twelve to fifteen hours a day. The young lives were spent in, at best in monotonous toil, at worst in hell of human cruelty.[32] In the same regard women were also exploited. They were hired to spin on the jenny (For weaving) in their homes because they had large number of kids within the family.

1.2.2 Political background

It is important for us to understand the political scene of the given context. John Wesley's lifetime (1703-1791) was not an era of political crisis but of political stability. Wesley's early years were stirred by victories of Duke of Marlborough; his ministry began as the political powers made a final effort to crush the Jacobite cause at Culloden in 1745. Jeremy Black opines that, "there were bitter political and religious disputes in Eighteenth Century Britain. The succession was the cause of division and instability until the crushing of Bonnie Prince Charles, elder son of the Jacobite claimant to the throne, at Culloden in 1746. Though, William III (1689-1702) and George I (1714-1727) George II (1727-1760) relied heavily on the Whigs[33] (*The **Whigs** were a political faction and then a political party in the parliaments of England, Scotland, and the United Kingdom. Between the 1680s and 1850s, they contested power with their rivals, the Tories*).

Eighteenth century Britain was free from the revolutionary atmosphere that prevailed in the 17th century. The country became rich through trade and people enjoyed life. At the same time, power of the king continued to decline. It was seen that king's minister became real policy maker. In 1707, the Act of Union formally united England and Scotland. In 1714, when Queen Anne the last of Stuarts (*a member of the royal family that ruled in Scotland from 1371 to 1714 and in England from 1603 to 1714*) died, the Parliament chose the German speaking elector of Hanover who was crowned as George I. He was succeeded by his son George II who like his father had no interest in the affairs of the Britain. The most powerful political leader of this time had been Sir Robert Walpole (1676-1745), the first Prime Minister, who developed the idea of cabinet. Those who were strongly attached to tradition and the monarchy were known as Tories. The Tories were supported by gentry, the landed aristocracy and the Angelical Church.

Political life and wealth were also interrelated in the achievement of power. These factors influenced each other which had resulted in status, honor and social power. Politicians understood that wealth meant power and it was always used to get power. Through their political influences they often got the wealth they looked

---

[31] J. H. Plumb, *England In the Eighteenth Century (1714-1815*, 85-89.

[32] T. S. Ashton, *The Industrial Revolution, 1760-1830*, 78.

[33] Jeremy Black, *The Politics of Britain* (United Kingdom: Manchester University Press, 1993), 17.

for. Robert Walpole was considered as the chief political symbol that was a picture of deism and at some point time encouraged slavery where the foundations were laid on corruption. Walpole financial reforms aroused resentment because political bribery and corruption were common features of that time. It was also seen that the widespread of corruption had disturbed the political life of the society.[34] Kings and queens were no longer considered as representative of God in the given context. People were in dilemma that who was the real ruler of the world. The political life of Wesley's time was such that people were in great distress and broken attitude. When people needed bread they were offered stone and when needed the living water they were supplied with river inks. Thus whosoever had wealth, and higher social status could influence the regulation of Parliament for their personal gains. It is clear that the fundamental configuration of power and politics was not egalitarian, it was hierarchical in nature, and male dominated which had no scope for women or poor people. The wealthy landlords maintained their hold upon political power because it was not possible for common man to compete with them. Throughout the whole of the eighteenth century, almost all writers who had occasion to speak of the general condition of society joined in one wail of lament over the irreligion and immorality that they saw around them.

1.2.3 The Great Awakening and Cultural Changes

The Great Awakening is in the 18th century, the same time as the Enlightenment. As faith increased, doubt and unbelief also increased. The spread of the printed page made the Great Awakening possible. People were in touch with one another through writing letters and publishing newspapers. Examples are George Whitefield's *Evangelical Magazine,* Thomas Prince's *Christian History,* James Robe's *Christian Monthly History,* and John Wesley's *Armenian Magazine.* Whitefield's sermons and other writings were widely published in both America and England. Benjamin Franklin helped Whitefield through publishing. After Whitefield preached to a group that Franklin estimated to be 30,000 in Philadelphia, a vision for an academy/college emerged to educate the youth of the city. This later became the University of Pennsylvania. George Whitefield was also involved in social ministry with his orphanages. His preaching was a model for others who were seeking revival in America.

Jonathan Edwards (1703-1758) was the theological genius of the Great Awakening. Jonathan Edwards's maternal grandfather was Solomon Stoddard. Edwards was a Congregationalist. Born the fifth child and only son to Rev. Timothy and Esther Stoddard Edwards. No doubt, Edwards was a precious

[34] Joseph Basappa Suray, *Towards a Theology of Universality: John Wesley's Socio-Economic, Political & Moral Insights on British Class & Indian Caste Distinctions*, 49-50.

child, studying Latin at 6 and reading Greek and Hebrew at 13. He was only 12 when he began his studies at Yale, graduating in 1720 (age 16). He was born again (converted) in May or June 1721. Edwards's first ministry was at an English Presbyterian church in New York (1722). He returned to complete his master's thesis at Yale (1723). Ordained at his grandfather's church in 1727, while serving as an assistant pastor. Married to Sarah Pierpont on July 28, 1727. In 1729, his grandfather (pastor of the "mega-church" in New England, with 700 members) passed away, the 25-year-old Edwards became the Senior Pastor. Revival came to Northampton in 1734, when Edwards was in his early 30s. He wrote a report of the revival in *A Faithful Narrative of the Surprising work of God* (1737). *A Faithful Narrative...* "The Distinguishing Marks of a Work of the Spirit of God" "In the apostolic age, there was the greatest outpouring of the Spirit of God, that ever was; both as to his extraordinary influences and gifts, and his ordinary operations, in convincing, converting, enlightening, and sanctifying the souls of men. But as the influences of the true Spirit abounded, so counterfeits did also abound: the devil was abundant in mimicking, both the ordinary and extraordinary influences of the Spirit of God. . . ." In 1741, Edwards preached a powerful sermon (his most famous one). It was titled "Sinners in the Hands of an Angry God."[35]

As senior pastor, Edwards began to place more demands on the church membership. His grandfather had been very open toward conversion and participation in the sacraments, but Edwards was more conservative. This led toward a confrontation between pastor and congregation. Edwards was forced to leave in 1750. Although, several large churches wanted Edwards to be their pastor, he decided to preach at a mission in Stockbridge, Massachusetts to the Housatonic Indians (Native Americans). He preached through an interpreter and continued his philosophical/theological writings. He wrote *Freedom of the Will* (1754). He is considered to be America's greatest philosophical theologian because of this book. In 1757, he was called to be the President of the College of New Jersey (later Princeton), but served only three months before his death.[36]

---

[35] Jonathan Edwards: America's greatest theologian, http://www.christianitytoday.com/history/people/theologians/jonathan-edwards.html (accessed on 12/11/16).

[36] George Marsden's *Jonathan Edwards: A Life* (New Haven: Yale University Press, 2003), 10-25.

Chapter 2

Biographical Note on John Wesley

2.1 John Wesley (1703-1791)

A. Skevington Wood opines that "John Wesley was destined to be an evangelist. Along with George Whitefield and his own brother Charles, he was called by God to lead the mission to Britain. Within twenty years, however, Charles was to retire almost completely from active campaigning. Whitefield died in 1770, worn out by his herculean labors. But John battled on for over fifty years, and lived to see the tide turned and a nation awakened."[37] John Wesley famously proclaimed a form of Christian perfectionism. He predicted that personal holiness would strengthen society, deepen the commitment of Christians, and even establish Christ's kingdom on earth. **John Benjamin Wesley**, born on June 17th, 1703 at Epworth Parsonage he was the fifteenth of the Rector's nineteen children. He received the names of two brothers, John and Benjamin, who had died in infancy, but he never used the second name. John Wesley's life has amazing and surprising background. He was the fifteenth child in a family of nineteen. At the time of his birth there were six children in the Rectory; the rest were dead. Samuel, the only boy, was thirteen years old, and was preparing to enter Westminster School the following year. Charles Wesley was not born for more than four years afterwards.

The children were taught to fear the rod when they were only a year old and to cry softly. By this means the Epworth Parsonage, though full of children, was as quiet as if there had not been one in the house. As soon as possible, the little table and chairs were set near the family dinner-table, where they could be easily overlooked. The children were taught to ask softly for anything they wanted and to eat whatever was provided for the family. As soon as they could handle a knife and fork they sat at the table with their parents. No eating or drinking between

[37] A. Skevington Wood, *The Burning Heart: John Wesley*, 83.

meals was allowed. Evening prayers were over at six o'clock. The children then had supper, and at seven o'clock were prepared for bed. First, the youngest was undressed and washed, then the rest in turn. All were in bed by eight.

In Eighteenth century Britain God raised up a number of notable Christian leaders and John Wesley was one of these. His life was one committed to the Lord's service. His personal characteristics of courage, loyalty, perseverance and a deep commitment to serving God and man were matched by his gifts as a preacher and organizer.[38] Like the others of the Epworth family, John Wesley was small in stature. Barely five feet six and weighing only fifty five kilos he was yet muscular and strong. Bright hazel eyes, fine features, an aquiline nose, a fine forehead, and a clear complexion combined to make his face arresting. Contemporaries have said that his eyes retained their bright and penetrating quality even to his last years. Meticulous as to personal appearance and habits, he never appeared other than neatly dressed.[39]

It is said that on February 9, 1909 six year old "Jackie" by which he was addressed by family members was dramatically saved. A fire had broken out in the rectory in the midnight. Most of them escaped fire either by staircase or windows. Young John Wesley was left asleep in bed. When he woke up he saw the fire and could not rescue himself since being very small. He was lifted safely from the roof. Later on John Wesley referred himself as "a brand plucked from the burning."[40] Epworth, the Lincolnshire town which is honored as the birthplace of John and Charles Wesley, was then a market-town of about two thousand inhabitants. It is the principal place in a strip of land once enclosed by five rivers—the Idle and Torr, on the west and south; the Trent, on the east; the Ouse, the Don, and the broad tidal estuary of the Humber, to the north. This was the Isle of Axholme. Three of the rivers are now only to be traced by the willow trees which mark their former Channels. The fine old church at Epworth, with its massive tower, has been made familiar by the well-known picture of Wesley preaching on his father's tomb. It stands on rising ground, and when seen from the old Market Place appears to command the town. It is dedicated to St. Andrew.

The Parsonage in which John and Charles Wesley were born was destroyed by fire February 9th, 1709. It was a three-storied building of timber and plaster, thatched with straw, and had seven principal rooms, a kitchen, hall, parlour, buttery, with three large upper rooms and some others for common use. A small garden, a thatched barn, a dovecot, and other outside premises were attached. The whole covered about three acres. In this old house John Wesley was born and taught to read. At the age of six years he was rescued from a fire that destroyed

---

[38] Isser Woloch, *Eighteenth Century Europe: Tradition and Progress 1715-1789* (New York: WW Norton and Company, 1982), 298.

[39] John Wesley, *Journal of John Wesley* (Chicago: Moody Press, 1951), 11.

[40] Albert C. Outler, ed., *John Wesley* (New York: Oxford University, 1964), 6. Cf. also Bruce L Shelley, *Church History in Plain Language* (Dallas: Word Publishing, 1995), 333.

the rectory. From that point on he believed that only God's providential care had saved him.[41] John Wesley, son of an Anglican rectory was raised in a large family by godly parents. His father Samuel was a committed Anglican churchman, but both his paternal grandfather and great grandfather were dissenting ministers ejected from their parishes in 1662. His maternal grandfather, Samuel Annesley, was an eminent nonconformist minister. His mother, Susannah, was a devoted Christian mother to whom he continued to look for guidance throughout his life. The Wesley's were a family that had taken their religion seriously for generations.

John Wesley's parents, Samuel and Susanna Wesley, both were of strong character and convictions. Samuel Wesley father and grandfather both were of puritan minded clergymen who had lost their position in the Church of England because of their refusal in 1662 to abide by the English Prayer book.[42] Samuel and Susanna had 19 children and John Wesley was one among the 19 of which ten only survived. John Wesley's mother Susanna herself was 25th child of her father Dr. Samuel Annesley. A history of Wesley family shows that he had a preaching legacy from his forefathers, who were firm in the faith and convictions.[43] John Wesley's great grandfather, Bartholomew was born about 1595 and died about 1680. His only child John after some studies at Oxford became the minister of Winterborn Whitchurch in Dorset on the invitation of the people there. After his appointment there it seems he offended some local people by discarding the liturgy and was summoned by then Bristol Bishop Dr. Gilbert Ironside for interrogation in relation to his deviation from the order of worship. After that he had challenged the bishop and went on to preach about Christ. Grandfather of John Wesley had two sons Mathew who was a physician in London and Samuel who became the rector of Epworth. Samuel Wesley got married in 1688 to Susanna, the youngest daughter of Dr. Samuel Annesley, who was known and well honored as nonconformist divines of his day.[44] His ancestry includes monks, priests, a crusader, a chaplain to King Edward the IV and others.

2.2 John Wesley's Education/Scholarship

In Wesley's own writings we find the mention that on January 28th, 1714, he was nominated by the Duke of Buckingham on the foundation of Charterhouse. His Grace, who was at that time Lord Chamberlain, had long been a friend of the Wesley's. This nomination introduced John Wesley to that famous school for which he cherished a life-long affection. He was send to the Charterhouse School in London.[45] While John Wesley was at Charterhouse, he was a Gown-boy for almost six years from 1714-1720. His father had advised John that he should jog

[41] Albert C. Outler.

[42] V. H. H. Green, *John Wesley* (London: Thomas Nelson and Sons Ltd., 1964), 9.

[43] H. G. Mithra, *Wesley's Philosophy of Education for Socio-Spiritual Change*, 28.

[44] W. L. Doughty, *John Wesley Preacher* (London: Epworth Press, 1955), 1-5.

[45] Albert C. Outler, ed., *John Wesley*, 6.

around the garden in the morning at least 3 times which helped him to keep good health. He had almost six years of training under Dr. Thomas Walker and later Andrew Tooke who succeeded him as schoolmaster. This training in real sense laid the foundation for his further scholarship.[46] The system of fagging (A student at a boarding school who is required to perform menial tasks for a student in a higher grade) seems to have been in full force. During Wesley's schooldays his life was one of much hardship. His height was five foot six inches and he weighed only 55 kilograms. The elder boys took the food from the juniors, and so had to face many times hunger. In spite of all these struggles he got distinction as a scholar while at Charterhouse.[47]

About that time, Wesley entered Charterhouse, his brother Samuel returned from Oxford to his old school at Westminster as usher. He seems to have married in 1715, and lived close to Dean's Yard. Charles, their youngest brother, came up to Westminster School in 1716, so that the three Wesley's were all in London together for four years, until John went to Oxford in 1720. (In June 1720 he entered Christ Church, Oxford. In 1724, he graduated as bachelors of Arts and 1727 he received Masters of Arts degree. In March 1726 he was elected as a fellow of Lincoln College, Oxford which gave him privilege to have a room at the college and regular salary). At the age of 17 John Wesley entered at Christ Church, one of the Oxford's largest and known colleges. This was a great delight for him because his father, grandfather and great grandfather were the alumni of Christ Church College. He was ordained deacon in Christ Church Cathedral on Sunday, September 19th, 1725, by Dr. Potter, then Bishop of Oxford, who also admitted him to priest's orders in the same place on September 22nd, 1728.[48] After finishing his master's degree he returned to Epworth, his father had requested him to assist him in serving Neighboring cure of Wroote. Wesley served as Parish curator for two years. He returned to Oxford in 1729 at the request of the Rector of Lincoln College to be a junior fellow.

He was ordained as a deacon on holy orders which were a necessary step to become a fellow and tutor at the universality. At the age of 21 he received his bachelors of Arts and at the age of 24 he received his Masters of Arts studies degree in 1727. During his post graduate studies he was offered to join Lincoln College which gave him name and financial stability.[49] His studies at Oxford were not only about divinity but involved metaphysics, ethics, logic, natural philosophy

---

[46] H. G. Mithra, *Wesley's Philosophy of Education for Socio-Spiritual Change*, 30. Cf., also John Telford, *The Life of John Wesley* (London: Charles H. Kelly, 1900), 16.

[47] John Wilkins Sigsworth, *World Changer: Karl Marx and John Wesley*, 6.

[48] John Telford, *The Life of John Wesley*, 17.

[49] John Telford.

and different languages. This gave him opportunity to moderator classes and become Greek lecturer.[50]

Christ Church was known for its library and John Wesley took his first degree from there itself. It is said that when they travelled from Epworth to Oxford which was really far they used the time by reading things one by one.[51] John Wesley apart from English knew ten languages such as Arabic, Latin, Hebrew, Greek, etc. He was interested in all kinds of books including church history, Church Fathers, reformation time theologians and classical writers. He liked Ignatius and Polycarp and mastered the literature of medieval mysticism which focused on union with God. He was aware of the teaching of deism and devoted himself to ancient classics and dramas and tragedies such as Shakespeare. He was also known to the scientific writing of Francis Bacon (1561-1626), Isaac Newton (1643-1727), Benjamin Franklin (1706-1790) and others. He loved poetries also and regarded Milton's *Paradise Lost* as one of the finest poem of the world.[52] He was also keenly interested with the study of medicine in order to become updated. Wesley's writings are all didactic, intended for a popular audience; he produced grammars, extracts from the classics, histories, biographies, and a vast number of hymns. He died on March 2, 1791.[53] John Wesley was widely acknowledged as a leader, administrator and a great scholar. He was addressed as the greatest captain of men in his century by Leslie Stephen. His family took advice from him in many matters even though he was younger in his family.

2.3 John Wesley's Character

John Wesley was a man of his day, speaking the language of his day as well as brought up in the cultural milieu of his country. He believed in ghosts. He thought that earthquakes were direct divine judgment against sin and public repentance could prevent them.[54] John Wesley was small in stature but very impressive in appearance. The good part of his life was that he was alert and vigorous to do things for the Lord. He was frail and in his life he had much sickness. John Telford describes an incident which describes the character of John Wesley. In the April of 1712, John and four more of the Parsonage children had the small-pox. "Jack has borne his disease bravely, like a man, and indeed like a Christian, without any complaint, though he seemed angry at the small-pox when they were sore, as

[50] V. H. H. Green, *The Young Mr. Wesley* (London: Edward Arnold Ltd., 1961), 125. Cf., also Mildred Bangs Wynkoop, *A Theology of Love* (Kansas City: Beacon Hill Press, 1972), 60.

[51] John Wilkins Sigsworth, *World Changer: Karl Marx and John Wesley*, 18.

[52] John Wilkins Sigsworth, *World Changer: Karl Marx and John Wesley*, 19.

[53] Brian Stableford, "Guide to Literary Masters & Their Works, of John Wesley," http://web.a.ebscohost.com/lrc/detail/detail?vid=4&sid=3d280652-becd-4260-a4dd-6db9bfbcd50e%40sessionmgr4003&hid=4204&bdata=JnNpdGU9bHJjLXBsdXM%3d#AN=1033311LM78379790307789&db=lkh (accessed on 19/07/16).

[54] Mildred Bangs Wynkoop, *A Theology of Love: The Dynamism of Wesleyanism*, 63-64.

we guessed by his looking sourly at them, for he never said anything."[55] He was a disciplined child and well mannered in house as well outside. He had long flowing curly hair which later on became grey eventually giving him apostolic look. Some people had commented that he grew his hair to avoid the barber's fees. At the old age he had less hair and so he had used a wig. He was known for his neatness and sense of well dressing. He avoided expensive dressings such as buckles, silk and velvet. His journal talks that he had undergone around 69 different attacks of sickness in his life time. Despite of his weak body, his look was both cheerful and serene but some time he was caught up with depression.[56]

John Wesley loved children and wherever he went or visited, kids came to him played with him as a friend. In recognition and affection towards them he either handshake with them or kissed them. Even though, John Wesley is known as serious person he had used humors in his discussion with people around. After their father's death in 1735, the Wesley brothers went as missionaries to Georgia, where John became embroiled in an unfortunate love affair with Sophia Hopkey. He accused her of breach of promise when she married another man in 1737, apparently weary of waiting for him to propose, and the community protested when he tried to exclude her from services. Few clergymen would allow Wesley access to their pulpits, so he began preaching in the open at Bristol in 1739, where he founded the first Methodist chapel.

In 1749, Wesley wanted to marry Grace Murray, heard him preach in the open air at London and accepted the Lord. Mrs. Murray's husband who was a ship captain died on the voyage. Wesley came close to Murray and had reason to marry her. She had kept house for him in Newcastle, but in a bizarre twist on the Hopkey affair, Charles, who disapproved of the match because of her low background presided over her marriage to another man named John Bennet. Instead, Wesley married a widow of a London Merchant, Mary Vaizelle, on February 19, 1751, but the marriage was a disaster. According to W. H. Fitchett, all of John Wesley's love affairs were disasters but his marriage was a tragedy.[57] So his personal and emotional life was really in mess. At some point of time John Wesley lacked the conjugal virtues basically at the time when he married. Inspite of all the ups and downs he had made very clear that he would not leave his travelling and preaching assignments. Apart from his some downfalls in relation to his marriage he was without any doubt a disciplined person. He is said to have covered 250,000 miles and preached 40,000 sermons, often awaited by crowds of strong thousands.

2.4 John Wesley's Theological Roots

As we discussed about the understanding of John Wesley it is important for us to also know the formative impact on him. Without any doubt one thing could be

[55] John Telford, *The Life of John Wesley*, 20.

[56] John Wilkins Sigsworth, *World Changer: Karl Marx and John Wesley*, 25-26.

[57] W. H. Fitchett, *Wesley and His Century* (Cincinnati: Jennings and Graham, 1966), 95.

affirmed that his parents Samuel and Susanna's religious influenced had shaped Wesley's early days and ministry. Wesley's parents from different religious and theological backgrounds trained him at home and later helped him to face the challenges when he was there at Christ Church Oxford. His parents Angelical and Puritans influences impacted Wesley a lot. John Wesley's family background had really helped him to develop his theological framework.[58] While he was getting ready for his ordination he often discussed with his mother on the nature of Christian faith. John Wesley was not very convinced about the stand that God would be held responsible for human sin and the concept of few being chosen while the most of them being destined for the doom. He believed that God's universal love was given equally to all humanity and there was no partiality in this regard.

Religious training began as early as possible. Even before they could kneel or speak, they were taught to be quiet at family prayers and to ask a blessing by signs. As soon as they could speak they repeated the Lord's Prayer morning and evening. A prayer for their parents, some collects, Catechism, and Scripture, were added as soon as they were able to learn them. No profane or rude words were ever heard in the Parsonage. The children were taught to ask quietly for what they wanted. Crying never won anything in this home. No one was allowed to speak to the servants without saying, "Pray give me such a thing." The little people were always expected to say "*Brother* John" or "*Sister* Kezzy." The code of honour observed among them allowed no promise to be broken, no gift reclaimed. No one attempted to take what belonged to his brother or sister. Confession of a fault always averted punishment, so that many temptations to falsehood were removed.

David Hampton opined that "Wesley is a man of the Enlightenment in his concern.... His desire that all men should be saved not just the Calvinist views that few would be saved. His strong opposition to slavery shows his thoughts were equivalents if enlightenment optimism."[59] In his letter to his mother on 29th of July, 1725 he had questioned the Calvinist idea of Predestination. He raised the question that the everlasting purpose of God to deliver some from damnation means others are excluded from deliverance. How can it be justified with the divine justice and mercy of God where majority of the human world would be born to eternal death? How can God be the author of sin and injustice? The doctrine of predestination contradicts with the concept of universal love and goodness of God.[60] John Wesley had the Armenian background he struggled with the concept of predestination in relation to the character of God. His

[58] Joseph Basappa Suray, *Towards a Theology of Universality: John Wesley's Socio-Economic, Political & Moral Insights on British Class & Indian Caste Distinctions*, 130-131.

[59] David Hampton, *Methodism and Politics in British Society* (London: Hutchinson, 1985), 22.

[60] Joseph Basappa Suray, *Towards a Theology of Universality: John Wesley's Socio-Economic, Political & Moral Insights on British Class & Indian Caste Distinctions*, 132-133.

mother anyhow held the view of predestination but with the understanding of God's foreknowledge. His parental understanding of grace helped him to see that everyone has the opportunity either to improve their fate or destroy their situation. John Wesley emphasized that grace and salvation were offered as a gift from God for all equally.

2.4.1 John Wesley: A Theologian

Leon O. Hynson sees John Wesley as a person of every context and time and says that theologically he was a skillful thinker who held the thread between God's sovereignty and human responsibility. Faith and works was showed as going together hand in hand. He also opines that he was folk theologian who spoke to all class of people whether simple or wise or rich/ poor.[61] He was concerned for people irrespective of any class or status. Wesley in fact had not made any systematic efforts to write a systematic Theology.[62] He is more seen as a great revivalist rather than in strict sense theologian. Wesley's theological discussion and sermons were grounded in life situation of his time. His theological response and application was on the basis of eighteenth century socio-political and the religious context could be compared at some extent with the contextual theology in contemporary world. In order to supplement the discussion, we could say that theological development is not the sole efforts of a person only in isolation. Instead it is the efforts of both thinker and the church in which context he/she lives.

John Wesley's theological discussions for sure were his theological response to the social and religious issues which existed in England. In this regard Howard Snyder had opined that' for in Wesley, Theology and Practice really were one. From the beginning, his theological work grappled with the practical issue. His theology was shaped by his experience and made sure his actions were grounded in sound doctrine."[63] He was considered as one the greatest theologian of the eighteenth century. Albert Outler had addressed him as greatest Angelical theologian of his century as well a champion of social reformation. He was the theologian of the whole church whose theology may be taken as a model for ecumenical dialogue.[64] His theology was considered as practical theology which was rooted in practical circumstances of society. His anti-slavery stand was primarily the result of his practical understanding of holiness. Concern for the lower class was one of the major features of John Wesley's theological thinking. Wesley's social concern and ethical preaching was mainly focused towards individual and then for the larger social system. Wesley's efforts to transform the society had reached to all class of people. His life and work have had an enormous influence on modern

---

[61] Leon O. Hynson, *To Reform the Nation* (Michigan: Francis Asbury Press, 1984), 25.

[62] Howard A Snyder, *The Radical Wesley* (USA: InterVarsity Press, 1980), 4.

[63] Howard A Snyder, 5.

[64] Joseph Basappa Suray, *Towards a Theology of Universality: John Wesley's Socio-Economic, Political & Moral Insights on British Class & Indian Caste Distinctions*, 138.

Christianity, including his teaching on Holiness of Sanctification and Christian perfection. It stir up wide spread revivals in England, United States and other European countries and its impact was far reaching.[65]

2.5 John Wesley and Holy Club

Whilst serving as his father's curate his brother Charles started what came to be called a "Holy Club" at Oxford. The club aimed to encourage serious attention to religious duties. The members, firstly led by Charles and later John Wesley, rose early, read their New Testament in Greek, fasted two days a week, took frequent Communion, observed all Church festivals and visited the sick and prison inmates. During Wesley's absence, his younger brother Charles (1707–88) matriculated at Christ Church. Along with two fellow students, he formed a small club for the purpose of study and the pursuit of a devout Christian life. On Wesley's return, he became the leader of the group which increased somewhat in number and greatly in commitment. The group met daily from six until nine for prayer, psalms, and reading of the Greek New Testament. They prayed every waking hour for several minutes and each day for a special virtue. While the church's prescribed attendance was only three times a year, they took communion every Sunday. They fasted on Wednesdays and Fridays until three o'clock as was commonly observed in the ancient church. In 1730, the group began the practice of visiting prisoners in jail. They preached, educated, and relieved jailed debtors whenever possible, and cared for the sick.

It was through this ministry that George Whitefield was introduced to John Wesley. Despite this strenuous and consistent approach John Wesley still lacked an inner spiritual peace.[66] Given the low ebb of spirituality in Oxford at that time, it was not surprising that Wesley's group provoked a negative reaction. They were considered to be religious "enthusiasts" who in the context of the time meant religious fanatics. University wits styled them the "Holy Club," a title of derision. Currents of opposition became a furor following the mental breakdown and death of a group member, William Morgan. In response to the charge that "rigorous fasting" had hastened his death, Wesley noted that Morgan had left off fasting a year and a half since. In the same letter, which was widely circulated, Wesley referred to the name "Methodist" which "some of our neighbors are pleased to compliment us." That name was used by an anonymous author in a published pamphlet (1733) describing Wesley and his group, "The Oxford Methodists" which later was used as nickname. Later in the Club's history, six years after its inception, George Whitefield became a member and gladly adopted their ascetic mode of life.

---

[65] Sunil Thomas, "Wesleyan Tradition on Holiness and its Significance," *Bethany Journal of Theology 6/2* (September, 2014): 67.

[66] Bruce L. Shelley, *Church History in Plain Language* (Dallas: Word Publishing, 1995), 333.

2.6 John Wesley: Mission to Savannah and Georgia

In 1735, John Wesley accepted a position as chaplain in the new colony of Georgia. The death of Samuel the Rector on April 23, 1735, unsettled John, and the meeting between General James Oglethorpe and himself caused him to accept the offer of a chaplaincy in the colony of Georgia. His father had been one of the first supporters of this new colony. A charter had been obtained from George II in June, 1732, creating the narrow strip of country between South Carolina and Florida into a British colony. It lay between the river Savannah on the north and the Alabama on the south, with a coast line of rather more than sixty miles. This territory was vested in twenty-one trustees, of whom Colonel (afterwards General) Oglethorpe was the chief. As a Member of Parliament, he had interested himself greatly in the sufferings of small debtors, and had obtained a committee to inquire into the state of the prisons. Many unfortunate debtors were, thus, released. Oglethorpe's practical sympathy led him to devise some means of support for his new constituency. The colony was therefore founded for the benefit of the poor, and he became its governor. On the outward sea journey a raging storm was encountered which terrified Wesley. At the same time he was deeply touched by the inner peace and assurance of a group of Moravian Christians who were fellow travelers.[67]

Both he and his brother Charles had gone to Georgia believing that they would be bringing the Gospel to native Indians. Georgia therefore marks a third stage in his spiritual pilgrimage. Whatever his motives, none could deny his apostolic zeal in his daily religious services and in the frequent celebration of Holy Communion. A plaque outside the Protestant Episcopal Church in Savannah makes John Wesley the founder of Sunday Schools in America, and certainly he gave much time to the instruction of the young. He ministered to French and German colonists by conversing with them in their own language, their dreams of reaching "unspoiled children of nature", however, were exploded as they found a world of violence and sin unresponsive to the high-church approach of John. Finally, in Georgia was laid the foundation of the system of classes which later became a distinguishing mark of the British Methodism. Wesley arrived in the colony in February 1736. He approached the Georgia mission as a High Churchman, seeing it as an opportunity to revive "primitive Christianity" in a primitive environment. Although, his primary goal was to evangelize the Native Americans, a shortage of clergy in the colony largely limited his ministry to European settlers in Savannah. While his ministry has often been judged to have been a failure in comparison to his later success as a leader in the Evangelical Revival, Wesley gathered around him a group of devoted Christians who met in a number of small group religious societies. At the same time, attendance at church

[67] Kenneth Scott Latourette, *A History of Christianity* (London: Eyre and Spottiswoode Ltd, 1955), 1024.

services and communion increased over the course of nearly two years in which he served as Savannah's parish priest. An unhappy love affair and the aftermath ended his ministry and he returned to London in 1738. It has been mostly recognized that one of the most significant accomplishments of Wesley's Georgia mission was his publication of a *Collection of Psalms and Hymns*. The *Collection* was the first Anglican hymnal published in America, and the first of many hymn-books Wesley published. It included five hymns he translated from German.

2.7 John Wesley and the Moravians

There were a number of Moravians on the ship "Simmonds" on which Wesley sailed to Georgia, and his contacts with these people constituted another important factor in his conversion and subsequent life. Wesley was amazed by the display of peace and the level of faith these Moravians possessed. During times of great distress and rough seas on the voyage across the Atlantic Ocean, while Wesley and many of the other passengers on board were greatly shaken, the Moravians seemed unafraid. In the midst of the psalm wherewith their service began, the sea broke over, split the main-sail in pieces, covered the ship, and poured in between the decks, as if the great deep had already swallowed us up. A terrible screaming began among the English.

The Germans calmly sung on. I asked one of them afterwards, 'Was you not afraid?' He answered, 'I thank God, no.' I asked, 'But were not your women and children afraid?' He replied, mildly, 'No; our women and children are not afraid to die.' From them I went to their crying, trembling neighbors, and pointed out to them the difference in the hour of trial, between him that feared God, and him that feared him not. At twelve the wind fell. This was the most glorious day which I have hitherto seen. There is little doubt that Wesley was impressed by what he saw in the behavior of the Moravians, including their children. He was greatly impressed with the unperturbed behavior of the Moravians in a storm and learned that even their women and children were not afraid because of their faith. Later one of their Leaders, August Gottlieb Spangenburg asked him pointedly, "Do you know Jesus Christ?" Wesley replied, "I know that He is the Savior of the world." "But," persisted the Moravian, "Do you know he has saved you?" Wesley replied in the affirmative, but he confessed in his Journal, "I fear they were vain words." This episode created a spiritual dissatisfaction in Wesley's heart which eventually, and under the tutorship of another Moravian, Peter Bohler, led to his evangelical awakening.

Wesley's mission in Georgia was not successful and even he regarded it as a failure. Nevertheless, his usefulness in the colony was strictly limited and his mission ended in a near fiasco. His rigid High Churchmanship divided the people and turned many against him.[68] Wesley allied himself with the Moravian

[68] Maldwyn L. Edwards, "John Wesley," httpwww.enterhisrest.orghistorybio_john_wesley.pdf (accessed on 01/08/16).

society in Fetter Lane. In 1738 he went to Herrnhut, the Moravian headquarters in Germany, to study. On his return to England, Wesley drew up rules for the "bands" into which the Fetter Lane Society was divided and published a collection of hymns for them. He met frequently with this and other religious societies in London but did not preach often in 1738, because most of the parish churches were close to him.

Wesley was unhappy about the idea of field preaching as he believed Anglican liturgy had much to offer in its practice. Earlier in his life he would have thought that such a method of saving souls was "almost a sin." He recognized the open-air services were successful in reaching men and women who would not enter most churches. From then on he took the opportunities to preach wherever an assembly could be brought together, more than once using his father's tombstone at Epworth as a pulpit. Wesley continued for fifty years – entering churches when he was invited, and taking his stand in the fields, in halls, cottages, and chapels, when the churches would not receive him. Late in 1739, Wesley broke with the Moravians in London. Wesley had helped them organize the Fetter Lane Society, and those converted by his preaching and that of his brother and Whitefield had become members of their bands. But he believed they fell into heresy by supporting quietism, so he decided to form his own followers into a separate society. "Thus," he wrote, "without any previous plan, began the Methodist Society in England." Formed similar societies in Bristol and Kingswood, and wherever Wesley and his friends made converts.

In London he came into contact with a group of Moravians under the leadership of Peter Bohler. Bohler impressed on him his need of a strong personal faith in Jesus Christ that would enable him to overcome sin and attain true holiness. John Wesley had long known of the doctrine of justification by faith but had considered it pure doctrine rather than a personal experience of God's forgiveness. In 1738, at their Aldersgate Street rooms he was suddenly and wonderfully converted. As he placed his trust in Christ and received assurance that his sins were forgiven, he experienced at last the peace he had been striving for all those years.[69] As he contemplated the future direction of his life he travelled to Germany to observe firsthand the Moravian community. The warm fellowship and enthusiastic singing of hymns bound their community together. Wesley later adopted their use of small groups to facilitate study, worship and prayer in his own "societies."

The Moravians[70] impression of peace during Atlantic storm had really impacted Wesley's life very much which had helped him to witness the work

---

[69] Bruce L Shelley, *Church History in Plain Language,* 335.

[70] The brief history of Moravians will help to understand the impact of it on John Wesley. Towards the latter part of 17th century Philip Spener rallied the devotional circles within Lutheranism in order to get back the personal piety (who is also known as founder of Pietism) Spener focused more of immediate inspiration. And they rarely celebrated the Eucharist. His thought anyhow had

of God. His attachment with Peter Bohler had really helped for the evangelical conversion of John Wesley which also led him to break away from mysticism. The Moravians were to serve as a kind of decompression chamber for John Wesley where they had held the Lutheran doctrine of justification by faith. It is believed that the Moravians influenced and attracted him from mysticism. The Moravian synthesis of mystical piety and reform theology appealed to Wesley and fulfilled his longing. Spangenberg and Bohler combined a strong sense of mystical piety with internal witness of the Holy Spirit received through faith in Jesus Christ. The Moravian understanding of that there would be no salvation by any action or works attracted Wesley very much. Bohler had sensed the need of Wesley and provided with that view. Bohler like Wesley and mystics emphasized holiness as a fruit of faith not the cause. He stressed the means of justification more than the need result of sanctification. Yet, John Wesley was drawn to Bohler because he could develop upon a new foundation justification by faith and still retain holiness and perfection as the need of religion.[71]

John Wesley and his brother Charles were sent by the Society for the Propagation of the Gospel to Georgia, where both of them developed their powers as preachers. Upon their passage they fell into the company of several Moravian brethren, members of the association recently renewed by the labors of Count Zinzendorf. It was noted by John Wesley in his diary that, in a great tempest, when the English people on board lost all self-possession, these Germans impressed him by their composure and entire resignation to God.[72] He also marked their humility under shameful treatment. He had greater influence on him by these friends also.

Wesley allied himself with the Moravian society in Fetter Lane. In 1738 he went to Herrnhut, the Moravian headquarters in Germany, to study. On his return to England, Wesley drew up rules for the "bands" into which the Fetter Lane Society was divided and published a collection of hymns for them. He met frequently with this and other religious societies in London but did not preach often in 1738, because most of the parish churches were closed to him. Wesley's Oxford friend, the evangelist George Whitefield, was also excluded from the churches of Bristol upon his return from America. Wesley was unhappy about the idea of field preaching as he believed Anglican liturgy had much to offer in its

impacted A. H. Francke who took the spirit of pietism to Halle. Moravians owed their existence as a system of thought to Spener and Pietists. The Moravians had no creed as such their particular brand of spirituality primarily emphasized a high degree of spiritual discipline. In many ways Moravians involved a reaction against the deistic thought which offered Christianity without Christ. Robert G. Tuttle, *John Wesley His Life and Theology*, 220.

[71] Robert G. Tuttle, 221-222.

[72] *Fox's Book of Martyrs: An Account of the Life of John Wesley*, http://www.umcmission.org/Find-Resources/John-Wesley-Sermons/The-Wesleys-and-Their-Times/Account-of-the-Life-of-John-Wesley#sthash.aVwDAMGg.dpuf, (accessed on 11/07/16).

practice. Earlier in his life he would have thought that such a method of saving souls was "almost a sin".

He recognized the open-air services were successful in reaching men and women who would not enter most churches. From then on he took the opportunities to preach wherever an assembly could be brought together, more than once using his father's tombstone at Epworth as a pulpit. Late in 1739 Wesley broke with the Moravians in London. Wesley had helped them organize the Fetter Lane Society, and those converted by his preaching and that of his brother and Whitefield had become members of their bands. But he believed they fell into heresy by supporting quietism, so he decided to form his own followers into a separate society. "Thus," he wrote, "without any previous plan, began the Methodist Society in England." He soon formed similar societies in Bristol and Kingswood, and wherever Wesley and his friends made converts.

2.7.1 Wesleyanism and Pietism

Pietism was a response to both rationality (philosophers) and dogmatism (theologians). It was an attempt to restore the "heart" to Christianity. "Pietism" usually refers only to the German movement led by Spener and Francke. Philipp Jacob Spener (1635-1705) is called the "father" of Pietism. He was Born and raised in Alsace. Studied at the best universities and received a doctorate in theology. Spener became pastor of a church in Frankfurt who also founded "colleges of piety" (small groups for prayer and Bible study). 1675 – Spener published his *Pia Desideria* (Pious desires). In his book, Spener, discussed the priesthood of believers and placed less emphasis on the division between laity and clergy. He recommended that all students of theology be tested to make sure that they are "true Christians." *Pia Desideria* was published in 1675 (in Frankfurt). He had six "simple proposals : 1. Intensive study of the Bible. 2. More laity involved in the church. 3. Emphasis on the practical (rather than intellectual). 4. Show love (charity) in religious discussions. 5. Reorganization in theological education and more of a devotional life among students and faculty. 6. Revival of preaching (with an aim to edify). Spener believed that preaching should not be a way of showing off a Pastor's knowledge, but a means of calling people to obey God's Word. He called for the Reformation to be completed, not to stop at doctrinal debates. Not everyone agreed with Spener views. Spener emphasized the need for both justification and sanctification in the Christian life. Many of his hearers thought that he was closer to Calvin than Luther. Spener also stressed biblical prophecy, especially the book of Revelation. The end was near. Christ was coming soon! The real question was, "Does Christianity call people to live a radically different kind of life?" "Or, is Christianity only a message to make good people better?"

Another person who contributed was August Hermann Francke (1663-1727) who was Spener's best student, and so the torch was going to be passed. Francke was a professor at the University of Halle. Francke wrote, "Suddenly, God heard me. As easily as one turns a hand, my doubts vanished. In my heart I was certain of the grace of God in Jesus Christ. Since then I was able to call God, not only 'God,' but also "Father." Sadness and anxiety immediately left my heart. And I was suddenly overcome by a wave of joy, such that I praised and magnified God aloud, who had granted me such grace." What does he mean by a "wave of joy?" Pietism taught that people must have a living and personal experience of faith. It didn't matter when or how it happened. People should all have real faith in the living Savior. People who had this kind of real faith began to join together in meetings that were "colleges of piety." Spener and Francke were both Lutherans, so early Pietism had a greater impact on Lutheranism in Germany. However, others were also influenced. Reformed Pietism began with German Reformed Christians but spread to other nations, especially the Netherlands and the British colonies in North America (USA and Canada).

Wesley eventually returned to England from Georgia in February of 1738. Upon his return to the European continent, he made an effort to continue his correspondence with the Moravians and Peter Bohler. Finally, in hope of learning more from "those holy men who were themselves living witnesses of the full power of faith...," Wesley travelled to Germany in July of 1738. There Bohler greeted him and introduced him to the leader of the Moravians, Count Nicholas Von Zinzendorf. Count Zinzendorf's (1700-1760) godfather was Spener. Zinzendorf came from a well-to-do family with a firm faith in Christ. He is what you would call "a Christian from his mother's womb." He realized that he could not point to a conversion experience. He had always been a Christian. Zinzendorf studied at the University of Halle (a student of Franck) and later at Wittenberg. In Dresden, he met a group of Moravians who were exiled from their native land. Zinzendorf founded a community for them at Herrnhut. He also joined the community. In 1731, he met a group of Eskimos who had been converted by the Lutheran missionary Hans Egede. Herrnhut became a mission training center. It was Zinzendorf's commitment to missions, guided by his Pietistic religious views he had first embraced during his childhood that led to the creation of a Moravian missionary movement. Peter Bohler had become an integral part of this movement.[73] The Moravians and Count Zinzendorf definitely played a significant role in shaping Wesley's views on the value and absolute necessity of the need for spiritual formation for children. It was Zinzendorf's commitment to missions, guided by his Pietistic religious views he had first embraced during his childhood that led to the creation of a Moravian missionary movement. Peter Bohler had become an integral part of this movement.[74]

[73] A. Servington Wood, *Count Von Zinzendorf, Introduction to the History of Christianity*, Tim Dowley, ed. (Minneapolis: Fortress Press, 2002), 483.

[74] G. Dan Harris, *The Early Influences of John Wesley, Concerning His Views of the Ministry to Children, The Moravians*, http://works.bepress.com/gdanharris/4/ (accessed on 21/07/16)

John Wesley was exposed to theological influence of German pietism which had viewed that salvation is by grace through faith not by good works. His theological views were changed as a result of Moravians influences but he didn't change his church affiliation/ denomination until his death. His spiritual and theological foundation was laid by both his family heritage and parents. His association with Oxford community had deepened his convictions as Anglican Christian.[75]

[75] H. G. Mithra, *Wesley's Philosophy of Education for Socio-Spiritual Change*, 55.

Chapter 3

Influencing Factors on John Wesley

John Wesley was to become a great theologian but theology was not his greatest strength. Wesley's most significant contribution to the eighteenth century and a church as a whole lies in his ability to organize people in a body that would sustain both them and the movement called eighteenth century Evangelical Revival. Our task is to see the influences that have kept on John Wesley which made him to function as theologian as well as evangelist. We need to see what the motivations principles were for John Wesley which made him firm. In other word we need to see how John Wesley did theology who became a person who changed the history of nation at some point of time. His practical theology enabled him to gear the attention of the people and served them.

As the discussion is about the influences or impacts on John Wesley it is needed to focus on the ideology and philosophy existing in eighteenth century. The beginning of the Eighteenth century was a breeding ground for theological schizophrenia that means there were two schools of thought existing side by side in that time. On the one hand there were people (to use the Aristotelian model) who thought that reality had to do only with those things which is perceivable by sense experience. Matters which could be touched, or smelled or heard, or tasted or seen were real. Since matter was the only reality one had to reason to faith. That showed that reason lead to faith. This brought over different thoughts such as Deism which asserted goodness of man and he could himself find his way to faith. In other words, it exalted reason over faith. The Church of England also at some point of time was also in it approach like Aristotelian in nature.[76] Through its Armenian doctrine it taught that man (since original sin affected him only from neck down, corrupting his heart but not his intellect) had the freedom to reason

[76] Robert G. Tuttle, *John Wesley His Life and Theology*, 71.

his way to faith.[77] Although his heart was prone to evil, his mind was left free to reason with the heart and respond to God by faith once the call was understood.

The second school of thought included those (to use the Platonic model) who thought that reality had to do with ideals. Matter even though it could be perceived by sense experience, was an illusion. Since reality had to do with ideals which was not perceived by sense experience, understanding came by faith which means faith leads to reason. This view also had its footing in eighteenth century context. Mysticism basically was Platonic in nature and in its approach to God. They believed that reality was non sensory and so it is received only by mystical experience.[78] There was another group of people who still believed that both heart and the intellect were corrupted by sin and only by the grace of God in faith would bring understanding.

It is said that John Wesley not only influenced the eighteenth century, but eighteenth century also influenced John Wesley very much. Both Aristotelian model and deism as prevailing philosophy on one hand and Puritans background of his parents on the other hand impacted him immensely. A significant part of influence surrounding Wesley's home environment was great amount of devotional readings. Reading at the Epworth rectory consisted mostly of the Puritan divines and mystics.[79] While John Wesley was a boy there were many reading at his home from Richard Baxter, John Bunyan, George Fox and others. Thus, John Wesley's High Church/ Puritan/ Mystical heritage had influenced him a lot. The ascetic element was very much prevalent in that context which demanded disciplined living and moral vigor.[80]

As in the **High Church (there** was a strong emphasis on asceticism as the handmaid to reason. Since the intellect was not corrupted by sin, it could instruct the believer through self denial and mortification. This rigorism leads to focus on sacraments as the means of grace) **and Puritan traditions** (they also focused on disciplined living and moral rigorism) spiritual exercise and self denial were starting of true religion. In the broader understanding the real fear for John Wesley was not exactly the sin but it was death. He was looking for the assurance the

[77] Armenian theology argues for a degree of free will, over and against the views of strict Calvinism, which had its acceptance in the Church of England.

[78] The basis of mystical theology is meditation which is directly applied to souls which might be elevated towards God. Several layers or levels of mystical consciousness are involved. The first stage is purgative stage which is preceded by some type of religious awakening or experience which involves ascetic living just like a preparation for the athlete. The rigid discipline which would purify the body was required. The second stage was illuminative which demanded a concentration on God. It is a faith on God beyond reason. During this time God send some sparks into the soul which gives the mystic experience. The third stage is unitive which is a mystical path could lead for a person to be closer to God.

[79] John A. Newton, *Susanna Wesley and Puritan Tradition in Methodism* (London: Epworth Press, 1969), 43.

[80] Robert G. Tuttle, *John Wesley His Life and Theology*, 73-74.

inward witness. Thus, the two things which could be clearly seen as a influence on John Wesley were Puritanism and Mysticism. Puritans taught that faith itself was the assurance of things hoped for and evidence of things not seen. Repent and believe was the formula for faith. Mystics talked about a union with God where a person could have a constant awareness of God's presence in his life and well as in the world. It is said that Wesley made religion the business of his life and started the process of cleaning himself so that God could love him. But his wait became a long time since God touched him and allowed him to shun all his self righteousness and rely on him fully. The Aldersgate experience changed his life which ultimately led for the Evangelical Revivalism. We will try to see first the major influence on John Wesley who was his mother Susanna Wesley and then look into his Aldersgate experience.

3.1 The Mother: Susanna Wesley (1669-1742)

Susanna Wesley as often was called the "Mother of Methodism." In a biological sense this is true, for she was the mother of John and Charles as well as sixteen or seventeen other children, ten of whom survived infancy. She was also the spiritual mother, for her influence on the education, theology and world view of her sons was strong and continued to be a challenge to them throughout their lives. She was a prolific writer. She was never published, but she wrote great devotions for her children, letters, and other intellectual treatises on God, the Bible and the life of a Christian. She desired more than perhaps anything to live a godly life, pleasing to God and was passionate to train her children up in the way that they should go. She was born as **Susanna Annesley**, was the daughter of Dr. Samuel Annesley and Mary White, and the mother of John and Charles Wesley. One of the major impacting factors for John Wesley was his mother Susanna Wesley. Susanna Wesley was the 25th of 25 children.

Her father, Dr. Samuel Annesley, was a dissenter of the established church of England. At the age of 13, Susanna stopped attending her father's church and joined the official Church of England. She and Samuel Wesley were married on 11 November, 1688. Samuel was 26 and Susanna was 19. Ten of the 19 kids born to Susanna Wesley survived infancy and she was the sole responsible person for their education. She had refused to send them to the local schoolmaster, John Hollan because she felt he was not fit and incompetent. Her servants did the house work while she taught the ten children on regular school day schedule.[81] The frequent absences of her husband on church business left the management of the household in her hands. The village was often cut off by floods and communication with the outside world was the exception.

[81] Wesley Tracy, "Christian Education in the Wesleyan Mode", In *Wesleyan Theological Journal* 17/1 (March, 1982): 44.

3.1.1 Educating Children

Susanna ran a strict, ordered household and homeschooled all of her children. She knew Latin, Greek, and French (most likely) as well as philosophy and politics. She taught her children for six hours a day (9am-12pm and 2-5pm) and each of her children began their schooling the day after their fifth birthday, with each child expected to learn the alphabet on their first day. Each week, she spent an hour with each child, to know them and their desires better and to talk with them about spiritual matters to direct each child's path. She also spent at least one hour a day in private prayer, often at the kitchen table with her apron pulled up over her head - a sure sign to her children not to disturb her.[82]

She had made her habit to talk with individual kids one evening a week separately. Thursday evening was devoted to John Wesley and he was so much blessed that he had asked his mother to pray for him on that day regularly. One of the good things what she did that she had developed by herself the text books for teaching children such as Exposition of the Apostles Creed, Exposition of the Ten Commandments and others.[83] Under no circumstances were the children permitted to have any lessons until they had reached their fifth year, but the day after their fifth birthday their formal education began. They attended classes for six hours and on the very first day they were supposed to learn the whole of the alphabet. All her children except two managed this feat, and these seemed to Susanna to be very backward. The children got a good education. Daughters included, they all learnt Latin and Greek and were well tutored in the classical studies that were traditional in England at that time.

Religious training began as early as possible. Even before they could kneel or speak, they were taught to be quiet at family prayers and to ask a blessing by signs. As soon as they could speak they repeated the Lord's Prayer morning and evening. A prayer for their parents, some collects, Catechism, and Scripture, were added as soon as they were able to learn them. No profane or rude words were ever heard in the Parsonage. The children were taught to ask quietly for what they wanted. Crying never won anything in this home. Confession of a fault always averted punishment, so that many temptations to falsehood were removed. The children were taught to fear the rod when they were only a year old and to cry softly. By this means the Epworth Parsonage, though full of children, was as quiet as if there had not been one in the house. As soon as possible, the little table and chairs were set near the family dinner-table, where they could be easily overlooked.

The children were taught to ask softly for anything they wanted and to eat whatever was provided for the family. As soon as they could handle a knife and fork

[82] Inspiring Women - Susanna Wesley, http://lizparnell.com/articles/64-womanhood-and-motherhood/247-inspiring-women-susanna-wesley (accessed on 22/07/16).

[83] Elmer E. Towns, ed., *A History of Religious Educator* (Grand Rapids: Baker Book House, 1975), 214.

they sat at the table with their parents. No eating or drinking between meals was allowed. Evening prayers were over at six o'clock. The children then had supper, and at seven o'clock were prepared for bed. First, the youngest was undressed and washed, then the rest in turn. All were in bed by eight. Mrs. Wesley's first care was to teach her children obedience. She knew that this was not only the way to rule well her large household, but also to secure the happiness of her boys and girls. "I insist," she says in her interesting letter, "upon conquering the will of children betimes, because this is the only strong and rational foundation of a religious education, without which both precept and example will be ineffectual. But when this is thoroughly done, then a child is capable of being governed by the reason and piety of its parents, till its own understanding comes to maturity, and the principles of religion have taken root in the mind." One result of this training was seen in times of illness. There was no difficulty in getting these model children to take even the most unpleasant medicine.[84]

There were certain guidelines put forth by Susanna Wesley for the kids to be followed such as : 1. Eating between meals not allowed. 2. As children they are to be in bed by 8 p.m. 3. They are required to take medicine without complaining. 4. Subdue self-will in a child, and those working together with God to save the child's soul. 5. To teach a child to pray as soon as he can speak. 6. Require all to be still during Family Worship. 7. Give them nothing that they cry for, and only that when asked for politely. 8. To prevent lying, punish no fault which is first confessed and repented of. 9. Never allow a sinful act to go unpunished. 10. Never punish a child twice for a single offense. 11. Comment and reward good behavior. 12. Any attempt to please, even if poorly performed, should be commended. 13. Preserve property rights, even in smallest matters.[85] During a time when her husband was in London, defending a friend against charges of heresy, he had appointed a locum to bring the message. The man's sermons revolved solely around repaying debts. The lack of diverse spiritual teaching caused Susanna to assemble her children Sunday afternoon for family services. They would sing a psalm and then Susanna would read a sermon from either her husband's or father's sermon file followed by another psalm. The local people began to ask if they could attend. At one point there were over two hundred people who would attend Susanna's Sunday afternoon service while the Sunday morning service dwindled to nearly nothing.[86] She loved the kids but at the same time disciplined them on time.

---

[84] John Telford, *The Life of John Wesley* (London: Charles H. Kelly, 1900), 29. media.sabda.orgalkitab-6wh3-refjt-tlow.pdf.

[85] H. G. Mithra, *Wesley's Philosophy of Education for Socio-Spiritual Change*, 51. See also http://www.raisinggodlychildren.org/2011/03/16-house-rules-by-susannah-wesley-john-wesleys-mom.html#sthash.tRjXByNj.dpuf (accessed on 22/07/16).

[86] Ingvar Haddal, *John Wesley* (New York: Abingdon Press, 1961), 14.

3.1.2 Strong and Highly Committed

Susanna exhibited early the independence of thought and action which characterized her throughout her life. Despite the dedicated and sacrificial commitment to the Dissenting tradition shown by her father, Susanna made the decision at the age of thirteen to step away from her family's identification and return, on her own, to communion with the Church of England.[87] Susanna, who was wise, educated at home and beautiful, married a minister of the Church of England, Samuel Wesley when she was just 19 years old. Her life was filled with struggles that sadden my heart yet her resilience and dedication to both God and her family are an incredible inspiration. Her family was plagued by financial troubles *her entire life*. This was not due to any frivolous spending or extravagance on the part of the Wesley's. The life of a clergyman was a meager living at best and with 10 children to feed and clothe, the Wesley's seemed always to be in want. One of the prayer of Susanna Wesley was, "Help me, Lord, to remember that religion (Christianity) is not to be confined to the church, nor exercised only in prayer and meditation, but that everywhere I am in Thy Presence." Susanna continued to speak into the lives of her children until her dying day on all matters of faith, theology and personal relationships.

She corresponded frequently and often at great length, her seventy-three extant letters (most of them to her sons) revealing an active interest in theological issues as well as in family concerns. She also composed three pieces of religious instruction: an exposition of the Apostles' Creed, an incomplete commentary on the Decalogue, and a dialogue on natural and revealed religion—all for the use of her children, particularly the girls. Her devotional journal, filled with the results of her thrice-daily periods of meditation, usually consists of spiritual self-examination but occasionally reflects on a book she has been reading.[88] We find in her letters, journals, and other writings that she was a serious, highly intellectual woman with strong, developed opinions which played a profound role in an age in which women were not given an equal voice with Men. Charles Wallace opined that it was a deeply formed sense of self; a Puritan self-understanding that ultimately values foe individual and empowers her when in conflict with 'the world,' however, at might be construed.[89]

It is not surprising that Susanna's letters to John are the most abundant of all that have been preserved. Throughout her letters she shows the same quality of affection and deep interaction that she reveals in her letters to Charles and Samuel. Indeed, Susanna was willing to engage in theological contemplation with her son,

---

[87] Charles Wallace, Jr., ed., *Susanna Wesley: The Complete Writings* (New York: Oxford University Press, 1997), 71.

[88] Charles Wallace Jr., "Some Stated employment of your mind: reading, writing and religion in the life of Susanna Wesley," *Church History*, 58/3 (September, 1989): 355.

[89] Charles Wallace, Jr., "Susanna Wesley's Spirituality: The Freedom of a Christian Woman," *Methodist History* 22/3 (1984): 158-163.

interacting with him about readings in spirituality and theology John was curious about his mother's opinions on topics, affirmed that she knew it well.[90] She died on July 23, 1742 and was buried in London's Bunhill Fields, where John Bunyan and Isaac Watts are also buried. Susanna Wesley was a woman of her age. She is known as a wife and mother, a wife to an oft-tempestuous pastor and a mother to significantly more children than is common in our era. She handled both of these roles with patience and perseverance. Susanna has served as a decisive if not always prominent p art o f Wesley studies. It is for this reason that Susanna should be further studied for who she actually was and how she thought, as a real person, not as a caricature. She was, in m any ways, a conventional woman of her age but, in m any other ways; she was an extraordinary woman unique to her age. She was extremely well read and showed continued evidence of intellectual engagement with main key thinkers of that time, whether in philosophy or religion. Her letters show both foe evidence of her learning and her tendency toward intellectual sparring, not for its own sake but as a way of better determining the truth about God and life.

3.2 The Aldersgate Experience

The High Church background along with Puritans influences had raised many questions within John Wesley. His desire for assurance of salvation became an obsession. From the early age John Wesley was reminded of the result of sin. It was simply that Wesley did not want to die a sinner he had great fear about this. Some of his fears were cleared in his stay at Chapterhouse where he became well acquainted with death in the infirmary. He was always reminded that he was a sinner and mortal. Although he was not a blatant sinner, at the same time he was also not a saint.[91] His religious conversion was brought forth by the influences he had in his life. Wesley was looking for the assurance the inward witness. His religious experience had revived his fear of death. The change of heart in 1725 was a religious conversion which later on leads for the Aldersgate experience. John Wesley wanted to clean himself so that God might love him. Wesley had to wait for thirteen years for another touch of God after which he let aside all pretention of self righteousness in order to follow naked, the naked Jesus. God then breathed into John Wesley the spirit of new life and the great revival was on.

Prior to Aldersgate, Wesley's primarily concern was with imitating the suffering of Christ. He stressed the incarnation not the cross, as the main focal point of Christianity. He emphasized man's reconciliation to God, Not God's reconciliation to man. After Aldersgate experience he emphasized the victorious Christ and cross as atonement of sin. The difference in thinking could be very clearly seen in his sermons before and after Aldersgate experience. John Wesley was

---

[90] Charles Wallace Jr., "Some Stated employment of your mind: reading, writing and religion in the life of Susanna Wesley," 354-356.

[91] Robert G. Tuttle, *John Wesley His Life and Theology*, 74-75.

fully changed and after this experience he was a different person. The Aldersgate experience shows the complete spiritual reconstruction. Wesley returned to England in deep spiritual dejection, which our fathers would probably have called "conviction for sin," though he was certainly no sinner if the term implies moral wrong doing. But he reproached himself over and over again, declaring that he was "carnal sold under sin," in a "vile abject state of bondage to sin," and "altogether corrupt and abominable."[92]

In London he came into contact with a group of Moravians under the leadership of Peter Bohler. Bohler impressed on him his need of a strong personal faith in Jesus Christ that would enable him to overcome sin and attain true holiness. John Wesley had long known of the doctrine of justification by faith but had considered it pure doctrine rather than a personal experience of God's forgiveness. On May 24th, 1738 at their Moravians meetings at Aldersgate Street rooms he was suddenly and wonderfully converted. As he placed his trust in Christ and received assurance that his sins were forgiven, he experienced at last the peace he had been striving for all those years.[93] To the experience about which he wrote what are perhaps his most famous words: "In the evening I went very unwillingly to a society in Aldersgate Street, where one was reading Luther's preface to the Epistle to the Romans. About a quarter before nine, while he was describing the change which God works in the heart through faith in Christ, I felt my heart strangely warmed. I felt that I did trust in Christ, Christ alone for salvation, and an assurance was given me, that he had taken away my sins, even mine, and saved me from the law of sin and death."

It was the watershed of Wesley's whole career and it gave him charter and compass for a course from which he never deviated. Even more, it gave him the spiritual energy for his pilgrim's progress, so that never again was he Christian with a burden on his back. Until his dying day Wesley dated his experience, his message, and his doctrine back to this date of 1738. Daniel L. Burnett writes: "The significance of Wesley's Aldersgate Experience is monumental. It is the fundamental point in his life and the Methodist movement. Without it the names of Wesley and Methodism would likely be nothing more than obscure footnotes in the pages of church history."[94]

Although Aldersgate was inevitable, it was also absolutely necessary for John Wesley both as Christian and as an evangelist. Aldersgate experience made him more useful and active. Aldersgate made John Wesley a Christian in the full sense of the word and directed his hold on the needs of the people. Aldersgate experience was necessary for the revival because without which he would have not known things apart from himself. Aldersgate was not only necessary for him

---

[92] Maldwyn L. Edwards, *John Wesley,* httpwww.enterhisrest.orghistorybio_john_wesley.pdf (accessed on 01/08/16).

[93] Bruce L Shelley, *Church History in Plain Language* (Dallas: Word Publishing, 1995), 335.

[94] Frederick A. Dreyer, *The Genesis of Methodism* (Pennsylvania: Lehigh University Press, 1999), 27.

personally, but for his ministry among people also. Wesley for thirteen years tried to find peace but he was not fully at the receiver end. Reason alone could not help him to have the assurance of faith. His High Church tradition was also of little help which meant means of grace of alone. Even the mystic's ideology could not help much (internal works-righteousness alone). With all these experiences he was ready for a change. John Wesley was tossed by various winds of doctrine. His attachment with Moravians and introduction with Peter Bohler are important for his evangelical conversion. The background to Aldersagte experience was laid by Peter Bohler and his discussion with Wesley. He accepted justification by faith and retained holiness and perfection as the end of religion. Now he was able to understand faith in the evangelical reform sense. Salvation and faith presumed God's initiative. By 1725 Wesley craved for holiness which was fulfilled only through faith in Christ. Aldersgate linked his understanding of work of the Holy Spirit to God through justification by faith. Wesley prior to Aldersgate, had no power, no peace, no joy, no heart, no expectation to see God at work among people. But after that all changed and God touched and life ignited.

3.2.1 John Amos Comenius (1592-1670)

Jan Amos Komensky was born in Nivnitz a village near western Moravia. Later he Latinized his name as it was the norm of the day to Comenius. After his studies in Europe he had come back to Moravia where he taught and became the bishop of Moravian Brethren. He was a Christian educator par excellence. He is also accreted with many books. John Wesley had visited Herrnhut in Germany and saw Moravian schools in action. It may be noted that John Wesley would have taken some principles from the writings of Comenius which was The Great Didactic. **John Locke (1632-1704) :** He was an English philosopher and educator who had influenced Wesley. He hailed from the materialistic rationalism.[95] For him, individual's consciousness is both the source and the criterion of all truths. Many writings of John Wesley are writings which shows some similarities that he was influenced by Locke.

3.3 George Whitefield (1714-1770)

George Whitefield was born in Southgate Street, Gloucester, England. The youngest of seven children, he was born in the Bell Inn where his father, Thomas Whitefield and Elizabeth Edwards, was a wine merchant and innkeeper. His father died when George was two and his widowed mother Elizabeth struggled to provide for her family. Eight years later, Whitefield's mother married a second time. Hard times forced young Whitefield to leave school for a short period to serve as a "common drawer" at the bar of the Bell Inn and to assist in duties there. During his years at the Free Grammar School of Gloucester he had "won a name for himself through his prowess in elocution and recitation." Whitefield,

[95] C. B. Eavey, *History of Christian Education* (Chicago: Moody Press, 1966), 167.

therefore, as a youth of some ability, was not to be kept from his education. At about the age of seventeen "he paid a visit to an elder brother in Bristol, when he heard the sermon which first awoke his soul to serious thought for God."[96]

As he thought he would never make much use of his education, at about age 15 George persuaded his mother to let him leave school and work in the inn. In 1732 at age 17, George entered Pembroke College at Oxford. He was gradually drawn into a group called the "Holy Club" where he met John and Charles Wesley.[97] At an early age, he found that he had a passion and talent for acting in the theatre, a passion that he would carry on with the very theatrical re-enactments of Bible stories he told during his sermons. It is said that he often skipped school to practice for his schoolboy performances. He was educated at the Crypt School, Gloucester, and Pembroke College, Oxford. As his business at the inn had become poor, Whitefield did not have the means to pay for his tuition. He therefore entered Oxford as a helper, the lowest rank of students at Oxford. In return for free tuition, he was assigned as a minister to a number of higher ranked students. His duties included teaching them in the morning, helping them bathe, taking out their garbage.[98] Forced to leave school because of poor health, George returned home for nine months of recuperation. Far from idle, his activity attracted the attention of the bishop of Gloucester, who ordained Whitefield as a deacon, and later as a priest, in the Church of England. Whitefield finished his degree at Oxford and on June 20, 1736, Bishop Benson ordained him. The Bishop, placing his hands upon George's head, resulted in George's later declaration that "My heart was melted down and I offered my whole spirit, soul, and body to the service of God's sanctuary." During his years at Oxford, Whitefield met Charles and John Wesley and was exposed to their seriousness of commitment. He was particularly moved by a small book loaned to him by Charles Wesley entitled *The Life of God in the Soul of Man,* written by Henry Scougal. While reading it he realized that union with God "meant that he must be a new creature." But it was not until he read a book by Joseph Hall entitled *Contemplations on the New Testament* that he experienced in his own life that keynote message of his later preaching—that is, that man is justified before God not by works but by faith.[99]

Whitefield was an astounding preacher from the beginning. Though he was slender in build, he stormed in the pulpit as if he were a giant. Within a year it was said that "his voice startled England like a trumpet blast." At a time when London had a population of less than 700,000, he could hold spellbound 20,000 people at a time at Moorfields and Kennington Common. For thirty-four years his preaching resounded throughout England and America. In his preaching ministry

---

[96] M. L. Loane, *Oxford and the Evangelical Succession* (London: Butterworth, 1950), 19.

[97] http://www.ccel.org/ccel/whitefield (accessed on 29/08/16).

[98] https://en.wikipedia.org/wiki/George_Whitefield (accessed on 29/08/16).

[99] J. Pollock, *George Whitefield and the Great Awakening* (New York: Doubleday, 1972), 17-19.

he crossed the Atlantic thirteen times and became known as the 'apostle of the British empire.'[100] Late 1736 and early 1737 saw the rise of Whitefield's popularity as he preached as often as five times each week while he anxiously waited to be taken to his American parish. It was during these early months of Whitefield's preaching ministry that he began to pray and preach extemporaneously.[101] He says that Whitefield had an early affinity for the stage, and as a result of this influence, he 'became an actor-preacher' who 'produced a new philosophy of preaching' that 'adopted the assumptions of the actor. 'Whitefield wanted to be a star, and the particular egotistical self-promotion he displayed in his career was very much in the manner of the great actor.' Stout sees in Whitefield the 'protomodern figure,' who exploited new media and the marketplace mentality, and he anticipates modern evangelists, particularly those in the 'electronic church.'[102]

3.3.1 George Whitefield's Evangelistic Endeavor

Whitefield preached his first sermon at St. Mary de Crypt Church in his home town of Gloucester, a week after his ordination. In 1738 he went to Savannah, Georgia, in the American colonies, as parish priest. While there he decided that one of the great needs of the area was an orphan house. He decided this would be his life's work. He returned to England to raise funds, as well as to receive priest's orders. While preparing for his return he preached to large congregations. At the suggestion of friends he preached to the miners of Kingswood, outside Bristol, in the open air. His contemporary Augustus Toplady (1740–1778) remembered him as "the apostle of the English Empire." He was Anglo America's most popular eighteenth-century preacher and its first truly mass revivalist.[103] Whitefield was a gifted preacher with a golden voice. He could make people faint when he pronounced "Mesopotamia."

The newspapers made fun of him, because of his crossed eyes. During Whitefield's second trip to the North American colonies, he began preaching in all the colonies, from north to south. All together, Whitefield made 7 trips to North America. He died on the 7th trip and is buried in Newburyport, Massachusetts (USA). He had a powerful and beautiful voice. People could hear him without a PA system. Whitefield was the main international instrument of God in the first Great Awakening. No one else in the 18th century was anointed like this in America and England and Wales and Scotland and Ireland. The impact of George Whitefield, the Wesley's, and the Great Awakening in England changed the face of the nation. He never went through a sermon without weeping sometimes

[100] Harry S. Stout, *The Divine Dramatist: George Whitfield and the Rise of Modern Evangelicalism* (Grand Rapids: Eerdmans, 1991), 59.

[101] J. Pollock, *George Whitefield and the Great Awakening,* 42.

[102] Harry S. Stout, *The Divine Dramatist: George Whitefield and the Rise of Modem Evangelicalism* (Grand Rapids: Eerdmans, 1991), xix-xxiii.

[103] J. Pollock, *George Whitefield and the Great Awakening,* 42.

he exceedingly wept, stamped loudly and passionately, and was frequently so overcome, that, for a few seconds.[104] There is no disagreement that God uses ***natural*** vessels to display his ***supernatural*** reality. And there is no disagreement that George Whitefield was a stunning natural vessel. He was driven, affable, eloquent, intelligent, empathetic, single-minded, steel-willed, venturesome, and had a voice like a trumpet that could be heard by thousands outdoors — and sometimes at a distance of three kilometers.

He was a firm Calvinist in his theology yet unrivaled as an aggressive evangelist. Though a clergyman of the Church of England, he cooperated with and had a profound impact on people and churches of many traditions, including Presbyterians, Congregationalists, and Baptists. Whitefield, along with the Wesley's, inspired the movement that became known as the Methodists. Whitefield preached more than 18,000 sermons in his lifetime, an average of 500 a year or ten a week.[105] In 1740, for over a month he preached almost every day in New England to crowds up to 8,000 people. That was when the population of Boston, the largest city in the region, was not much larger than that.[106] It is also said that there were times when he preached to the crowd of 20,000 or even more.[107] He was extremely a man of one thing, who was engaged always about his Master's business. From Sunday mornings to Saturday nights, from 1 January to 31 December, except only when he was sick, he was almost incessantly preaching Christ and going about the world entreating men to repent and come to Christ and be saved.

Whitefield accepted the Church of England's doctrine of predestination and disagreed with the Wesley brothers' views on the doctrine of the Atonement. He regularly preached in the open air before spellbound crowds of 10,000 even 30,000. He did these 40 to 60 hours per week, given to quantity of sermons preached, the masses of people who heard and responded to his message, tile wide variety of his popular appeal, and the single-mindedness of his evangelistic purse, Whitefield stands as one of the pre-eminent evangelists in the history of the Christian church.[108]

The Anglican Church did not assign him a pulpit, so he began preaching in parks and fields in England on his own, reaching out to people who normally did

---

[104] Harry S. Stout, *The Divine Dramatist: George Whitfield and the Rise of Modern Evangelicalism*, 41.

[105] Arnold Dallimore, *George Whitefield: The Life and Times of the Great Evangelist of the Eighteenth-Century Revival,* Vol. 2 (Westchester, Illinois: Cornerstone Books, 1979), 522.

[106] Mark Noll, *The Old Religion in a New World: The History of North American Christianity* (Grand Rapids: Eerdmans, 2002), 52.

[107] Michael A. G. Haykin, ed., *The Revived Puritan: The Spirituality of George Whitefield* (Dundas, Ontario: Joshua Press, 2000), 32-33.

[108] David Crump, "The Preaching of George Whitefeild and his use of the Mathew Henry's Commentary," *Crux* 25/3 (September, 1989): 19.

not attend church. Like Jonathan Edwards, he developed a style of preaching that raised emotional responses from his audiences. His success in communicating to the young and poorly educated as well as the rich and prestigious was due, at least in part, to his ability to simplify his message. But Whitefield had charisma, and his voice his small stature, and even his cross-eyed appearance all served to help make him one of the first celebrities in the American colonies. Although, Whitefield did not invent the concept of the new birth, he constructed his own meaning of the conversion process proclaiming that salvation transcended traditional church boundaries.[109] The open-air preaching of Whitefield allowed more people to hear the gospel than any other means in the eighteenth century would have permitted. Crawford opines that Whitefield was an evangelist with an extraordinary call to preach to all who would listen. Instead of leading to religious awakening and moral reformation a specific community over which he exercised recognized spiritual authority, he traveled from place to place, seeking to transform the entire nation. The phenomena associated with the Methodist revival were the itinerant preacher, large outdoor religious gatherings, and the organization of the awakened into religious societies.[110]

3.3.2 Evangelical Movement

The religious impulses lay behind the evangelical movement that was born in English Christianity during the 1730's when John and Charles Wesley drew closer at Oxford University, the company of students scornfully labeled "Methodists" One was the Anglican morals that Started John Wesley on his spiritual pilgrimage. Inspired by his parents, particularly his mother Susanna, Wesley soon concluded that the call to righteousness that pervades the Old and the New Testaments was the central theme of Scripture. He read such works as Jeremy Taylor's *Holy Living* and *Holy Dying* and William Law's *Plain and Serious Call to a Devout and Holy Life.* And he set out in earnest to find by God's grace that "holiness", without which no man shall see the Lord.

The second inclination was the persisting force of Puritanism, the English version of Calvinism that in the preceding century had turned the nation first to prayer and then to political revolution. The Puritan movement subsided with the restoration of the Stuart monarchy in 1660, and the crowning of William and Mary twenty-eight years later reinforced the growing aversion to all forms of intense piety. But in Presbyterian Scotland and among the dissenting Baptists, Presbyterians, and Congregationalists of England and America Puritan fervor and moral seriousness persisted. Meanwhile, George Fox's Society of Friends propagated on both sides of the Atlantic their radical commitment to moral

---

[109] Jerome Dean Mahaffey, "George Whitefield Homiletic Art: Neo-sophism in the Great Awakening," *Homiletic,* 31/1 (April-May, 2006): 13.

[110] Michael Crawford, *Seasons of Grace: Colonial New England's Revival Tradition in Its British Context* (New York and Oxford: Oxford University Press, 1991), 165.

discipline and their belief that the light of Christ, usually identified with the Holy Spirit, awakened the conscience, or "seed," that remained alive in fallen human hearts. The third inclination stemmed from German Pietism. This movement of prayer, Bible study, and corporate discipline brought laypersons and pastors into hundreds of local associations that were intent on renewing the spiritual life of the established Lutheran or Calvinist churches.[111]

[111] Timothy L. Smith, "George Whitefield and Wesleyan Perfectionism," *Wesleyan Theological Journal*, 19/1 (March-April, 1984): 63.

Chapter 4

Theology of John Wesley

Kenneth J. Collins argues that Wesley crafted a theology that was extremely practical and organized around the Order of Salvation (*Ordo Salutis).* The order of salvation is a theological term outlining God working in the process of salvation that liberates man from sin. It makes sense that the theology of Methodism's founder would emerge into a practical and invitational construct, since Wesley's mission was a powerful evangelical revival in conflict with a nominal folk Christianity that infected much of eighteenth century England.[112] Drawing the relation between the suffering servant of Isaiah 53 and Christ, Wesley reveals that at Calvary, the lamb of God bore 'those punishments by which our peace, our reconciliation to God, was to be purchased. John Wesley's views on justifying faith depicted Martin Luther and John Calvin understanding. Wesley's own new birth experience occurred at Aldersgate in 1738 while listening to a reading of Luther's preface of the Epistle to the Romans.

4.1 The Understanding of Scripture

The Bible is Wesley's constant and ultimate source of knowledge and authority. His credo that "I am a man of one book" is seen throughout his sermons. John Wesley sees scripture alone as the authority for Christian faith and practice. Revelation: in Wesley's understanding revelation is a communication of divine message from God to God's chosen messengers, prophets, evangelists and apostles. Wesley tries to minimize the contribution of human efforts in this process. He almost comes close to the dictation theory of revelation in his discussions. He believed that scripture is free from error (infallibility). The scripture are God's testimony and therefore, they are without error. Thus, scripture alone need to determine

[112] Ray Nothstine, "The Theology of John Wesley", http://www.acton.org/pub/religion-liberty/volume-18-number-2/theology-john-wesley (accessed on 05/09/16).

Christian teaching. Scriptures are source of truth as well as norm for the truth.[113] While Wesley held to the authority of Scripture alone, Scripture did not stand alone, but was held in tension with four other factors: reason, Christian antiquity, the Church of England, and experience.

Each particular text of scripture is best read in the light of other correlated passages. Scripture is the best expounder of scripture. Scripture interprets scripture. The church needs to be judged by scripture, not the scripture by the church. The scriptures are the touchstone where Christians examine all real or supposed revelations.[114] Scripture remains forever and the Old and the New Testament is most solid and precious system of divine truth. It is the fountain of heavenly wisdom.[115] The Bible is not written by good people or the bad people but it is breathed out as God's own Word. It is given by divine inspiration. On corrupting the scripture he writes that: the corrupters are predisposed to blend scripture with political interests, economic motives who dilute the word of God either with errors of others or fancies of their brain. Sometime they pervert the sense of scripture by taking it out of context. They also try to reduce certain norms of the scripture.[116]

Wesley set forth five constituent elements of serious meditation of scripture such as:-

1. Setting apart a set time for daily scripture study
2. Read the Hebrew Bible in relation to New Testament. Reading both with single eye to know the whole will of God.
3. Have a constant eye to the analogy of faith where we find relationship with original sin and justification by faith, new birth and others.
4. Reading of scripture should be surrounded by prayer
5. Pause frequently for honest self examination.[117]

Wesley never preached from the apocrypha, even though it was included in the KJV during his time. The Wesley's (John and Charles) utilized a number of translations, including: the Geneva Bible, Luther's German Bible, and others. The Wesley's studied the Greek and Hebrew texts, they considered the primary languages more authoritative than the KJV. Wesley firmly held that scripture was inspired, however, he believed that it was not always exact on "tangential

---

[113] Scott J. Jones, *John Wesley's Conception and Use of Scripture* (Nashville: Abingdon Press, 1995), 34-38.

[114] Thomas C. Oden, *John Wesley's Scriptural Christianity: A Plain Exposition of his Teaching on Christian Doctrine* (Michigan: Zondervan Publishing House, 1994), 58.

[115] Robert W. Burtner & Robert E. Chiles, eds., *John Wesley's Theology* (Nashville: Abingdon Press, 1982), 18.

[116] Thomas C. Oden, *John Wesley's Scriptural Christianity: A Plain Exposition of his Teaching on Christina Doctrine*, 63. Cf., also Robert W. Burtner & Robert E. Chiles, eds., *John Wesley's Theology*, 22.

[117] Ibid., 60.

matters" (genealogies, for example). Wesley argued that the Bible was "infallibly true." The word "inerrancy" was not in use in his time. Wesley believed that the inspiration of the Holy Spirit was key to understanding the Bible. "We need the same Spirit to understand the Scripture which enabled the holy men of old to write it." Wesley preached nearly the entire Biblical canon, including extensive Old Testament preaching. There are records that show he preached from all books except: Esther, Song of Songs, Obadiah, Nahum, Zephaniah, Philemon, and 3 John. Wesley read the Bible in conference with others. "If any doubt still remains (understanding a difficult passage)." Wesley valued the writings of early Christian writers, particularly those of the first three centuries of the church.[118] He is known as the man of one book. He himself asserted that, "My ground is the Bible. Yea I am Bible-bigot. I follow it in all things, both great and small."[119] The Christian rule of right and wrong is the Word of God, the writings of the Old and New Testament. Wesley read the Bible in conference with the "Rule of Faith." He held strongly to the Apostle's Creed. What the historical church had spoken on certain matters (such as the Trinity) was important in his thinking.

Wesley focused on the value and nature of creation. He believed that God wanted to redeem all of creation. Wesley was convinced that God's love for all of humanity was the central teaching of scripture. He described 1 John 4:19 as "the sum of the whole gospel." We love him because he first loved us. He called First John "the compendium of all the Holy Scriptures." He also frequently referred to Psalm 145:9. The Lord loves to all, and his mercy is over all his works. Wesley's favorite passages (as evidenced by the frequency he preached from them) were the book of First John, the book of Romans, 1 Corinthians 13, and Matthew 5-7 (The Sermon on the Mount). Wesley read the Bible because it was the guide to Christian belief, the guide to Christian behavior, and hope and sustenance for the believer.

Wesley recognized that readers often labor to understand particular scriptures, and that a central resource is consulting other parts (or books) of the one Book. He encouraged his followers to read a portion of ***both*** Testaments each morning and evening, rather than confining themselves to favored portions of Scripture. He also modeled conferring with the whole Bible. One commitment that Wesley's Anglican upbringing nurtured was a higher emphasis than in some other Protestant circles for studying God's revelation in the natural world (the "book of nature") alongside of studying Scripture. Wesley's central interest in studying the natural world was to strengthen the faith awakened by Scripture and deepen our appreciation of God's power, wisdom, and goodness.[120] Wesley believed, first of all, that the living core of the Christian faith was revealed in "scripture" as the sole

[118] Randy Maddox, "The Rule of Christian Faith, Practice, and Hope: John Wesley on the Bible," *Methodist Review,* 3 (2011): 1-3.

[119] Robert W. Burtner & Robert E. Chiles, eds., *John Wesley's Theology,* 20.

[120] http://www.catalystresources.org/how-john-wesley-read-the-bible/ (accessed on 06/09/16).

foundational source. The centrality of scripture was so important for Wesley that he called himself "a man of one book." However, doctrine had to be in keeping with Christian orthodox "tradition." So, tradition became in his view the second aspect of the so-called diamond. Furthermore, believing, as he did, that faith is more than merely an acknowledgment of ideas, Wesley as a practical theologian, contended that a part of the theological method would involve "experiential" faith. In other words, truth would be verified in personal experience of Christians (over all, not individually), if it were really truth.[121]

Tradition, experience, and reason, however, are subject always to scripture, each of the "legs" of the Wesleyan Quadrilateral must be taken in balance, and none of the other three apart from scripture should be viewed as being of equal value or authority with scripture. None of these should be taken in isolation without the balancing effect of the others, and always Scripture should have the central place of authority. Wesley insisted that scripture is the first authority and contains the only measure whereby all other truth is tested. It was delivered by authors who were divinely inspired. It is a rule sufficient of itself. It neither needs, nor is capable of, any further addition. It would take a high view of the authority and inspiration of Scripture, within that contending for reliable access to divine revelation. It would foster a ready use of all relevant approaches to knowledge outside of Scripture, correlating them with Scripture. It would seek out the whole message of Scripture, focusing on its soteriological content. It would use the best critical tools. And it would aim at articulating the understanding of the whole Christian church.[122]

4.2 The Understanding of Human being

Human being is said to be creature that uses language to convey ideas. By means of rational language he can and does communicate with other creatures. He is also capable of entering into a meaningful dialogue. Man made in the image of God seems to refer that he experiences any communication, to establish a rapport with God or even to reject that fellowship.[123] Wesley's doctrine of man receives full meaning when seen in its relation to salvation. The image of God which is defaced by sin is restored by the redemptive process. Wesley distinguishes between the guilt of sin, which is forgiven in justification and the depravity or power of sin which is removed in sanctification.

Wesley's Theology of Man made in the image of God becomes clearer only when it is understood in terms of his describing man's total depravity and its effects upon man in God's presence. Although, fall of man have many good

[121] Donald A. D. Thorsen, *The Wesleyan Quadrilateral: Scripture, Tradition, Reason & Experience as a Model of Evangelical Theology* (Nappanee, Indiana: Francis Asbury Press, 1997), 127.

[122] William J. Abraham, "John Wesley's Conception and Use of Scripture," *Wesleyan Theological Journal* 33/1 (Spring, 1998): 7-8.

[123] Mildred Bangs Wynkoop, *A Theology of Love: The Dynamism of Wesleyanism,* 104-105.

natural gifts to perform all possible good deeds, while standing face to face in God's presence he has nothing to plead. Man is totally helpless before God. This dimension is clearly stated by Wesley, although the fall of man affects the total loss of the moral image but the natural image is still retained. He further interprets such original righteousness in term of man's relationship to God. According to Wesley the true image of God is that ...man was God's vicegerent upon earth, the prince and governor of this lower world; all the blessings of God flowed through him to the inferior creatures... man is capable of God; the inferior creators are not. Despite his fallen nature, man has a capacity to desire and know God only because he is created in order to have a personal relationship with his Creator. So, then, the meaning of the fall of man is that he is separated or fallen away from such relationship, which utterly marred the meaning of his existence. In general, the image of God in man is not completely ruined.

4.2.1 The Image of God

In the image of God man was made holy, merciful and perfect. God made him to be image of his eternity, an incorruptible picture of his glory. Let us make man in our image, after our likeness. So God created man in his own image, in the image of God created him:" (Gen. 1:26, 27) -- Not barely in his *natural image,* a picture of his own immortality; a spiritual being, endued with understanding, freedom of will, and various affections; -- nor merely in his *political image,* the governor of this lower world, having "dominion over the fishes of the sea, and over all the earth;" -- but chiefly in his *moral image;* which, according to the Apostle, is "righteousness and true holiness." (Eph. 4:24) in this image of God was manmade. "God is love:" Accordingly, man at his creation was full of love; which was the sole principle of all his tempers, thoughts, words, and actions. God is full of justice, mercy, and truth; so was man as he came from the hands of his Creator. God is spotless purity; and so man was in the beginning pure from every sinful blot; otherwise God could not have pronounced him, as well as all the other work of his hands, "very good."[124]

He was expected to be as pure as God was pure. He was away from sin and inwardly as well as outwardly sinless and undefiled. He loved the God with all his heart, mind, soul and strength. He was given the perfect law to be obeyed and no allowance was made for any falling short. He was induced with a will, liberty or freedom of choice without which that could just a piece of marble.[125] He chose to do his own will, rather than the will of his creator. He was not deceived, but knowingly and deliberately rebelled against his Father and King. In this moment he lost the moral image of God and in part the natural. Wesley argues, And God, "the three-one God," said; "Let us make man in our image, after our

[124] Kenneth J. Collins & Jason E. Vickers, eds., *The Sermons of John Wesley: A Collection for the Christian Journey*, The New Birth (Nashville: Abingdon Press, 2013), 157.

[125] Robert W. Burtner & Robert E. Chiles, eds., *John Wesley's Theology,* 109-110.

likeness. So God created man in his own image," (Gen. 1:26,27): not barely in his natural image, a picture of His own immortality; a spiritual being, endued with understanding, freedom of will, and various affections; nor merely in his political image, the government of this owner world, having "dominion over the fishes of the sea, and over all the earth": but chiefly in his moral image: which, according to the Apostle, is "righteousness and true holiness." Wesley understands of man and his relationship with both God and fellow being has serious implications due to the fall. Since his mind had been corrupted, the works of his hands were also corrupt and failed to honor his creator.[126]

4.2.1.1 John Wesley's Sermon on the Image of God

This sermon on the image of God is said to be first of his sermon because it was his first University sermon preached at St. Mary on Nov. 15, 1730. The subject matter is Creation and talks about the salvation and thus is said to be first of its kind. In this sermon he lays basics of doctrine of humanity where human beings are seen as compound of matter and spirit. For Wesley image of God was as righteousness and true holiness. Wesley had seen the image of God in three ways: natural, political and moral images given more stress on the moral images. Humans are seen as having will and liberty. Human were given power to discern truth from falsehood. They were also bestowed with a perfect will and perfect freedom which ultimately seen as ultimate happiness. Wesley raises the question that how human being lost their perfection? He says that liberty required some tests which lead for the true choice before human being. Adam ate the forbidden fruit which had many greater effects on him. The basic effect what we see was loosing of immortality. The understanding was destroyed and slowly ignorance began to increase. The perfect will which was given to human came under subjection of imperfection, anger and shame. The result of this subjugation leads for sadness and ultimately loosing peace.[127]

Later he himself raises the question that how human being could recover the previous status of freedom. He say that Jesus Christ who conquered over death the one who could again make us whole and restore us previous status. The very basic recovery that we become humble we know our status what we are and thus reforms our will and do charity in line with the word of god. Thus, the law of spirit allows human being free from the bondage of sin and death. He is having passion for the human being and would want the people know Christ personally and come back to him. He says who does not accept the invitation of Jesus is still under the bondage and is in sad condition. They need to be helped and allowed to come out of that condition. He talks about the responsibility of believers that they

[126] Joseph Basappa Suray, *Towards a Theology of Universality: John Wesley's Socio-Economic, Political & Moral Insights on British Class & Indian Caste Distinctions*, 150-151.

[127] Kenneth J. Collins & Jason E. Vickers, eds., *The Sermons of John Wesley: A Collection for the Christian Journey* (Nashville: Abingdon Press, 2013), 1-9.

should talk and preach about the Jesus Christ and let them see the love of Christ so that they could come to the fold of God and be restored. In the light of this there are few questions brought forth such as: Is the image of God still distorted or recovered? Why after accepting Christ Christian leaders continue to do evil things and are hungry for power and wealth?

4.2.2 John Wesley's view on Fall

John Wesley viewed that "On the day he disobeyed he did die: he died to God, the most dreadful of all deaths. He lost the life of God and he was separated from him, in union with whom he lived before. He lost the knowledge and love of God both without which the image of God could not exist. He was deprived at the same time and became unholy and unhappy. Here, he had sunk into pride and self will which is the image of evil and into sensual appetites and desires."[128] Man's liberty included a power of choosing refusing either good or evil. By one Adam as being the representative of mankind sin entered into the world which was actual sin, its results and a sinful nature. By this death entered into the world but before this it did not entered. So death came upon all men even the infants were included. In the same way as sin as sin entered by one man so by one man's righteousness life entered into the earth. So life passed upon all men through second Adam by faith and in that all are justified. Adam's sin imputed to all mankind means: in Adam all die. Our bodies became mortal; our souls died which showed disunity from God. So whole humanity is born with sinful nature and we had become the children of wrath, liable to death eternal.[129] Paul A. Mickey affirms that Wesley believed in original sin, where humanity cannot save itself. It cannot experience the grace of God apart from divine initiatives… this pervasive curse of original sin not limited to only individual beings. It extends beyond each person, corrupting all social relations.[130]

4.2.3 The Concept of Free Will

Wesley understood free will as a fundamental aspect of humankind in God's creation he suggested that because of sin, free will was forcing man to continue disobey God in order to please himself. People deliberately decided to do evil rather than please God by doing good. His understanding of man as God's creature led Wesley to be concerned about the social evils that were barriers to the growth of human love.[131] This free will of man was used to gain prosperity at the expense of his fellow man. But Wesley emphasized that man, by having freedom,

---

[128] Mildred Bangs Wynkoop, *A Theology of Love: The Dynamism of Wesleyanism,* 107-108.

[129] Mildred Bangs Wynkoop, 117.

[130] Paul A. Mickey, *Essentials of Wesleyan Theology* (Michigan: Zondervan Publications, 1980), 83.

[131] Joseph Basappa Suray, *Towards a Theology of Universality: John Wesley's Socio-Economic, Political & Moral Insights on British Class & Indian Caste Distinctions,* 154.

could depart from selfishness and with total obedience dedicates to love God. Describing man as God's creature without any discrimination; Wesley emphasized his worth and dignity as equal throughout the human race. Wesley's concern was not only salvation for sinful man; he wanted to see human being redeemed from the unjust and degrading conditions of slavery. Wesley also noted that the whole of mankind had a special place and great value in the sight of God.

According to Wesley, Adam was created in the image of God; therefore, he reflected initially the perfect nature of his creator. Evidently, before his fall, man was in harmony with God in every respect. Man was the medium through whom God could reflect his own image. He was also considered to be the mirror, in which God's beauty was to be seen in its fullness. God's love accordingly, man at his creation was full of love; which was the sole principle of all his tempers, thoughts, words, and action. God is full of justice, mercy, and truth; so was man as he came from the hands of his Creator.[132] Christianity is essentially a social religion, and to turn it into a solitary religion is indeed to destroy it... that it cannot exist at all without society, without conversing with fellow being.[133] Wesley affirmed time and again that God, the creator cared for his creation, with eternal power. The love of God poured out in the heart produced love for God and for neighbor.

4.2.4 Understanding of Original and Actual Sins

Wesley understands that from the original sin comes up the actual sins which is clearly found in James 1:14. He also mentions Matthew. 15:19 where it says, "Out of the heart precede evil thoughts, murder, adulteries, fornications, thefts, false witness, and blasphemies." In his view actual sin proceeds from original, evil works from an evil heart. He also believes that from the branches of this tree only evil can come out and so the fruit also is the same of the tree.

4.2.4.1 Wesley's Sermon on Original Sin - (Gen. 6:5) 1749

Wesley had published one of the largest works on the doctrine of original sin in 1757. Wesley had taken up two basic thoughts of Augustinian doctrine of original sin which is Universality where all have sinned Rom. 3:23, and total depravity where all thoughts seems to be evil Gen. 6:5. It seems that Wesley would have followed Mathew Henry at some point which talks about bitter root and corrupt spring. In this sermon he begins with asking the question what are human beings like before the flood? Before the flood God saw that wickedness of man was great, he also saw the imagination all human heart and whole imagination human being heart was evil in nature.

He then goes on to ask that are the people same as before the flood? He goes back to the Bible and says that scripture gives us no reason to think that they

---

[132] Joseph Basappa Suray, 155.

[133] Philip S. Walson, *The Message of Wesley* (London: The Epworth Press, 1964), 188.

were good. The present plight of human being is very clearly seen in the daily experience of people.

When God opened the eyes of human being it was observed that we were helpless without God. Since we were having no knowledge of, we seemed to be having no love for God and no reverence for him. This also showed that we did not even have fear towards God. In this sense all the people of the world is in the state of being atheist. In their natural status they are born as idolater and all human races had developed pride among them which kept them away from God. Satan had put his own seal on our image and we had no more of our will to control because it was controlled by the Satan. People began loving their own will and world and thus ended up in the self praise. The people of other faiths are ignorant of the entire depravation of human being. All who deny the depravity of soul could be seen as heathens. God heals this depravity or ignorance or atheism by providing his knowledge through Jesus Christ. If there was no fall this would have been not needed.[134] The ultimate goal of religion is to get back to God and renew our hearts in the image of God. This is what recalled and challenged that renew our minds in the likeness of Christ. In present context can we talk about the concept of original sin when people are more of self active? Is workable or we talk about Christ and his grace to people of other faiths around the globe?

4.3 John Wesley's Understanding of Justification

Justification is an acquittal, an exoneration, a setting right, a correcting. Justification is unnecessary if there is nothing wrong, nothing off center, nothing out of balance in the first place. Thus, the study of John Wesley's doctrine of justification opens with a synopsis of his anthropology, in the light of The Human Problem. The good news from God for humans is that in Christ Jesus a way to become justified has been provided. At the heart of John Wesley's doctrine of salvation, "Justification by Faith" was a "landmark sermon" and one of the eight that he considered be the Christian church stands or falls with it. It is evident that justification in not being made actually just and righteous. This is sanctification which is indeed, in some degree, the immediate fruit of justification, but it is a distinct gift of God. The term justification in wider sense includes sanctification. It is to see that God esteems us better than we really are, or believes us righteous when we are unrighteous.[135] It was likely preached the first line on May 28, 1738, at the Long Acre Chapel in London and several years later on top of his father's tomb at Epworth on June 8, 1742, it did not appear in print until 1746. Wesley demonstrated the significant influence of both the English and continental Reformation on his thinking in this sermon by affirming that faith is the "only

[134] Kenneth J. Collins & Jason E. Vickers, eds., *The Sermons of John Wesley: A Collection for the Christian Journey*, 10-17.

[135] Robert W. Burtner & Robert E. Chiles, eds., *John Wesley's Theology*, 163.

necessary condition of justification and pointing that it is the glory of God's 'free grace' to justify the ungodly."[136]

4.3.1 John Wesley's view of Anthropology

John Wesley's doctrine of salvation is controlled by his doctrine of sin. He traces the necessity for the new birth back to the fall. The controlling concept is that of the image of God and the effects that sin had upon it. Wesley analyzed the image of God as comprising three aspects. The natural image was "a picture of His own immortality; a spiritual being, endued with understanding, freedom of the will, and various affections." The political image was man as governor of this world. Most important was the moral image; in Paul's words "righteousness and true holiness."[137] Thus, was man created "able to stand, and yet liable to fall." Fully warned of the consequences of disobedience to the Creator, Adam nonetheless willfully rebelled against his Sovereign. Adam chose to be governed by his own will rather than the will of God. "In that moment he lost the moral image of God, and, in part, the natural "("On the Fall of Man," II.6)." The natural consequence of this is, that every one descended from him comes into the world spiritually dead, dead to God, wholly dead in sin; entirely void of the life of God; void of the image of God, of all that righteousness and holiness wherein Adam was created. Instead of this, every man born into the world now bears the image of the devil, in pride and self-will; the image of the beast in sensual appetites and desires. This, then, is the foundation of the new birth—the entire corruption of our nature."[138]

Along with the idea of salvation justification by faith was his master piece. He viewed that God justifies not the righteous but ungodly who receives the seal of the Spirit. For Wesley the question how a sinner could be justified is of great importance because that is the heart of all but that has not been taken into serious considerations. He lays down the basic ground of justification by faith. He begins by telling that human were made in the image of God and were holy and perfect. He gave a perfect law and looked for obedience from human being. Very clearly it was told that 'don't eat the fruit of the tree.' Human beings were happy and holy in their original state but as soon as they disobeyed him they sinned and death entered into the world. In order to redeem the humanity he send his son and through the death of His son he reconciled the world to himself again. Being saved to Wesley implied that a sinner has been "saved (to comprise all in one word) from sin." Being saved from sin assumes what is generally thought of as "justification." Justification (taken in and of itself, apart from the rest of God's saving acts) occurs when a "sinful man find(s) favor with God." The sinful man

---

[136] Kenneth. J. Collins and Jason E. Vickers, eds., *The Sermon of John Wesley: A Collection for the Christian Journey*, 134.

[137] Kenneth. J. Collins and Jason E. Vickers, eds., The New Birth 1.1, 157.

[138] Kenneth. J. Collins and Jason E. Vickers, eds., The New Birth, 1.4, 158.

has been pardoned for all of his sins. "Justification," which taken in its *largest* sense, implies a deliverance from guilt and punishment, by the atonement of Christ actually applied to the soul of the sinner now believing in him, and a deliverance from the power of sin, through Christ "formed in his heart."[139]

John Wesley clearly speaks of Justification by faith saying, "By justifying faith I mean that faith which whosoever hath is not under the wrath and the curse of God. By a sense of pardon I mean a distinct, explicit assurance that my sins are forgiven. I allow: (1) that there is such an explicit assurance: (2) that it is the common privilege of real Christians; (3) that it is the proper Christian faith, which purifies the heart and overcomes the world. But I cannot allow that justifying faith is such an assurance, or necessarily connected therewith."[140] The sinner would continue in this state of conviction and repentance until God saw fit to grant him full justifying faith. At that point, the sinner has his eyes fully opened and truly "sees" God. He realizes that his sins are forgiven by the "testimony of God's Spirit." He has that inward assurance. He is now free to love God and he begins to see the fruits of being forgiven (faith, hope, and love). And thus, by the "witness of his own spirit" he has the assurance that he had been born from above. The sinner is now properly "saved," not only from the wrath of God, but more importantly (at least in Wesley's understanding) from the power of sin.[141]

4.3.2 General Ground of the Doctrine of Justification

In the image of God was human made; holy as he that created him is holy, merciful as the author of all is merciful, perfect as his Father in heaven is perfect. To the human this upright and perfect God gave a perfect law, to which he required full and perfect obedience, to the entire law of love which was written in his heart. Such then was the state of human in paradise. By the free, unmerited love of God he was holy and happy; he knew, love, enjoyed God, which is life everlasting. Human did disobey God, 'And in that day he was condemned by the righteous judgment of God. Being already dead in spirit, dead to God, dead in sin, he hastened on to death everlasting, to the destruction both of body and soul in the fire never to be quenched. In consideration of this as by the offence of one judgment come upon all human to condemnation, even so by the righteousness of the one the free gift come upon all human unto justification.' So that for the sake of his well-beloved Son, of what he hath done and suffered for us, God now vouchsafes on one only condition both to remit the punishment due to our sins,

---

[139] Albert C. Outler, ed., *The Works of John Wesley: Sermons,* Vol. 1 (Nashville: Abingdon Press, 1984), 121-124.

[140] Frank Baker, ed., *The Works of John Wesley, Letters,* Vol. 26 (Oxford: Clarendon Press, 1982), 254-5.

[141] Scott Thomas Kisker, "Justified but Unregenerate? The Relationship of Assurance to Justification and Regeneration in the thought of John Wesley". *Wesleyan Theological Journal,* 28/1 (March-May, 1993): 55.

to reinstate us in his favor, and to restore our dead souls to spiritual life, as the earnest of life eternal.[142]

The twin human problems of alienation from God and from other people are intransigent to human solution. The good news of the gospel of grace is that in Christ Jesus a solution has been provided: atonement is an historic fact; reconciliation is a potential reality, and restoration to the image of God is the gift and the goal for human beings. What we discern in Wesley's atonement theology is a distinction between objective and subjective aspects of the atonement. To describe the former he employed the traditional concepts of satisfaction, ransom, sacrifice, and substitution. Among these the most important was satisfaction. John Wesley believed that God was morally offended by human sin. The divine wrath meant an angry God. Sin was an affront to God and a failure of man to fulfill his role in the scheme of creation. The justice of God required that the affront be propitiated. The morality of God required that the failure be corrected. Man, however, had no way to correct this situation for which he alone was responsible. He could neither allay nor flee the wrath of God.[143]

4.3.3 Meaning of Justification

It implies what God does for us through his Son; the other what he works in us by his spirit. The plain scripture notion of justification is pardon, the forgiveness of sins. It is that act of God the Father whereby, for the sake of the propitiation made by the blood of his Son he 'showed forth his righteousness (of mercy) by the remission of the sins that are past. This is easy natural account of it given by St. Paul throughout his whole epistle. So he explains it himself, more particularly in this and in the following chapter. In the next verses but one to the text, 'blessed are they (saith he) whose iniquities are forgiven, and whose sins are covered. Blessed is the human to whom the Lord will not impute sin.' To him/her that is justified or forgiven God 'will not impute sin' to his/her condemnation.[144] The plain scriptural notion of justification is pardon, the forgiveness of sins.

Perhaps Wesley's most famous statement concerning what justification is *not* includes the following: Least of all does justification imply, that God... esteems us better than we really are, or believes us righteous when we are unrighteous. Surely no. The judgment of the all-wise God is always according to truth. Neither can it ever consist with His unerring wisdom, to think that I am innocent, to judge

[142] Albert C. Outler & Richard P. Heitzenrater, eds., *John Wesley's Sermons: An Anthology* (Nashville: Abingdon Press, 1991), 112-113.

[143] Charles W. Brockwell, Jr., "John Wesley's Doctrine of Justification," *Wesleyan Theological Journal*, 18/2 (September-December, 1983): 20-21.

[144] Albert C. Outler & Richard P. Heitzenrater, eds., *John Wesley's Sermons: An Anthology*..., 114-145.

that I am righteous or holy, because another is so.[145] Wesley defines "salvation" as something attainable not merely in heaven, but also at the present time. Specifically, in Christ we are saved, first of all, from "the guilt of all past sin." Here for the first time Wesley cites Romans 3:25 to support what he means by justification: "[Christ] God hath set forth to be propitiation through faith in his blood, to declare his righteousness for (or by) the remission of the sins that are past." He adds that believers are also "saved from fear," i.e., "from fear of punishment; from fear of the wrath of God."[146]

4.3.4 The Term Human are Justified

Who are they that are justified? Apostle tells expressly, God, 'justified the ungodly; the ungodly of every kind and degree and none but ungodly. It is only sinners that have any occasion for pardon: it is in sin alone which admits of being forgiven. Forgiveness, therefore, has an immediate reference to sin and to nothing else. It is our 'unrighteousness' to which the pardoning God is 'merciful; it is our iniquity which he remembered no more. But on what terms then he or she is justified whose is altogether 'ungodly', and till that time 'worked not'? on one alone, which is faith. He 'believeth' in him that justified the ungodly,' and 'he that believeth is not condemned; yea, he 'is passed from the death unto life'. For 'the righteousness of God is by faith of Jesus Christ unto all and upon all them that believe;...whom God hath set forth to be a propitiation through faith in his blood', that 'he might be just, and the justifier of him which believeth in Jesus...Therefore, conclusion is that human is justified by faith without the deeds of the law'-without previous obedience to the moral law. The condition of justification, however, is not as radical as its work. The work of justification is Christ's and Christ's alone. The condition of justification is faith, and faith alone, which also comes directly from God as a gift—a sure confidence in the merits of Christ's passion. Yet there are degrees to this condition, and the justified sinner may not receive the full assurance of faith for quite some time, even though the condition might be evidenced to others by the fruits of the Spirit in a person's life. While the gift of full assurance should be expected, and indeed sought in prayerful expectancy, it should not therefore be confused with the work of justification, which is God's radical reconciliation in Christ of human beings radically alienated in sin.[147]

Faith, therefore, is the necessary condition of justification. Faith in general is a divine, supernatural 'evidence' or conviction 'of things not seen', not

[145] Albert C. Outler, eds., "Salvation by Faith," *The Works of John Wesley,* Vol. 1 (Nashville: Abingdon Press, 1984), 122.

[146] Ted M. Dorman, "Forgiveness of past sins: John Wesley on Justification," *Pro Ecclesia,* 10/3 (June, 2001): 279.

[147] David Lowes Watson, "The Much Controverted point of Justification by faith and the Shaping of Wesleyan's Evangelistic Message", *Wesleyan Theological Journal,* 21/1 (May-December, 1986): 10.

discoverable by our bodily senses as being either past, future, or spiritual. Justifying faith implies, not only a divine evidence or conviction that 'God was in Christ, reconciling the world unto himself', but a sure trust and confidence that Christ died for sins, that he loved me, and gave himself for me.[148] John Wesley argues that three things should go together in justification: Upon God's part, his great mercy and grace, upon Christ's part, the satisfaction of God's justice by offering his body and shedding his blood and upon our part, true and living faith in Jesus Christ. Thus in our justification it is not only God's mercy and grace but also his justice involved. In the whole process of justification faith alone is the condition and not good works.[149] It is very clear from it that faith is the presupposition of the Christian life as well as being justified. In the Indian context where multi-pluralistic context prevails this should be a clear call for the people of God that faith is the decisive in accepting Christ and not other peripheral things which at many points of time make blocks for people to come to Christ. There are many things which some time church requires from people and they fail to adhere with that norms and thus, they go back to the old faith.

Wesley's doctrine of justification is part of his comprehensive teaching concerning salvation. He analyzed the interaction between God and man into stages from repentance to final salvation. The progression as he saw it was: repentance, faith, justification and the new birth, life in the Spirit which produces sanctification and entire sanctification, final salvation. The several stages, however, were relational conditions, not static ones. The study of John Wesley's doctrine of justification begins with a review of his theological anthropology. He saw the image of God as having three parts: the natural, the political, and the moral. It was the moral image righteousness and true holiness) which suffered most from the fall of Adam. Owing to the disobedience of the first man all of humanity is under the condemnation of original sin. Salvation has two grand parts: justification and sanctification. It begins with justification and the regeneration which occurs at the same time. It continues to entire sanctification and final salvation. Justification restores us to the favor of God; sanctification restores us to the image of God. In justification righteousness is imputed to us; we are counted righteous for the sake of the merits of Christ and through faith in Him. In sanctification righteousness is actually imparted to us; we become righteous; we receive and grow daily in righteousness and true holiness. Justification is what Christ does *for* us; sanctification is what the Holy Spirit does *in* us. Faith is the only condition for justification. Regeneration is simultaneous with but separate from justification.

Wesley seems to have learned at Aldersgate that man is justified by grace alone and that this grace is given only through faith to humanity. It has been argued above that Wesley was in substantial agreement with both Luther and

[148] Albert C. Outler & Richard P. Heitzenrater, eds., *John Wesley's Sermons: An Anthology*..., 116-120.

[149] Robert W. Burtner & Robert E. Chiles, eds., *John Wesley's Theology,* 167-168.

Calvin at the point of claiming that man in himself is morally impotent and that justification is by grace alone. Being justified, however, does not mean being made actually righteous or just. It means precisely what it meant in the thought of the Reformers, namely, that we who have no righteousness are accounted as righteous. In more direct language, in John Wesley's view, it is to say that justification is the basis and beginning of the Christian life, that faith opens the way to the "new birth" and fullness of life in Christ, and that sanctification in holiness then follows.[150]

4.4 Christian Perfection and Sanctification

John Wesley's teaching on Christian perfection, influences on him from Pietism and its writings. He also maintained that Christian Perfection or entire sanctification is both gradual and instantaneous. John Wesley in his account of Sanctification addresses how it occurs – whether it is gradual or instantaneous, and whether it is ever complete. He uses the word 'Perfection' to refer to this instant and complete sanctification. Mark K. Olson argues that Wesley's "mature" theology embraced perfection as a distinct second work of grace, though not invariably an instantaneous work.[151] Through its "dialogue" with the seventeenth and eighteenth centuries, that we will be able to perceive the *nature and center* of the influence of the Early Church Fathers on Wesley's doctrine of Christian perfection. This is because Wesley, by birth and eventually by conviction, was a part of a church in which patristic concerns had long held a place of priority.[152]

Wesley conceives of Christian perfection in dynamic rather than static terms. Moral nature of such perfection is seen in the two basic areas in which Christians are or may be perfect in this life. First, there is a minimal level of moral perfection which Wesley ascribes to all believers: "A Christian is so far perfect as not to commit sin" at any stage of the Christian pilgrimage. Second, there is the full sense in which Christians can be perfect in this life, although, as the tenor of the second division of the sermon reveals, perfection in these terms is not the universal experience of all believers. The second or full sense of perfection apparently refers to deliverance from the sinful nature, for Wesley's statement that "My evil nature, the body of sin, is destroyed, most likely refers back to evil thoughts and evil tempers." Wesley's focus on this aspect of perfection is from a Christological perspective: Christ is (1) the Pattern for the perfection

---

150 Harmon L. Smith, "Wesley's Doctrine of Justification: Beginning and Process," *Duke Divinity School Bulletin*, 28/2 (May, 1963): 95.

151 Mark K. Olson, eds., *The John Wesley Reader on Christian Perfection: Developments in Doctrine and Theological System (*Fenwick, MI: Truth in Heart, 2008), 116.

152 John G. Merritt, "Dialogue Within A Tradition: John Wesley and Gregory of Nyssa Discuss Christian Perfection," *Wesleyan Theological Journal*, 22/2 (March-May, 1987): 92.

which involves freedom from the sinful nature and (2) the source of the virtuous expressions of that life.[153]

4.4.1 Christian Perfection

For Wesley, salvation was the total restoration of the deformed image of God in us, and its fullness was the recovery of our negative power not to sin and our positive power to love God supremely. Wesley chose to call that furthest reach of grace in sanctification and its triumphs in this life 'Christian Perfection', a position that he had stated earlier in 'The Circumcision of the Heart' (1733). Just as justification and regeneration are thresholds for the Christian life in earnest ('what God does for us'), so also sanctification is 'what God does in us', fulfilling the human potential according to his primal design. Few Christians had ever denied some such prospect after death; few, in the West at least, had ever envisioned it as a realistic possibility in this life.

Wesley maintained that he had no difficulty in harmonizing 'Christian perfection' with his later emphases on 'faith alone' and 'assurance.' Many Protestants were bound to see in the Wesleyan doctrine, despite all its formal disclaimers, a bald advertisement of spiritual pride and implicit works-righteousness. Even the Methodists, working from their own unexamined Latin traditions of forensic righteousness, tended to interpret 'perfection' in terms of a perfected spiritual elitism and so misunderstood Wesley and the early Eastern traditions of teleos as a never ending aspiration for all of love's perfecting fullness. Thus, 'Christian Perfection' came to be the most distinctive and also the most widely misunderstood of all Wesley's doctrines. He continued to teach it, as the farthest horizon of his vision of Christian existence, an idea with radical implications for personal ethics and for social transformation as well.[154]

It is with this inner moral situation perceived following the co-commencement of justification and sanctification which Wesley calls "the gradual work of sanctification" is supposed to deal. The focus of this gradual work of sanctification is the deepening radical treatment "of our evil nature which has as its objective an increasing death of sin" (which, in light of the immediate context, may be assumed to be the sinful nature and the inner stirrings which it prompts) and, conversely, an increasing alive-ness to God. This is done through the enablement of the Holy Spirit within the context of the life of discipleship.

4.4.1.1 The Nature of Christian Perfection

John Wesley believed that the ultimate goal in life was the fullest possible love of God and neighbor—the restoration of the image of Christ in the life of every believer. This restoration is a journey birthed by grace, nurtured by grace, and

---

[153] John G. Merritt, 105.

[154] Albert C. Outler & Richard P. Heitzenrater, eds., *John Wesley's Sermons: An Anthology*, "Christian Perfection," 69.

reaching its ultimate goal through grace: Christian perfection.[155] He also asserts that it is attainable in this life, runs great hazard of being accounted by them worse than a heathen man or a publican.[156] According to him "justification by grace through faith is a relative change in our status before God." But he adds an equal emphasis on the real change that takes place in our hearts, lives, and loves as we become new creatures in Christ. Rather than viewing salvation as a static act of God at some point in the past, he interprets salvation as a therapeutic process. It begins with justification and new birth (through faith/trust in Christ) and continues as the transformed person grows in grace toward entire sanctification (active love in every thought, word, and action). The purpose of a life reclaimed by faith alone, in other words, is the restoration of God's image, namely love, in the life of the believer.[157]

He defined perfection in terms of love, love to God and man. Perfection was to "love nothing, but for his sake," to please God, not self.[158] One of Wesley's most succinct definitions of Christian perfection appears in "The Scripture Way of Salvation": "It is love excluding sin; love filling the heart, taking up the whole capacity of the soul. It is love 'rejoicing evermore, praying without ceasing, in everything giving thanks." This definition conjoins two dimensions: 1) an ability to love God and others wholeheartedly and 2) an exclusion of sin from the life of the believer. Wesley believed and taught that both dimensions can be realized in this life—in an instant, and by a simple act of faith. But, consistent with his characteristic emphasis on the dynamic nature of the way of salvation, he also insisted that the gracious gift of God that can be received in a moment through trusting faith is never a static or finished state.[159]

In order to summarize his perception on Christian Perfection let us see his quotation- 'Christian Perfection does not imply (as some men seem to have imagined) an exemption either form ignorance, or mistake, or infirmities, or temptations. Indeed, it is only another term for holiness. They are two names for the same thing. Thus, every one that is holy is, in the Scripture sense, perfect. Yet we may observe that neither in this respect is there any absolute perfection on earth. There is no perfection of degrees, as it is termed; none which does not admit of a continual increase. So that how much any man has attained, or in how

---

[155] Randy L. Maddox and Paul W. Chilcote, *A Plain Account of Christian Perfection* (Kansas: Beacon Hill Press, 2015), 7.

[156] Albert C. Outler & Richard P. Heitzenrater, eds., *John Wesley's Sermons: An Anthology*, 70.

[157] Randy L. Maddox and Paul W. Chilcote, *A Plain Account of Christian Perfection,* 7.

[158] Edward W. H. Vick, *John Wesley's Teaching Concerning Perfection* (Michigan: Berrian Spring, 1994), 8.

[159] Randy L. Maddox and Paul W. Chilcote, *A Plain Account of Christian Perfection,* 8.

high a degree so ever he is perfect, he hath still need to "grow in grace," and daily to advance in the knowledge and love of "God his Savior."[160]

Wesley's expectations regarding Christian perfection also made a significant contribution to his feelings of failure in North America. It was not until 1740 (after his return to England from Georgia) that Wesley was encouraged to publish his thoughts on Christian perfection. His sermon "Christian Perfection" was printed soon after. His goal in that sermon was to show "In what sense Christians are not [and] in what sense they a Christian can be perfect in godly love. However, the expectation which Wesley expresses varies from the standard of Christian perfection he seems to have applied to First Peoples in Georgia when he writes about First Peoples as debased, drunk, uneducated human beings who even with the light and knowledge of Christ preached to them would be unable to attain perfection or sanctification in Wesley's own lifetime. His definition of sin in *Plain Account* clarifies 'Voluntary transgression of a known law" as more than a mistake ("an involuntary transgression of a divine law, known or unknown," which could be committed even by a person filled with the love of God"). This suggests that he held the First Peoples he met accountable for their behavior as those who knew God's law but chose to disregard it."[161]

4.4.1.2 John Wesley's Sermon on the Christian Perfection: Phil. 3:12 (1741)

This deals with the concept of entire perfection. It also deals with the thought that what the gift of the son of God towards perfection. Those who are justified are not to continue to sin. Wesley very clearly brings a distinction between freedom from the guilt of sin which is justification and power of sin which is regeneration and being of sin which would be Christian perfection. Christian perfection means that we are not free from mistakes and best also can error and so there is no demand of that in real sense. He also very clearly asserts that we are neither free from temptation. He later begins to discuss that of mature Christians. Those who are born again should not continue to sin and thus they are made free from outward sin. In the present time Christian perfection is possible and it can be attained through faith in Christ. Christians are reed from evil thought and evil tempers also because we are crucified with Jesus Christ. So all the Christian should press forward to reach the goal and be fit for the calling what he has given to us together for the glory of God. "Perfection" comprehended three aspects: purity of intention; imitation of, or conformity to, Christ; and love to God and neighbour. By "purity of intention" Wesley meant "a wholehearted attitude to God unsullied by any kind

---

[160] Mildred Bangs Wynkoop, *A Theology of Love: The Dynamics of Wesleyanism*, 302, Cf. also Kenneth. J. Collins and Jason E. Vickers, eds., *The Sermon of John Wesley: A Collection for the Christian*, "Christian Perfection," 614.

[161] Heather A. Clements & Cassandra S. Sequivel, "John Wesley, First Peoples of North America and Christian Perfection," *Wesleyan Theological Journal*, 46/2 (March-May, 2011): 166.

of ulterior motive;" more pithily, "one design and one desire." Imitation of Christ was the formation of the new creation itself in those who abided in their Lord and who cherished his abiding in them. Love to God and neighbor was, however, the essence of Christian perfection. Any notion of inner sanctity which undervalued human fellowship Wesley regarded as a contradiction of God's work.

Thus, it is important for all of us that we are trying to reach towards the Christian perfection which our lord has kept for us.[162] In one of the most succinct definitions of Christian perfection, John Wesley continues this theme of love as he writes, What is Christian perfection? Loving God with all our heart, mind, soul, and strength. This implies that no wrong temper, not contrary to love, remains in the soul; and that all the thoughts, words and actions are governed by pure love.[163] Although, Wesley taught Christian perfection to the end and urged it upon his followers, he was "scrupulously careful never to claim it himself" and on one occasion made the vigorous disclaimer that I have not attained it. Perfection as the inward disposition only to love and therefore, genuinely to be loveable from God's point of view is the Wesleyan doctrinal hallmark of fame. It springs, clear and refreshing, from the same fountain of grace as the justifying faith of the Reformers. It but adds a further, and what appeared to Wesley an obvious, precept: God who is good enough to forgive sin is likewise great enough to transform the sinner into the saint and that within the confines of the same temporal existence and among the same pressing temptations which led him into sin.

4.4.2 Sanctification/Entire Sanctification

Entire Sanctification (holiness, perfection), as understood in the Wesley a tradition, refers to John Wesley's doctrine of spiritual transformation. It is understood as an experience of grace, subsequent to salvation, with the effect that the Holy Spirit takes full possession of the soul, sanctifies the heart, and empowers the will so that one can love God and others blamelessly in this life. One is justified and then sanctified—understood as communing with God with the result that the holiness of God is actually imparted, not just imputed on the basis of what Christ accomplished on the cross. The power of sin in the believer's life is either eradicated or rendered inoperative as one participates in the higher life of the divine. *The doctrine of entire sanctification admits to at least two models of interpretation: (1) instantaneous and (2) progressive perfection, involving (a) eradication of sin or (b) a blameless walk with God.[164]

---

[162] Kenneth. J. Collins and Jason E. Vickers, eds., *The Sermon of John Wesley: A Collection for the Christian,* 609-611.

[163] Kenneth. J. Collins and Jason E. Vickers, eds., *The Sermon of John Wesley: A Collection for the Christian,* 614.

[164] Michael J. Christensen, "Theosis and Sanctification: John Wesley's Reformulation of a Patristic Doctrine," *Wesleyan Theological Journal,* 31/2 (March-May, 1996): 86.

4.4.2.1 Entire Sanctification

John Wesley variously, but clearly, answers this question. It "does not imply an exemption either from ignorance, or mistake, or infirmities, or temptations. Indeed, it is only another term for holiness." It is "the loving God with all our heart, mind, soul, and strength." This implies that no wrong temper, none contrary to love, remains in the soul; and that all the thoughts, words, and actions are governed by pure love. "It is nothing higher, and nothing lower than this -- the pure love of God and man. It is love governing the heart and life, running through all our tempers, words, and actions." "The essence of Christian holiness is simplicity and purity, one design, one desire entire devotion to God." He defines it as experienced: "Many have (in 1761, at London) and many do daily experience an unspeakable change. After being deeply convinced of inbred sin, particularly of pride, anger, self-will, and unbelief, in a moment they feel all faith and love: no pride, no self-will, or anger: and from that moment they have continual fellowship with God, always rejoicing, praying, and giving thanks." "Till this universal change was wrought in his soul, all his holiness was mixed.

He was humble, but not entirely; his humility was mixed with pride; he was meek, but his meekness was frequently interrupted by anger, or some uneasy or turbulent passion. His love of God was frequently damped by the love of some creature; the love of his neighbor by evil surmising, or some thought, if not temper, contrary to love. His will was not wholly melted down into the will of God: now and then nature rebelled, and he could not clearly say, 'Lord, not as I will, but as Thou wilt.' His whole soul is now consistent with itself; there is no jarring string. All his passions flow in a continual stream with an even tenor to God. There is no mixture of any contrary affections; all is peace and harmony. After being filled with love, there is no more interruption of it than of the beating of his heart; and continual love bringing continual joy in the Lord, he rejoices evermore. And as he now loves God with all his heart, so Jesus now reigns alone in his heart, the Lord of every motion there." "Rapturous joy, such as is frequently given in the beginning of justification, or of entire sanctification, is a great blessing; but it seldom continues long before it subsides into calm, peaceful love." And in relation to judging whether we have attained it, he observes: "Not that 'to feel all love and no sin' is sufficient proof. Several have experienced this for a time before their souls were fully renewed. None, therefore, ought to believe that the work is done till there is added the testimony of the Spirit, witnessing his entire sanctification, as clearly as his justification."[165]

---

[165] D. A. Whedon, *Entire Sanctification of John Wesley's View* (London: Newby Books Noble Ind., 2015), 5.

4.4.2.2 Entire Sanctification and Regeneration

John Wesley says: "Sanctification begins in the moment a man is justified. Yet, sin remains in him, yea, the seed of all sin, till he is sanctified throughout." Again: "There does still remain, even in them that are justified, a mind which is in some measure carnal (so the apostle tells even the believers at Corinth, 'Ye are carnal'); a heart bent to backsliding, still ever ready to depart from the living God; a propensity to pride, self-will, anger, revenge, love of the world, yea, and all evil; a root of bitterness, which, if the restraint were taken off for a moment, would instantly spring up; yea, such a depth of corruption as, without clear light from God, we cannot possibly conceive."[166] Further: "We may learn the mischievousness of that opinion, that we are wholly sanctified when we are justified; that our hearts are then cleansed from all sin. It is true, we are then delivered from the dominion of outward sin; and, at the same time, the power of inward sin is so broken that we need no longer follow, or be led by it; but it is by no means true that inward sin is then totally destroyed, that the root of pride, self-will, anger, love of the world is then taken out of the heart.

At the very moment of justification we are born again; in that instant we experience that inward change from darkness into marvelous light; from the image of the brute and the devil, into the image of God; from the earthly, sensual, devilish mind, to the mind which was in Christ Jesus. But are we then entirely changed? Are we wholly transformed into the image of Him that created us? Far from it: we still retain a depth of sin, and it is the consciousness of this which constrains us to groan for a full deliverance to him that is mighty to save.[167] Hence, it is that those believers who are not convinced of the deep corruption of their hearts, or but slightly, and as it were, notionally convinced, and have little concern about entire sanctification." He also asserts "The contrary doctrine is wholly new; never heard of in the Church of Christ, from the time of his coming into the world till the time of Count Zinzendorf; and it is attended with the most fatal consequences."[168]

Mr. Wesley's views on this point exhibit no inconsistency, though they become more clearly defined after the commencement of the great revival. They may be stated briefly that a deep conviction of depravity is necessary. There is also need for entire devotion of the whole man to God's service and a hearty obedience to his whole will. Along with this simple and direct faith is needed. The conviction "implies no guilt, no sense of condemnation, no consciousness of wrath of God. It does not suppose any doubt of the favor of God, or any 'fear that hath torment.' It is a conviction wrought by the Holy Ghost, of the sin which still

---

[166] Kenneth. J. Collins and Jason E. Vickers, eds., *The Sermon of John Wesley: A Collection for the Christian,* "Scripture the Way of Salvation", 584.

[167] Kenneth. J. Collins and Jason E. Vickers, eds., *The Sermon of John Wesley: A Collection for the Christian,* "Scripture the Way of Salvation", 588.

[168] D. A. Whedon, *Entire Sanctification of John Wesley's View,* 6-7.

remains in our heart; of the carnal mind which 'does still remain even in them that are regenerate;' although it does no longer reign, it has not now dominion over them.[169] It is a conviction of proneness to evil, a heart bent to backsliding; of the still continuing tendency of the flesh to lust against the Spirit; of the tendency of our heart to self-will, to atheism, or idolatry, and, above all, to unbelief; of the sin still cleaving to all our words and actions; of our helplessness, of our utter inability to think one good thought or to form one good desire." When thus convinced, we must give ourselves unreservedly to the whole will of God, and at once and constantly hold ourselves "a living sacrifice."

We must look for the sanctifying Spirit, "not in careless indifference or indolent inactivity, but in vigorous, universal obedience; in denying ourselves, and taking up our cross daily, as well as in earnest prayer and fasting, and a close attendance on all the ordinances of God." That is, in the path of duty we shall find it. But "all who expect to be sanctified at all, except to be sanctified by faith. Meantime, they know that faith will not be given but to them that obey. Justification and sanctification are not two kinds of grace, but two dimensions of the experience of God's Love and grace.[170] With the Reformers, Wesley insisted that the Gospel included justification and sanctification (regeneration). Unlike the Reformers he claimed that sanctification could progress, by grace, until love flooded the believer's consciousness and became the "temper" which characterized motive and mission. He readily admitted that even within the love-saturated there remained buried sinfulness for which they had to pray for God's forgiveness. Wesley's "perfect" was much closer to the Greek *teleios*, meaning "mature" or "fulfilled."[171] Wesley always knew that the full flowering of God's grace *restored* men and women to authentic humanity; it did not render them superhuman or angelic. For this reason Wesley averred that the "entirely sanctified" were not lifted above finitude, not transposed beyond creatureliness. Accordingly, he told his readers that among the fully sanctified they would find errors arising from ignorance, mistakes due to poor judgment, defects in intellectual equipment, together with the personal and social complications arising from all of these.[172]

What, then, is sanctification in Mr. Wesley's teaching? If a man is given control over sin by justification, is not anything else superfluous? Is not justification itself synonymous with Christian perfection? So it would seem, but such is not the case in Wesley's teaching. Rather satisfaction is not a single act, like justification. God forgives a man of his sin in a definite moment. Then he is justified. But sanctification has to do with inner dispositions, feelings, and motives, the delicate

---

[169] Robert W. Burtner & Robert E. Chiles, eds., *John Wesley's Theology,* 183-184.

[170] Mildred Bangs Wynkoop, *A Theology of Love: The Dynamics of Wesleyanism*, 311.

[171] Victor Shepherd, "That We May Perfectly Love Thee: John Wesley And Sanctification," *Touchstone,* 6 /2 (May 1988): 35.

[172] Kenneth. J. Collins and Jason E. Vickers, eds., *The Sermon of John Wesley: A Collection for the Christian,* "Christian Perfection", 612.

and often unexpressed inclinations of the human heart. "As a man thinks in his heart, so is he." Sanctification, therefore, is a long process. Frequently its duration is a lifetime. Wesley tries to protect sanctification, like justification, from the encroachment of human accomplishment and merit and therefore, to make its claimants immune to pride and all its deceit. This he does by stating simply that it, too, is the direct gift of God, a peculiar sanctifying grace individuated as faith in the lives of the particular men and women who possess it. It is essential to full salvation, that is, acceptance by God into heaven in the end.[173]

4.5 John Wesley and Church

John Wesley always claimed to accept fully the teaching of the Church of England. But, in his preaching, he concentrated on the one aim of reviving personal religion, demanding of his listeners the same revolutionary change that had come over his own life. In 1742, he instituted class-meetings, with class-leaders, for devotions and mutual help, all classes being knitted together into his "Society of the people called Methodists." He would not call it a Church. The only "Church" he acknowledged was the Church of England.[174] Wesley would have sure believed the visible church is a congregation of faithful men in which the pure Word of God is preached and the sacraments be duly administered according to the Christ's ordinance in all those things that of necessity are requisite to the same.[175] The essential of visible church according to John Wesley needs to have: firstly, Living faith: without which indeed there could be no church at all, neither visible nor invisible. Secondly: preaching and consequently hearing, the pure word of God, otherwise faith would languish and die. Thirdly, a due administration of the sacraments, ordinary means where God increases faith.[176] Wesley believed that the necessity of mutual encouragement, mutual examination and mutual service, within the context of the means of grace, required more than hearing of the Word, the participation in sacraments. Wesley's view of holiness was woven into his ecclesiology. He believed that gathering together of believers into small voluntary societies for mutual discipline and Christian growth was essential to the church's life.[177] Wesley emphasized much on the classical Protestant view which had stressed on the necessity of the Church where faith is aroused by preaching of the Word of God.

---

[173] William R. Cannon, "John Wesley's Doctrine of Sanctification and Perfection," *The Mennonite Quarterly Review,* 35/2 (April,1961): 95.

[174] James T. Reuteler, *The Essentials of Methodism* (Colorado: Bible Studies Aurora, 2013), 21-23.

[175] Colin W. Williams, *John Wesley's Theology Today: A Study of the Wesleyan Tradition in the Light of Current Theological Dialogue* (Nashville: Abingdon Press, 1960), 141.

[176] Colin W. Williams, *John Wesley's Theology Today: A Study of the Wesleyan Tradition in the Light of Current Theological Dialogue*, 142.

[177] Colin W. Williams, *John Wesley's Theology Today: A Study of the Wesleyan Tradition in the Light of Current Theological Dialogue*, 151.

We find in Wesley an emphasis on the objective of holiness of the church, the fact that Christ is present in the church through the sacraments. He believed not only in preaching but also the true unity of the church which is vital for the church. he also believed that the objective holiness of the church should result in subjective holiness through the faith relationship.[178]

In replying to a Roman Catholic Bishop's *Caveat Against the Methodists,* Wesley set forth a description of the **true church** : "And such is the Catholic Church—that is, the whole body of men, endued with faith working by love, dispersed over the whole earth, in Europe, Asia, Africa, and America. And this church is 'ever one.' In all ages and nations it is the one body of Christ. It is 'ever holy, for no unholy man can possibly be a member of it. It is 'ever orthodox'; so is every holy man in all things necessary to salvation; 'secured against error' in all things essential 'by the perpetual presence of Christ; ever directed by the Spirit of Truth' in the truth that is after godliness."[179] John Wesley explained that a Church of Christ might be either a company of two or more Christian believers meeting together (a family or otherwise), a congregation of Christians meeting in a place, or several congregations in a town considered collectively, or all the congregations on earth as in Acts 20:28 where he declared it "undoubtedly means the catholic or universal Church, that is, all the Christians under heaven. The catholic or universal Church is, all the persons in the universe whom God hath so called out of the world as to entitle them to the preceding character; as to be 'one body' united by 'one Spirit,' having 'one faith,' one hope, one baptism; one God and Father of all, who is above all, and through all and in them all.[180]

John Wesley's view on "the Church" could be very clearly seen in John S. Simon's view which evidently reflects Archbishop Seeker's "Lectures on the Church Catechism." "The Church is defined as comprehending all good men in all ages, under every dispensation, who have believed and served Christ according to the degree of light which they had. It is the Catholic Church as distinguished from the Jewish Church, which embraced only one nation. It is the universal Church, which embraces all men in all nations. The Catholic faith is that form of doctrine which was delivered by the apostles. It can be learned with certainty only in the writings of the New Testament. Every Church or society of Christians which preserves this Catholic or universal faith is a part of the true or universal Church. In this sense, every individual Church which holds the essentials of Christianity is a Catholic Church."[181] The true church was a missionary church as was the primitive church. Wesley told his preachers their chief task was to save souls.

---

[178] Colin W. Williams, *John Wesley's Theology Today: A Study of the Wesleyan Tradition in the Light of Current Theological Dialogue*, 149.

[179] Roy S. Nicholson, "John Wesley and Ecumenicity," *Wesleyan Theological Journal,* 2/1 (April-May, 1967): 75-76.

[180] Robert W. Burtner & Robert E. Chiles, eds., *John Wesley's Theology,* 255.

[181] John S Simon, *John Wesley and the Methodist Societies* (London: Epworth Press, 1952), 280.

Parish boundaries established by centuries of ecclesiastical tradition would not be observed. Like the early apostles the Methodists would go anywhere the Spirit led to announce the joyful news of salvation.[182]

The ever-growing number of converts from his preaching of Free, Present and Full Salvation looked to Wesley as their spiritual leader; and he had no choice but to organize them in some way. But he had no thought of founding any new denomination or sect. He thought only of new life within the Church of which he was an ordained clergyman, the Church of England. "What may we reasonably believe," he wrote, to be God's design in rising up the preachers called Methodists? Not to form any new sect; but to reform the nation, particularly the Church; and to spread Scriptural holiness over the land." But 18th century Anglicanism did not want to be reformed. Anglican rectors refused the use of their churches to the revivalist preachers, and refused Communion to Methodists. John Wesley, therefore, ignored the authority of Anglican Bishops, and all diocesan and parochial limits. He sent his preachers where he would, and continued building up his Methodist Societies, which had no constitutional link with the Church of England, and any status or privileges within that Church.

He fell back upon a vague theory of the "Church Invisible." He viewed the Anglican Church as a visible legal and human organization only. For him, the Church of England was a legal establishment, so that, in disobeying the Bishops, he was violating legal authority only, and not spiritual authority. The latter authority he persuaded himself to have from the "Invisible Church," a mission from the invisible Head of the Church, Christ Himself, with whom he and his Methodists were united by invisible bonds of grace. And he persuaded himself that thus, his independent "Society" was in no way a separation from the Church of England. By 1744, the Wesleyan Methodist Society was effectively organized. In that same year, the first Wesleyan Conference resolved that they did not want a schism from the Church of England, and expressed the hope that they would be recognized as an auxiliary organization.[183]

4.6 John Wesley and Sacraments

John and Charles Wesley were sacramentalists. As loyal sons of the Church of England they cherished its traditions and found great comfort and direction in its institutions, especially the Book of Common Prayer (1549). Citations to this Book are abundant throughout their works and references to ideas informed by its contents can also be detected.[184] The basic discussion here is to understand John Wesley's view of the sacraments from his own writings. Wesley lived and served

[182] Luke L. Keefer, "John Wesley: Disciple of early Christianity," *Wesleyan Theological Journal*, 19/1 (April-May, 1984): 26.

[183] James T. Reuteler, *The Essentials of Methodism*), 51.

[184] Steven T. Hoskins, "Eucharist and Eschatology in the Writings of the Wesleys," *Wesleyan Theological Journal* 29/1-2 (August-January, 1994): 66.

God his whole lifetime in the Anglican Church. He took communion three times a week normally during his lifetime and urged his American ministers to administer the Supper every Sunday.[185] He was convinced that the New Testament Church partook of the Supper daily and believed that the primitive church should be a guide to the contemporary church. The doctrines of the Church of England were one of Wesley's standards; he professed never to have left them or her ministry.[186] John Wesley was not of a systematic theologian nor did he develop a dogmatic theology like Calvin.

A different approach to his sacramental theology is by means of an historical treatment since it shows the development of Wesley's thought as it was moulded by his religious experience, family and church background, theological debate and continuous study of Scripture.[187] The Angelical Church affirmation by and large was the affirmation of John Wesley himself. The Church believed that The sacrament must be understood, not in the sense of supernatural operations which in themselves confer on man the right to be justified by God regardless of his moral achievements, but rather as supernatural operations which enable man to perform moral acts and to achieve a quality of moral goodness which causes God to appropriate unto him the merits of His Son and to pronounce him justified.[188] The sacraments were the means for the release of supernatural power into natural channels and instruments for the achievement of moral goodness.

4.6.1 Understanding of Baptism

John Wesley in fact after his Aldersgate experience had a tough time but carried the both evangelical experience and sacramental heritage together. After Aldersgate experience Wesley did not over react; he did not abstain from the sacraments. Rather his conception of them changed. He still exhorted men to use the sacraments as means of receiving salvation. The new birth for Wesley was an inward thing, not to be equated with baptism as it was by many Anglican priests .John Wesley broadened his concept of the means of grace to include prayer, reading and hearing Scripture and Supper as the ordinary means.[189] There was change in Wesley's thinking and thus he began to be more ecumenical in his thinking. Irwin Reist summarizes the effect of Aldersgate upon Wesley as: 1) remember God is above means; 2) there is no automatic power in the means; 3)

---

185 William Turner, "New Strivings in Methodism" *Christianity Today*, 3/3 (November, 1958): 15.

186 John Wesley, *Explanatory Notes Upon the New Testament* (London: The Epworth Press, rep. 1954), 402.

187 Irwin Reist, "John Wesley's view of the Sacraments: A Study in the Historical Development of a Doctrine," *Wesleyan Theological Journal*, 6/1 (1971): 41.

188 W. R. Cannon, *The Theology of John Wesley: With Special Reference to the Doctrine of Justification* (New York: Abingdon-Cokesbury, 1956), 42.

189 P. L. Higgins, *John Wesley, Spiritual Witness* (Minneapolis: T. Denison and Co., 1960), 278.

seek God alone in the means; 4) use the means as means, not for their own sake; and 5) do not use the means as a source of religious pride.[190]

His view of baptism centers about Ephesians 4:5, Galatians 3:27, Romans 6:4, Matthew 16:16, Acts 22:16, and John 3:5. He viewed that there is one baptism which is the outward sign our one Lord who has been pleased to appoint of all that inward and spiritual grace which he is continually bestowing upon his church...a precious means whereby this faith and hope are given to those that diligently seek him. It is an outward sign and means of inward change brought by the Spirit (John 3:5). It is dying and rising with Christ (Rom. 6:4). Believers are to be baptized in token of their faith in Christ and are to testify to their faith in Christ by being baptized. Wesley is here true to his evangelical principle of the sacraments as instruments of divine grace when inward faith is present. John Wesley had believed that infant baptism was supported by Scripture. Baptism and teaching or evangelism of candidates is to be determined by the nature of things. Children are to be baptized before they are taught as the Jews circumcised their children. The effect of baptism is to engraft into Christ through faith from whence a man draws new spiritual life. The sacrament is a means by which through faith the work of the Spirit is accomplished.

Wesley looked upon Baptism as: "An Outward and Visible Sign of an Inward and Spiritual Grace." In terms of his Order of Salvation, Wesley identified Baptism as the Church's external affirmation and proclamation of Grace. Baptism is not only a sign of profession and mark of difference whereby Christians are distinguished from others that are not baptized; but it is also a sign of regeneration or the new birth. The Baptism of young children is to be retained in the Church. Methodist believed that water baptism was commanded by Jesus to be administered to believers as a symbol of the new covenant of grace. It signifies that we have accepted the benefits of Christ's atonement. By means of this sacrament, believers declare their faith in Jesus Christ as Savior.[191] Baptism signifies entrance into the Christian community, and is a symbol of repentance and inner cleansing from sin, a representation of the new birth in Jesus Christ, and a mark of Christian discipleship. Since children are accepted by Christ as heirs of the Kingdom of God, they may also be baptized, but their parents are to be believers and members of the Church themselves. The Church has a special responsibility to nurture and lead its children to confirm their faith and make a personal confession of faith in Christ.[192]

Baptism signifies entrance into the household of faith, and is a symbol of repentance and inner cleansing from sin, a representation of the new birth in

---

[190] Irwin Reist, "John Wesley's view of the Sacraments: A Study in the Historical Development of a Doctrine, 45.

[191] Frank Baker and Richard P. Heitzenrater, eds., *The Bicentennial Edition of the Works of John Wesley*, volumes-7 (Nashville: Abingdon Press, 1984), 83.

[192] James T. Reuteler, *The Essentials of Methodism* (Colorado: Bible Studies Aurora, 2013), 140.

Christ Jesus and a mark of Christian discipleship. We believe children are under the atonement of Christ and as heirs of the Kingdom of God are acceptable subjects for Christian Baptism. Children of believing parents through Baptism become the special responsibility of the Church. They should be nurtured and led to personal acceptance of Christ, and by confession of faith confirm their Baptism.[193] The matter of baptism is the water which has the natural power of cleansing and hence is fit for its spiritual use in cleansing. Just as Jews entered the covenant with God through circumcision, so Christians are admitted into the Church by baptism. Baptism could be administered by dipping, pouring, or sprinkling, for: 1) there is no express precept for one mode apart from the other; 2) there is no conclusive example against one apart from the other; 3) the word, baptize, does not mean necessarily to dip, to pour, or to sprinkle in and of itself.[194]

Wesley believed that infants should be baptized for the following reasons: 1) as taught in Deuteronomy 29:10-12, infants can make a covenant with God through their parents; 2)circumcision as the sign of the Old Covenant has been replaced by baptism as the sign of the New; 3) as Hebrew infants were circumcised, so infants of Christian parents being under the evangelical covenant should be baptized; 4) infants are guilty of original sin; 5) baptism washes away original sin; 6) therefore infants should be baptized; 7) the apostolic church baptized infants; 8) infants can come to Christ by no other way than baptism.[195]

The effects of baptism also present to us an irresolvable tension and contradiction in Wesley's thought. He declares that in baptism a man obtains the washing away of the guilt of original sin, by the application of the merits of Christ's death. By baptism we enter into covenant with God which he had made for the humanity. As circumcision was then a way of entering into the covenant, so baptism is now. By baptism we are admitted into the church and are made members of Christ who is the head. By baptism we who are by nature children of wrath are made the children of God.[196] By water then, as a means, the water of baptism, we are regenerated and born again; whence it is called by the apostles 'The washing of regeneration'...Nor does she the Church ascribes it to the outer washing, but to the inward grace, which added thereto, makes it a sacrament.[197]

John Wesley clearly says that baptism is not the new birth and so they are not one and the same thing. Baptism is more of external in nature and new birth is more of internal in nature. Baptism is a visible thing and new birth is invisible. Baptism is an act of man and new birth is a change which is brought by God himself in the soul. So a new birth may not be accompanied by baptism often. A

---

193 James T. Reuteler, *The Essentials of Methodism,* 141.

194 Robert W. Burtner & Robert E. Chiles, eds., *John Wesley's Theology,* 266.

195 John Wesley, "A Treatise on Baptism, " *The Works of John Wesley* (Grand Rapids: Zondervan Publishing House, n.d.), 193-195.

196 Robert W. Burtner & Robert E. Chiles, eds., *John Wesley's Theology,* 266-267.

197 John Wesley, "A Treatise on Baptism, " *The Works of John Wesley*, 81.

person may possibly be born of water and yet not born of the Spirit. So it is not necessary that who are baptized are born again. The life would show how much fruit is there on the tree.[198]

4.6.2 Understanding of the Lord's Supper

Lord Supper was central to the life of the great congregation where by the grace of his Spirit was conveyed to the souls of all the children of God.[199] For John Wesley Moravians thinking was same and he found in the Fetter-Lane Society of London (1 May, 1738) upon his return. Wesley exhorted the Society to keep close to the church and the ordinances, for some were holding that one could not be justified unless he would leave the sacraments and church. Wesley asserted very clearly that 1) the Supper gives preventing, justifying, or sanctifying grace; 2) the Supper is for all who want the grace of God; and 3) the only preparation necessary is a sense of worthlessness.[200] Wesley finally withdrew from the Society, but he had established his instrumental view of the sacraments. The sacraments and means are converting and confirming ordinances parallel to inward religion. Spiritual life then was Christ-centered and focused on the objective means of grace and centered in the life of the visible church. From this we could understand that John Wesley saw the Lord's Supper as a Sacrament in which Christ is truly present, conveying grace to the recipients.

In Wesley's view, Lord's Supper is to: 1. Represent the suffering of Christ which is past, therefore it is a memorial. 2. To convey the first fruits of these sufferings in present graces and therefore it is means. 3. To assure us of glory to come and so it is an unchanging pledge. It is **a memorial** because the basis of Lord's Super is that it directs our faith to the merits of the death of Christ by which we are alone saved. So it is not just a reminder of some event of the past, but the sacrifice of Christ is represented in the Lord's Supper so that our faith may be aroused by his present action. So Wesley memorial means recalled or brought back so that Supper is the extension of an act done in the past until its effects are a present power.[201] The real presence of Christ in the Supper was advocated by John Wesley. The nature of the presence of Christ cannot be interpreted in terms of substance, or act of consecration does not bring any change in the elements. Christ is present not in any physical way, but through the mediation of the Holy Spirit. Here Wesley focused on the need of the faith in terms of our plight.

---

[198] Robert W. Burtner & Robert E. Chiles, eds., *John Wesley's Theology*, 268-269.

[199] Colin W. Williams, *John Wesley's Theology Today: A Study of the Wesleyan Tradition in the Light of Current Theological Dialogue*, 158.

[200] Colin W. Williams, *John Wesley's Theology Today: A Study of the Wesleyan Tradition in the Light of Current Theological Dialogue*, 159.

[201] Colin W. Williams, *John Wesley's Theology Today: A Study of the Wesleyan Tradition in the Light of Current Theological Dialogue*, 160.

In Wesley's view Lord's Supper also shows the **eschatological sense**. John C. Bowmer shows three aspects of this eschatological reality to explain why the Supper was given to the dying person: first there was a believe that the Lord's Supper is the foretaste of the heavenly banquet. Second there was a belief in the Communion of Saints, and third that the Lord's Supper as heavenly food.[202] John Wesley saw the Lord's Supper as a main means for bringing that faith which prepares us for the final destiny. For Wesley, Holy Communion was the means of Grace through which we are remembered to the Real Presence of Jesus. The Supper of the Lord is not only a sign of the love that Christians ought to have among themselves one to another, but rather is a sacrament of our redemption by Christ's death; insomuch that, to such as rightly, worthily, and with faith receive the same, the bread which we break is a partaking of the body of Christ; and likewise the cup of blessing is a partaking of the blood of Christ..[203]

The body of Christ is given, taken, and eaten in the Supper, only after a heavenly and spiritual manner. And the mean whereby the body of Christ is received and eaten in the Supper is faith. The Sacrament of the Lord's Supper was not by Christ's ordinance reserved, carried about, lifted up, or worshiped. John Wesley believed the Lord's Supper to be "the grand channel whereby the grace of his Spirit was conveyed to the souls of all the children of God." Wesley believed and Christian tradition teaches that the Lord's Supper is the paramount means of grace. The sharing of bread and wine that re-present the body and blood of our Savior conveys forgiveness of sins, reconciliation, and healing that is tangible and real. Wesley puts it this way:

"The grace of God given herein confirms to us the pardon of our sins by enabling us to leave them. As our bodies are strengthened by bread and wine, so are our souls by these tokens of the body and blood of Christ. This is the food of our souls: this gives strength to perform our duty, and leads us on to perfection. If therefore we have any regard for the plain command of Christ, if we desire the pardon of our sins, if we wish for strength to believe, to love and obey God, then we should neglect no opportunity of receiving the Lord's Supper" (Sermon 101: The Duty of_Constant Communion,).[204]

John Wesley emphasized the early Church's daily use of communion and also encouraged it. For him, the Supper is a memorial of the death of Christ. The bread is a sign of Christ's body, broken for the sinner (I Cor. 16:24-25). The wine is a sign and memorial of Christ's blood which purchases salvation (Mark 14:24). Christ's use of the word "is" is figurative and not ontological. Just as the lamb

---

[202] John C. Bowmer, *The Sacrament of the Lord's Supper in Early Methodism* (London: Dacre Press, 1951), 145.

[203] Frank Baker and Richard P. Heitzenrater, eds., *The Bicentennial Edition of the Works of John Wesley*, volumes-7, 92.

[204] Albert C. Outler and Richard P. Heitzenrater, eds., *John Wesley's Sermon: An Anthology* (Neshville: Abingdon Press,1991), 504-506. Cf., also William Crockett, *Eucharist: Symbol of Transformation* (New York: Pueblo Publishing, 1989), 200.

was only figuratively the Passover, so the bread is not his real body. The blood of the New Testament is only the sign and seal of the New Testament, not the New Testament itself. The bread and wine signify or represent the body and blood. For Wesley, the custom of Scripture is to call the thing signifying by the name of the thing signified. The effect of the Lord's Supper is to confirm the new covenant. The cup is the means of partaking of the blessings purchased by the blood of Christ. The bread is the means of partaking of the blessing won by Christ's body. In John Wesley's view, Lord's Supper is the duty of every Christian to receive as often it could be. He gives reason why it is necessary for the Christian to partake in the Lord's Supper: firstly, it is mainly the command of the Lord where he said, "Do this in remembrance of me." Secondly there are great benefits of doing it which is forgiveness of the past sins, the present strengthening and refreshing of our souls.[205]

In the early Methodist movement, the Lord's Table became a high worship point. From Wesley's sermon *The Means of Grace,* we can affirm that a Wesleyan Eucharistic invitation should be an open one, extended to those who truly and earnestly repented of sin, is in love and charity with neighbor, and intended to lead a new life following the commandments of God. As a means of grace, the Eucharist is that table by which God confers mercy and forgiveness, strengthens our faith, and calls us to be agents of justice and love in the entire world.[206]

4.7 John Wesley Understanding of Salvation

In his view of salvation he shows a complete dependence on God with the idea of human's complete responsibility where God's plan is workable. Basic to this is also prevenient grace, enabling man to reject or to be taken over by God's Grace. Man is never fully devoid of grace and the grace he has makes him to act. For Wesley justification and sanctification are interwoven and thus faith is made conditional at some point. Wesley's interest in the order of salvation began early and remained with him in his several roles: as an Anglican spiritual director at Oxford, in Georgia, and over the United Societies. John Wesley had an intensely practical concern with the order of salvation in the Christian life. The controlling theological inquiry throughout his life was into the meaning of becoming and being a Christian.[207]

---

[205] Robert W. Burtner & Robert E. Chiles, eds., *John Wesley's Theology,* 263. Cf., also Bard Thompson, *Liturgies of the Western Church* (Philadelphia: Fortress Press, 1980), 412.

[206] Tercio Bretanha Junker, "Sacramental Spirituality: A Reflection on Wesleyan and Brazilian Methodist Eucharist Context," *Apuntes,* 33/4 (December, 2013): 130.

[207] David L. Cubie, "Placing Aldersgate in John Wesley order of Salvation," *Wesleyan Theological Journal,* 24 (1989): 33.

4.7.1 The Nature of Salvation

John Wesley had presented the order of salvation in three ways- that of repentance, of faith and of holiness.[208] John Wesley in His sermon, "On Working out our Own Salvation.," opines that, "*Salvation begins with what is usually termed(and very Properly) preventing grace, including the first wish to please God, the first dawn of light concerning his will, and the first slight transient conviction of having sinned against him. All these imply some tendency towards life; some degree of salvation; the beginning of deliverance from a blind, unfeeling heart, quite insensible of God and things of God. Salvation is carried out by convincing grace, usually in scripture termed as repentance; which brings a larger measure of self-knowledge and a farther deliverance from the heart of stone. Afterwards we experience the proper Christian salvation; whereby "through grace", we are "saved by faith;" consisting of those two grand branches, justification and sanctification. By justification we are saved from the guilt of sin, and restored to the favor of God; by sanctification we are saved from the power and root of sin, and restored to the image of God. All experiences as well as scripture show this salvation to be both instantaneous and gradual. It begins the moment we are justified, in the holy, humble, gentle, patient love of God and man. It gradually increases from that moment as "a grain of mustard–seed, which at, first, is the least of all seeds;" but afterwards puts forth large branches, and becomes a great tree, in another instant, the heart is cleansed from all sin, and filled with pure love to God and man. This love grows till we reach the stature of the fullness of Christ.*[209]

John Wesley's theology needs to be presented in the light of order of Salvation (*ordo salutis*). His definition of salvation is given in his sermon, "*Ye are saved through faith." What is salvation? The salvation which is spoken is and first, whatsoever else it implies, it is a present salvation. It is something attainable, yea, actually attained, on earth, by those who are partakers of this faith. Ye are saved (to comprise all in one word) from sin. This is the salvation which is through faith. This is that great salvation foretold by the angel, before God brought his First-begotten into the world: "Thou shalt call his name Jesus; for he shall save his people from their sins." And neither here, nor in other parts of holy writ, is there any limitation or restriction. All his people, or, as it is elsewhere expressed, "all that believe in him," he will save from all their sins; from original and actual, past and present sin, "of the flesh and of the spirit."*[210] The salvation which is through faith, even in the present world: a salvation from sin, and the consequences of sin, both often expressed in the word justification; which, taken in the largest sense, implies a deliverance from guilt and punishment, by the atonement of Christ actually applied to the soul of the

[208] Colin W. Williams, *John Wesley's Theology Today: A Study of the Wesleyan Tradition in the Light of Current Theological Dialogue*, 39.

[209] Kenneth. J. Collins and Jason E. Vickers, eds., *The Sermon of John Wesley: A Collection for the Christian,* "On Working out Our Own Salvation," 66.

[210] Kenneth. J. Collins and Jason E. Vickers, eds., *The Sermon of John Wesley: A Collection for the Christian,* "Christian Perfection," "Salvation by Faith," 129.

sinner now believing in him, and a deliverance from the power of sin, through Christ formed in his heart. So that he who is thus justified, or saved by faith, is indeed born again. He is born again of the Spirit unto a new life, which "is hid with Christ in God." John Wesley also includes the eternal destiny in salvation. Salvation is the total wok of God.[211]

4.7.2 Prevenient Grace

The central focus of Wesley's Theology is one of the saving work of Christ and the human appreciation of that work. The saving work of Christ begins with the first coming of grace in the soul which John Wesley called prevenient grace. This prevenient grace has great significance in his theology. This prevenient grace concept is said to be developed from his Angelical background and the clause of the Thirty Nine articles of the Church of England which pointed to this doctrine. His main thoughts could be found in one of his major theological writing. He said, *"the condition of man after the fall of Adam is such that he cannot turn and prepare himself, by his own natural strength and good works, to faith and calling upon God; wherefore we have no power to do good works pleasant and acceptable to God, without the grace of God by Christ preventing us, that we may have a good will, and working with us, when we have that good will.*"[212] John Wesley's Angelical tradition challenged him to develop his theology of the prevenient grace. Wesley was sure enough that God's grace was universally given to everyone equally without any discrimination. So for Wesley grace of God is granted to few and denied to others. He was very clear in his concept that the teaching of Calvin was limited to redemption of God and denied the universal love of God to people of all nations. This also denies the universal purpose of salvation for all.[213]

Because of original sin, the natural man is dead to God and unable to move towards God or respond to him. It is through the work of prevenient grace that he is given the power to respond or resist. Prevenient grace creates within us the power to accept faith or to refuse it. "It is God that works in us both to will and to do of his good pleasure." The meaning of these words may be made plainer by a small transposition of them: "It is God that of his good pleasure works in you both to will and to do." If God works in you, then work out your own salvation. The original word rendered, *works out*, implies the doing a thing thoroughly. *Your own*; for you must do this, or it will be left undone forever. Your *own salvation:*

---

[211] Robert W. Burtner & Robert E. Chiles, eds., *John Wesley's Theology*, 143-144.

[212] Thomas Jackson, ed., *The Works of John Wesley*, Vol. 8 (London: John Mason, 1829), 229, cited by Joseph Basappa Suray, *Towards a Theology of Universality: John Wesley's Socio-Economic, Political & Moral Insights on British Class & Indian Caste Distinctions* (New Delhi: Christian World Imprints, 2015), 160.

[213] Thomas Jackson, ed., *The Works of John Wesley*, Vol. 7, 381, Cf. also Kenneth. J. Collins and Jason E. Vickers, eds., *The Sermon of John Wesley: A Collection for the Christian*, "On Free Grace," 25-26.

Salvation begins with what is usually termed (and very properly) *preventing grace*; including the first wish to please God, the first dawn of light concerning his will, and the first slight transient conviction of having sinned against him.[214]

Gifts of grace are necessary to enable man to come to repentance and then to justification. What is meant here is that God directly intervenes in the lives of people seeking to bring them back to the road to salvation. So prevenient grace marks the beginning of God's work of salvation and this is available to all people.[215] According to Wesley, it seems that teaching of Calvin is not in line with the scriptural understanding. The gospel tells about a total and universally free redemption to all who are willing to accept it. It is God who quickens us we cannot quicken our souls. John Wesley in His sermon on Free Grace talked about the importance of God's love which has brought free grace through his son Jesus Christ available to all. *How freely does God love the world! While we were yet sinners, "Christ died for the ungodly." While we were "dead in our sin," God "spared not his own Son, but delivered him up for us all." And how freely with him does he "give us all things!" Verily, FREE GRACE is all in all!"*[216] *Man cannot achieve this grace by his good works in any way. John Wesley sees the Grace of God beyond the reach of people making it someone's; own property, "It is free in all to whom it is given. It does not depend on any power or merit in man; no, not in any degree, neither in whole, nor in part. It does not in anywise depend either on the good works or righteousness of the receiver; not on anything he has done, or anything he is. It does not depend on his endeavors. It does not depend on his good tempers, or good desires, or good purposes and intentions; for all these flow from the free grace of God; they are the streams only, not the fountain. They are the fruits of free grace, and not the root. They are not the cause, but the effects of it. Whatsoever good is in man, or is done by man, God is the author and doer of it. Thus is his grace free in all; that is, no way depending on any power or merit in man, but on God alone, who freely gave us his own Son, and "with him freely gives us all things."*[217] So for John Wesley the grace of God is the only source of human salvation. Hence, this grace does not depend on any power, or merits or righteousness in humankind no matter what so ever may be the status of person.

John Wesley is very strong in opposing the predestination thought and goes up saying that if this followed then our whole preaching is in vain. He says doctrine of predestination is not God's design or God's desire but it is man made thought.

---

[214] Kenneth. J. Collins and Jason E. Vickers, eds., *The Sermon of John Wesley: A Collection for the Christian,* "On Working out Our Own Salvation," 65-66.

[215] Colin W. Williams, *John Wesley's Theology Today: A Study of the Wesleyan Tradition in the Light of Current Theological Dialogue*, 42-43.

[216] Kenneth. J. Collins and Jason E. Vickers, eds., *The Sermon of John Wesley: A Collection for the Christian,* "On Free Grace," 22.

[217] Kenneth. J. Collins and Jason E. Vickers, eds., *The Sermon of John Wesley: A Collection for the Christian,* "On Free Grace," 22.

- * It tends to kill the areas of holiness; bad people could be diverted in wrong directions.
- * It destroys the sense of religion and keeps it static
- * It obstructs the work of the Spirit
- * Predestination kills our zeal for good works and makes us more passive
- * It also keeps on back the revelation of God
- * The New Testament talks that all should be saved not only few selected
- * Predestination represent Jesus as hypocrite and deceiver
- * This thought also dishonors father and nullifies all his attributes
- * Wesley says, he hates this thought because of this major reasons
- * Thus, he gives a call to repent and come on the right track to be in the fold of God.
- * Wesley and Calvinistic standpoint. Grace is not elected but it is for all.[218]

Wesley recognized that God's presence gratuitously springs up throughout human cultures and even in religions other than Christianity. One of the most distinctive features of Wesley's understanding of prevenient grace is that it conveys the efficaciousness of Christ's atoning work to all human beings. Prevenient grace qualifies all people to receive the redemption of God which brings the notion that all have the same value before God. John Wesley's theology of other religions could be seen as an inclusive one that maintains the finality and sufficiency of Christ alone for salvation, but, yet, allows for the possibility although not the certainty- of salvation among other religions. Inclusive theologies of religion are, therefore, very careful to hold together God's universal saving will that desires no one to be lost (1 Timothy 2:4), but, yet, allow that even though salvation is possible outside the fold of church and even beyond foe boundaries of Christianity, it never takes place apart from Christ.

The concept of prevenient grace suggests that the *atonement is unlimited;* any person or all people can be saved. It brings the thought that Christians have the responsibility to communicate the love of God to all human being. John Wesley very clearly states that the idea of predestination discourages people from having good intentions to do the good works.

This is very clearly seen in John Wesley's sermon on Free Grace "This uncomfortable doctrine directly tends to destroy our zeal for good works. And this it does, First, as it naturally tends (according to what was observed before) to destroy our love to the greater part of mankind, namely, the evil and unthankful. For whatever lessens our love, must go far lessen our desire to do them good. This it does, Secondly, as it cuts off one of the strongest motives to all acts of bodily mercy, such as feeding the hungry, clothing the naked, and the like, --

[218] Kenneth. J. Collins and Jason E. Vickers, eds., *The Sermon of John Wesley: A Collection for the Christian,* "On Free Grace," 20-21.

viz., the hope of saving their souls from death. For what avails it to relieve their temporal wants, who are just dropping into eternal fire?"[219] John Wesley very strongly comes against the idea of Predestination and says this doctrine at many points *destroys or shuns the concept of holiness.* This doctrine not only tends to destroy Christian holiness, happiness, and good works, but hath also a direct and manifest tendency to overthrow the whole Christian Revelation. The point which the wisest of the modern unbelievers most industriously labor to prove, is, that the Christian Revelation is not necessary.

John Wesley was not of the view that the people who are not in Christ are completely denied the grace of God. He believed that everyone is given some degree of prevenient grace from God, what they have is God given conscience. John Wesley brings the picture that Conscience is placed in the middle under God, and above man. It is a kind of silent reasoning of mind, where by those things which are judged to be right and approved with pleasure. This shows that conscience is given equally to all people in all ages in all places.[220] J. C. Logan opines that, while the natural condition of a person outside Christ is that their spiritual senses are clogged and they are in a condition of being *non posse non peccare*, everyone at least has enough of prevenient grace to have a conscience and be able to respond positively to the grace already working in them.[221] In Wesley's views, conscience is not exactly a natural human faculty but it is gift of God's prevenient grace at work in every person even before they could think of coming to Christ.

The doctrine of prevenient grace leads Wesleyans to support an intimate relationship between nature and grace and creation and redemption. Asserting that the Holy spirit is pervasively present in all creation and redemptively active in all cultures and religions. Wesleyans affirm, along with the biblical witness, that God has not left himself "without witness" (Acts 14:7)? prevenient grace is the category by which Wesleyans are able to embrace truth, beauty, and holiness wherever they are found. It is thus foe ubiquitous and gracious presence of God through foe agency of the Holy Spirit which insists John Wesley to say: "*Some great truths, as being and attributes of God, and difference between moral good and evil, are known, in some measure, to foe heathen world. The traces of them are to be found in all nations: So that, in some sense, it may be said to every child of man, "He hath showed thee o man, what is good; even to do justly, to love mercy and to walk humbly with thy God" ... there is no man that is in a state of mere nature; there is no man, unless he has quenched foe Spirit, that is wholly void of foe grace of God.... [This is] more properly termed "preventing grace." every man has a greater or lesser measure of this. ...Everyone has sooner or later good desires, although foe generality of men stifle*

219 Kenneth. J. Collins and Jason E. Vickers, eds., *The Sermon of John Wesley: A Collection for the Christian,* "On Free Grace," 26.

220 Robert W. Burtner & Robert E. Chiles, eds., *John Wesley's Theology,* 150.

221 J. C. Logan, *Theology of Evangelism in Wesleyan Heritage* (USA: Abingdon Press, 1994), 53.

them before they can strike deep root or produce any considerable fruit. Everyone has some measure of that light, some faint glimmering ray, which sooner later, more or less, enlightens every man that cometh into foe world."[222]

4.7.3 The Concept of Repentance

Wesley specifically taught that, "There is a repentance consequent upon, as well as a repentance previous to justification." For example, in his commentary on Matt. 3:8, he remarked: Repentance is of two sorts; that which is termed legal, and that which is styled evangelical repentance. The former ... is a thorough conviction of sin. The latter is a change of heart (and consequently, of life) from all sin to all holiness.[223] Wesley makes clear the thought in his sermon, **The Means of Grace,** "*We may observe there is a kind of order, wherein God himself is generally pleased to use these means in bringing a sinner to salvation. A stupid, senseless wretch is going on in his own way, not having God in all his thoughts, when God comes upon him unawares, perhaps by an awakening sermon or conversation, perhaps by some awful providence, or, it may be, an immediate stroke of his convincing Spirit, without any outward means at all. Having now a desire to flee from the wrath to come, he purposely goes to hear how it may be done. If he finds a preacher who speaks to the heart, he is amazed, and begins searching the Scriptures, whether these things are so The more he hears and reads, the more convinced he is; and the more he meditates thereon day and night. Perhaps he finds some other book which explains and enforces what he has heard and read in Scripture. And by all these means, the arrows of conviction sink deeper into his soul. He begins also to talk of the things of God, which are ever uppermost in his thoughts; yea, and to talk with God; to pray to him; although, through fear and shame, he scarce knows what to say. But whether he can speak or no, he cannot but pray, were it only in "groans which cannot be uttered." Yet, being in doubt, whether "the high and lofty One that inhabited eternity" will regard such a sinner as him, he wants to pray with those who know God, with the faithful, in the great congregation. But here he observes others go up to the table of the Lord. He considers, "Christ has said, 'Do this!' How is it that I do not I am too great a sinner. I am not fit. I am not worthy." After struggling with these scruples a while, he breaks through. And thus he continues in God's way, in hearing, reading, meditating, praying, and partaking of the Lord's Supper, till God, in the manner that pleases him, speaks to his heart, "Thy faith hath saved thee. Go in peace."*[224]

---

[222] Kenneth. J. Collins and Jason E. Vickers, eds., *The Sermon of John Wesley: A Collection for the Christian,* "On Working out Our Own Salvation," 64, 68.

[223] John Wesley, *Explanatory Notes Upon the New Testament* (San Francisco: E Thomas Press; reprint ed., Salem, OH: Schmul Publishers, 1976), 15, Cited by Kenneth J. Collins, "A hermeneutical model for the Wesleyan ordo salutis," *Wesleyan Theological Journal,* 19/2 (September-December, 1984), 27. Robert W. Burtner & Robert E. Chiles, eds., *John Wesley's Theology,* 152.

[224] Kenneth. J. Collins and Jason E. Vickers, eds., *The Sermon of John Wesley: A Collection for the Christian,* "The Means of Grace," 80.

John Wesley accepts that falling from faith at some point marks the life of all who are justified, but also he is convinced that in this life all believers may eventually receive the gift of perfection by which they will keep from falling out of the faith relationship. To keep the faith intact there is a need of constant watchfulness and attendance upon the means of grace. The Christian is aware that he is sinful but he does not dwell on that awareness. He seeks to open to Christ so that outward sin may be destroyed by the relationship with Christ and the inward sin may go off with the presence of Christ.[225] John Wesley says, by "means of grace" I understand outward signs, words, or actions, ordained of God, and appointed for this end, to be the ordinary channels whereby he might convey to men, preventing, justifying, or sanctifying grace. The chief of these means is prayer, whether in secret or with the great congregation; searching the Scriptures; (which implies reading, hearing, and meditating thereon;) and receiving the Lord's Supper, eating bread and drinking wine in remembrance of Him: And these we believe to be ordained of God, as the ordinary channels of conveying his grace to the souls of men.[226]

Instituted means of Grace means which are instituted by Christ. **Prayer** is the key to Christian life which helps to have a living relationship with God. It helps us to draw near to God. But failure to pray is the most common cause of wilderness state.[227] Prayer need to be kept as the constant basis of the daily life. Private prayer requires an intimate connection with the reading of the Scripture. Prayer is the lifting up of heart to God and all word without this would be hypocrisy. The aim of the prayer is to learn the constant company of Christ which would lead for praying without ceasing. Searching the Scriptures is indeed very important which allows to have the whole knowledge of revelation. The Lord's Supper needs to be observed at every opportunity. John lays much emphasis on fasting also. He had asked his followers to have fasting on Friday. The purpose of fasting is to wean the soul from its natural attachment to earthly things and to keep before us our spiritual journey. No extreme ascetic practices are required. He also has Christian Conference where he said that the early church was gathering together into small groups for fellowship and nurture. In this regard he saw the organization of his societies as an expression of one of the essential means of grace, which is vital element for the growth of the Christian life where believers bear the burden of one another.[228]

---

[225] Colin W. Williams, *John Wesley's Theology Today: A Study of the Wesleyan Tradition in the Light of Current Theological Dialogue*, 128-129.

[226] Kenneth. J. Collins and Jason E. Vickers, eds., *The Sermon of John Wesley: A Collection for the Christian,* "The Means of Grace," 73.

[227] Ibid., 75.

[228] Colin W. Williams, *John Wesley's Theology Today: A Study of the Wesleyan Tradition in the Light of Current Theological Dialogue*, 134-135.

4.7.4 The New Birth

It is believed that Wesley preached almost sixty times on topic new birth. For him the new birth concept was basics to the Christian faith. This thought is closely attached with original sin and so it was said know your disease and know your cure. Wesley affirms that the new birth is the gate or entrance to holiness which leads for the process of sanctification. So in the light of this regeneration becomes vital truth for happiness. For Wesley, if anything which needs to be taken seriously and fundamental that would be doctrine of justification and new birth. There are three basic questions which need to be talked about that is: why new birth is necessary, how new birth should take place and what would be the nature of new birth. The basic of this thought is that humans were made in the image of God but they did not live accordingly. The death came into and this shows the loss of life and image of God. In Adam all were born in sin and thus there is a need to be born again in the spirit. There should be an inward transformation and which would enable the human being to listen to the voice of God which was lost before. Life again comes into existence by the new birth experience. A person needs to be born again to have holiness which is vital to have contact with God.

John Wesley says that the foundation of the doctrine of the new birth is the moral image of God in which human was made. Before a child is born into the world he has eyes, but sees not; he has ears, but does not hear. He has a very imperfect use of any other sense. He has no knowledge of any of the things of the world, or any natural understanding. To that manner of existence which he then has, we do not even give the name of life. It is then only when a man is born, that we say he begins to live. For as soon as he is born, he begins to see the light, and the various objects with which he is encompassed. His ears are then opened, and he hears the sounds which successively strike upon them. At the same time, all the other organs of sense begin to be exercised upon their proper objects. He likewise breathes, and lives in a manner wholly different from what he did before. How exactly doth the parallel hold in all these instances! While a man is in a mere natural state, before he is born of God, he has, in a spiritual sense, eyes and sees not; a thick impenetrable veil lies upon them; he has ears, but hears not; he is utterly deaf to what he is most of all concerned to hear. His other spiritual senses are all locked up: He is in the same condition as if he had them not. Hence, he has no knowledge of God; no intercourse with him; he is not at all acquainted with him. He has no true knowledge of the things of God, either of spiritual or eternal things; therefore, though he is a living man, he is a dead Christian.[229]

But as soon as he is born of God, there is a total change in all these particulars. The "eyes of his understanding are opened;" (such is the language of the great Apostle;) and, He who of old "commanded light to shine out of darkness shining on his heart,

[229] Kenneth. J. Collins and Jason E. Vickers, eds., *The Sermon of John Wesley: A Collection for the Christian,* "The New Birth," 159-160.

he sees the light of the glory of God," his glorious love, "in the face of Jesus Christ." His ears being opened, he is now capable of hearing the inward voice of God, saying, "Be of good cheer; thy sins are forgiven thee;" "go and sin no more." This is the purport of what God speaks to his heart; although perhaps not in these very words. He is now ready to hear whatsoever "He that teaches man knowledge" is pleased, from time to time, to reveal to him. He "feels in his heart," to use the language of our Church, "the mighty working of the Spirit of God;" not in a gross, carnal sense as the men of the world stupidly and willfully misunderstand the expression; though they have been told again and again, we mean thereby neither more nor less than this: He feels, is inwardly sensible of, the graces which the Spirit of god works in his heart. He feels, he is conscious of, a "peace which passes all understanding." He many times feels such a joy in God as is "unspeakable, and full of glory." He feels "the love of God shed abroad in his heart by the Holy Ghost which is given unto him;" and all his spiritual senses are then exercised to discern spiritual good and evil. By the use of these, he is daily increasing in the knowledge of God, of Jesus Christ whom he hath sent and to all the things pertaining to his inward kingdom.[230]

4.7.4.1 The New Birth and Sanctification

The new birth is not the same as sanctification. This is indeed taken for granted by many; particularly by an eminent writer, in his late treatise on "The Nature and Grounds of Christian Regeneration." To wave several other weighty objections which might be made to that tract, this is a palpable one: It all along speaks of regeneration as a progressive work, carried on in the soul by slow degrees, from the time of our first turning to God. This is undeniably true of sanctification; but of regeneration, the new birth, it is not true. This is a part of sanctification, not the whole; it is the gate to it, the entrance into it. When we are born again, then our sanctification, our inward and outward holiness, begins; and thenceforward, we are gradually to "grow up in Him who is our Head." This expression of the Apostle admirably illustrates the difference between one and the other and farther points out the exact analogy there is between natural and spiritual things. A child is born of a woman in a moment, or at least in a very short time: Afterward he gradually and slowly grows, till he attains the stature of a man. In like manner, a child is born of God in a short time, if not in a moment. But it is by slow degrees that he afterward grows up to the measure of the full stature of Christ. The same relation, therefore, which there is between our natural birth and our growth, there is also between our new birth and our sanctification.

4.7.4.2 The Marks of the New Birth

How is every one that is "born of the Spirit," -- that is, born again, -- born of God What is meant by the being born again, the being born of God, or being born of the

[230] Kenneth. J. Collins and Jason E. Vickers, eds., *The Sermon of John Wesley: A Collection for the Christian,* "The New Birth," 160.

Spirit What is implied in the being a son or a child of God, or having the Spirit of adoption That these privileges, by the free mercy of God, are ordinarily annexed to baptism (which is thence termed by our Lord in a preceding verse, the being "born of water and of the Spirit") we know; but we would know what these privileges are: What is the marks of the new birth? The First of these, and the foundation of all the rest, is faith. So St. Paul, "Ye are all the children of God by faith in Christ Jesus." (Gal. 3:26.) So St. John, "To them gave he power" (exousian, right or privilege, it might rather be translated) "to become the sons of God, even to them that believe on his name; which were born," when they believed, "not of blood, nor of the will of the flesh," not by natural generation, "nor of the will of man," like those children adopted by men, in whom no inward change is thereby wrought, "but of God." (John 1:12,13.) And again in his General Epistle, "Whosoever believeth that Jesus is the Christ is born of God." (1 John 5:1.).[231]

The Second scriptural mark of those who are born of God is hope. Thus St. Peter, speaking to all the children of God who were then scattered abroad, saith, "Blessed be the God and Father of our Lord Jesus Christ, which, according to his abundant mercy, hath begotten us again unto a lively hope." (1 Peter 1:3.) Elpida zusan, a lively or living hope, saith the Apostle; because there is also a dead hope, as well as a dead faith; a hope which is not from God, but from the enemy of God and man; -- as evidently appears by its fruits; for, as it is the offspring of pride, so it is the parent of every evil word and work; whereas, every man that hath in him this living hope, is "holy as He that called him is holy:" Every man that can truly say to his brethren in Christ, "Beloved, now are we the sons of God, and we shall see him as he is," "purifies himself, even as He is pure."[232]

The Third scriptural mark of those who are born of God, and the greatest of all, is love; even "the love of God shed abroad in their hearts by the Holy Ghost which is given unto them." (Rom. 5:5.) "Because they are sons, God hath sent forth the Spirit of his Son in their hearts, crying, Abba, Father!" (Gal. 4:6.) By this Spirit, continually looking up to God as their reconciled and loving Father, they cry to him for their daily bread, for all things needful, whether for their souls or bodies. They continually pour out their hearts before him, knowing "they have the petitions which they ask of him." (1 John 5:15.) Their delight is in him. He is the joy of their heart; their "shield," and their "exceeding great reward." The desire of their soul is toward him; it is their "meat and drink to do his will;" and they are "satisfied as with marrow and fatness, while their mouth praises him with joyful lips."[233]

---

[231] Kenneth. J. Collins and Jason E. Vickers, eds., *The Sermon of John Wesley: A Collection for the Christian,* "The marks of the New Birth," 167.

[232] Kenneth. J. Collins and Jason E. Vickers, eds., *The Sermon of John Wesley: A Collection for the Christian,* "The marks of the New Birth," 169.

[233] Ibid., 171.

4.7.4.3 Baptism and the New Birth

John Wesley believed that baptism is normally the beginning of the Christian's new life. He believed also that it normally takes place in infancy, as infant baptism is in line with New Testament thought. As to the mode of baptism Wesley argued that while immersion was the ancient manner of baptizing sprinkling and pouring are recognized in Heb.10:22. If immersion symbolizes dying and rising with Christ, sprinkling symbolizes the outpouring of the Holy Spirit at Pentecost. Baptism is then a means by which God begins his work of regeneration in our heart. Baptism is God given sign which declares the fact that it is God who begins the work of regeneration in our lives, but God's purpose for us is to bring us to the consciousness of new birth. So John Wesley speaks of new birth in two ways/senses: first in preparatory sense that God enters the dead life of the unregenerate, bringing the grace without which it is impossible to know God, and secondly, in the sense of fulfillment, in which believer comes to conscious acceptance of Christ.[234]

4.8 The Doctrine of Atonement

Even though, John Wesley claimed that the atonement was crucial to his theology, he never articulated a systematic theory of the atonement. The cross functions in his order of salvation is in two ways. It plays a substitution role in the removal of sin and guilt and has a participatory function, through the work of the Holy Spirit, to affect holiness in the life of the believer. How does John Wesley understand the concept of the atonement? Even though he believes that it is the foundation for the order of salvation, he never developed a complete statement on atonement, nor did he publish a paper or sermon exclusively on atonement. Wesley avoids the debates over atonement theories because his primary concern is the creation of a theology to support his evangelistic movement.[235]

The doctrine of atonement no doubt is very important in John Wesley's thinking. John Wesley's understanding of atonement is closely connected with the concept of prevenient grace. In Wesley's understanding both doctrines are universal in nature which shows equality of all people in God's sight. In this regard the theology of atonement was a source of divine grace by which human being is rescued from the clutches of sins and reconciled to God. In the created order man is under divine condemnation and thus it is not possible for man to stand before God as righteous.[236] In Wesley's view, man's sin caused God to be angry with humankind. But God has provided the grace by which human being

[234] Colin W. Williams, *John Wesley's Theology Today: A Study of the Wesleyan Tradition in the Light of Current Theological Dialogue*, 118-119.

[235] Alan C. Clifford, *Atonement and Justification, English Evangelical Theology, 1640-1790* (Oxford: Clarendon Press, 1990), 132.

[236] Joseph Basappa Suray, *Towards a Theology of Universality: John Wesley's Socio-Economic, Political & Moral Insights on British Class & Indian Caste Distinctions*, 172.

could be restored to his favor through the death of Christ upon the cross. This grace reaches out to whole humanity. Colin Williams cites the Wesley's quote where John Wesley had agreed with Quaker Barclay: That all mankind by nature is separated from God and evil in his sight, that God gave his son to die for every man and that Christ enlightens every man who comes to him, that this benefit of Christ's death extends even to those who are excluded from the direct knowledge of Christ.[237] In order to assess John Wesley's understanding of atonement the two views can be taken in consideration: The Moral influence theory, Substitution theory.

4.8.1 The Moral Influence Theory

In John Wesley's view man was unable to raise himself towards God, but Christ's life and death had brought man closer to God. John Wesley spends lots of time for the exposition of the sermon of the mount which is more of the example which Christ has given to follow. Christ is the one who through his life, teaching and death has set a pattern to guide us and follow his path. He is revealer of that holiness without which no person would see Lord. John Wesley believed that because of our sin, God was really angry with us. But his anger is subsided and Christ is accepted on our behalf, and by the suffering and death on our behalf God is reconciled.[238] Cross becomes an objective event in which God provides his Son as a sacrifice to atone for humankind. So it is by depending upon the atonement of Christ we could be reconciled to God and thus it becomes a pattern for all of us. As Stephen Long suggests, Wesley is best seen as a moral theologian for whom primary obstacle is guilt.[239] The way of the cross is still a way the Christians must follow. The life of Christ, which leads to cross, is then the way which needs to be followed. The Moral influence theory seems to be drawn firmly into John Wesley's picture of the Christian life.[240]

4.8.2 The Penal Substitution Theory

The atonement's primary function is the removal of guilt so that we can become holy, and substitution atonement is the best interpretation of the cross for this purpose. Wesley's view of the atonement as penal substitution comes from the Reformation Anglicanism of the Edwardian Homilies and the *Book of Common Prayer.* From these Wesley claims that the death of Christ is "a full, perfect and

---

[237] Colin W. Williams, *John Wesley's Theology Today: A Study of the Wesleyan Tradition in the Light of Current Theological Dialogue*, 74-75.

[238] Colin W. Williams, *John Wesley's Theology Today: A Study of the Wesleyan Tradition in the Light of Current Theological Dialogue*, 80.

[239] D. Stephen Long, *John Wesley's Moral Theology* (Nashville: Kingswood Books, 2005), 22.

[240] Colin W. Williams, *John Wesley's Theology Today: A Study of the Wesleyan Tradition in the Light of Current Theological Dialogue*, 83.

sufficient sacrifice, oblation and satisfaction.[241] It is a full and perfect sacrifice in that it does not require additional work on our part. It is a sufficient sacrifice in contrast to the image of the Catholic mass as a sacrifice. It is oblation in that it cost God something and it is satisfaction because it is propitiation for our sins.[242] After John Wesley's Aldersgate experience he preached sermon on "Justification by Faith," which was a landmark sermon because it is the first, full articulation of his order of salvation. Here, John Wesley sees Christ as a "second general parent and representative of the whole human kind. As such, Christ is the Second Adam who has "tasted death for every man." As our representative, Christ satisfied the just requirement for which human was to be punished for sin. The effect of this was that God will not punish us; we are put in good standing with God, and our dead souls are restored to eternal life.

The cross is propitiation for the human beings because the divine justice done to Christ is the divine mercy shown to whole human race. The driving force behind his cuddle of penal substitution theory is the centrality of the doctrine of justification. Substitutionary atonement makes justification possible because human beings are pardoned by virtue of "the merits of Christ's death and Passion" and faith is the "way of obtaining a share in his merit. Without the atonement as the objective foundation, our justification is either an illusion or relies upon our own works. For John Wesley, substitutionary atonement reveals that there is nothing we can do to get our salvation. John Wesley's embrace of penal substitution shows the importance of grace in his theology and is the back bone for his order of Salvation (*ordo salutis*).[243]

For John Wesley, righteous expressed in the atonement is to mean nothing less than justification." The righteousness of Christ (be it "active" or "passive") does not fulfil- "satisfy" – the requirements of the law for us, which would make us exempt from having to obey the law. Instead, the righteousness of Christ must also be implanted in us after the pardon has been given- "imputed" - to us. Regarding this implanted righteousness of Christ, Wesley believes "*His divine righteousness belongs to his divine nature, as he is even, He that exists; "over all, God blessed for ever;" the Supreme; the Eternal; "equal with the Father, as touching his Godhead, though inferior to the Father as touching his manhood." Now this is his eternal, essential, immutable holiness; his infinite justice, mercy, and truth; in all which, he and the Father are one. But I do not apprehend that the divine righteousness of Christ is immediately concerned in the present question. I believe few, if any, do now*

[241] Kenneth J. Collins, *The Scripture Way Salvation* (Nashville: Abingdon, 1997), 83-84.

[242] Darren Cushman Wood, "John Wesley Use of Atonement," *Asbury Journal*, 62/2 (2007): 57-58.

[243] Kenneth. J. Collins and Jason E. Vickers, eds., *The Sermon of John Wesley: A Collection for the Christian*, "Justification by faith," 137.

contend for the imputation of this righteousness to us. Whoever believes the doctrine of imputation, understands it chiefly, if not solely, of his human righteousness."[244]

The human righteousness of Christ belongs to him in his human nature; as he is the "Mediator between God and man, the Man Christ Jesus." This is either internal or external. His internal righteousness is the image of God, stamped on every power and faculty of his soul. It is a copy of his divine righteousness, as far as it can be imparted to a human spirit. It is a transcript of the divine purity, the divine justice, mercy, and truth. It includes love, reverence, resignation to his Father; humility, meekness, gentleness; love to lost mankind, and every other holy and heavenly temper; and all these in the highest degree, without any defect, or mixture of unholiness. The death of Christ pleased God and became the only basis for the forgiveness of sins. So human being could be reconciled with God only by depending upon Christ as the atonement of sins. John Wesley had affirmed that the redemption which is provided in Christ helps human being to perform acts of mercy, love and justice.

4.9 John Wesley and Ethics

The Christian religion is a redemptive religion. It has ethical implications. This means that it makes a practical difference in the lives of people. In the Christian thinking, religion without ethical consequences would be meaningless. So, the morals and ideals of Christian life are the continuous efforts to grow in faith. For John Wesley entire sanctification is an event which is brought by God in the human soul on the basis of faith. Christian perfection is a process, resulting in an objective life of holiness which is never completed but in the process of development. Christian perfection itself talks about obligation under grace but at the same time it has to be carried out towards perfection. The atonement of Christ is needed for both of the process. For the regulation of the life within the given framework of society John Wesley had indicated many duties and marks of character for which a Christian is expected to follow. John Wesley's practical ethics is primarily seen as individualistic in nature; his social ethics is an extension of this applied individual ethics.[245] I would be drawing most of the thoughts from his sermons "Upon our Lord's Sermon on the Mount" to discuss Ethics.

4.9.1 The Christian Life

It is impossible for any that have it, to conceal the religion of Jesus Christ. This our Lord makes plain beyond all contradiction, by a two-fold comparison: "Ye are the light of the world: A city set upon an hill cannot be hid." Ye Christians "are the light of the world," with regard both to your tempers and actions. Your holiness makes you as conspicuous as the sun in the midst of heaven. As ye cannot go out of the world, so

---

[244] Albert C. Outler & Richard P. Heitzenrater, eds., *John Wesley Sermons: An Anthology*, "The Lord of Righteousness," (Nasville: Abingdon Press, 1984), 383-384.

[245] Robert W. Burtner & Robert E. Chiles, eds., *John Wesley's Theology*, 223.

neither can ye stay in it without appearing to all mankind. Ye may not flee from men; and while ye are among them, it is impossible to hide your lowliness and meekness, and those other dispositions whereby ye aspire to be perfect as your Father which is in heaven is perfect. Love cannot be hid any more than light; and least of all, when it shines forth in action, when ye exercise yourselves in the labor of love, in beneficence of every kind. As well may men think to hide a city, as to hide a Christian; yea, as well may they conceal a city set upon a hill, as a holy, zealous, active lover of God and man.[246]

So impossible it is, to keep our religion from being seen, unless we cast it away; so vain is the thought of hiding the light, unless by putting it out! Sure it is, that a secret, unobserved religion, cannot be the religion of Jesus Christ. Whatever religion can be concealed is not Christianity. If a Christian could be hid, he could not be compared to a city set upon an hill; to the light of the world, the sun shining from heaven, and seen by all the world below. Never, therefore, let it enter into the heart of him whom God hath renewed in the spirit of his mind, to hide that light, to keep his religion to himself; especially considering it is not only impossible to conceal true Christianity, but likewise absolutely contrary to the design of the great Author of it. This plainly appears from the following words: "Neither do men light a candle, to put it under a bushel." As if he had said, As men do not light a candle, only to cover and conceal it, so neither does God enlighten any soul with his glorious knowledge and love, to have it covered or concealed, either by prudence, falsely so called, or shame, or voluntary humility; to have it hid either in a desert, or in the world; either by avoiding men, or in conversing with them. "But they put it on a candlestick, and it gives light to all that are in the house:" In like manner, it is the design of God that every Christian should be in an open point of view; that he may give light to all around that he may visibly express the religion of Jesus Christ.[247] Thus, it is very clear from John Wesley's understanding of the Christian life that Christians are to be clear and portray the life and example of Jesus Christ in their life.

Wesley clearly maintained that Christianity is a social Religion and turning into a solitary would destroy the whole meaning of Christianity. Christianity cannot live without a society and believers need to interact with godly and ungodly both. He maintained that Christians are both salt and light their witness should be outside the four walls of the church. He said a secret and unobserved religion cannot be a religion of Jesus Christ. In this context, Wesley clearly says "let your light shine to people." Thus, Christianity is essentially a social religion and cannot be hidden or concealed. It has to reach to people and be a peacemaking tool. It has to interact with the world and people. It should be related to the present context of society and be an example for the world. He further goes on to say that religion

---

[246] Kenneth. J. Collins and Jason E. Vickers, eds., *The Sermon of John Wesley: A Collection for the Christian,* "Upon our Lord's Sermon on the Mount-4" faith," 519.

[247] Kenneth. J. Collins and Jason E. Vickers, eds., *The Sermon of John Wesley: A Collection for the Christian,* "Upon our Lord's Sermon on the Mount-4," 519.

cannot be hidden/ or invisible. It is to shine and let people get rid of the darkness. In other words, Christianity is to dispel the blindness of the world and proclaim the love of Christ. All should be done in order to glorify God and God alone. I think message is very clear where Wesley affirms that the basics of Christianity are not to be hidden but to be demonstrated among the people. The love of Christ should be viable to the people of other faiths and they should come to Christ for what he has done for the world.

John Wesley while talking on being humble opines that, "Christian meekness implies, the being without zeal for God, any more than it does ignorance or insensibility. No; it keeps clear of every extreme, whether in excess or defect. It does not destroy but balance the affections, which the God of nature never designed, should be rooted out by grace, but only brought and kept under due regulations. It poises the mind aright. It holds an even scale, with regard to anger, and sorrow, and fear; preserving the mean in every circumstance of life, and not declining either to the right hand or the left. Meekness, therefore, seems properly to relate to ourselves. But it may be referred either to God or our neighbor. When this due composure of mind has reference to God, it is usually termed resignation; a calm acquiescence in whatsoever is his will concerning us, even though it may not be pleasing to nature; saying continually, "It is the Lord; let him do what seemed him good." When we consider it more strictly with regard to ourselves, we style it patience or contentedness. When it is exerted toward other men, then it is mildness to the good, and gentleness to the evil."[248]

Let thy religion be the religion of the heart. Let it lie deep in thy inmost soul. Be thou little, and base, and mean, and vile (beyond what words can express) in thy own eyes; amazed and humbled to the dust by the love of God which is in Christ Jesus. Be serious. Let the whole stream of thy thoughts, words, and actions flow from the deepest conviction that thou stands on the edge of the great gulf, thou and all the children of men, just ready to drop in, either into everlasting glory or everlasting burnings! Let thy soul be filled with mildness, gentleness, patience, long-suffering towards all men; -- at the same time that all which is in thee is a thirst for God, the living God; longing to awake up after his likeness, and to be satisfied with it! Be thou a lover of God and of all mankind! In this spirit do and suffer all things! Thus show thy faith by thy works; thus "do the will of thy Father which is in heaven!" And, as sure as thou now walk with God on earth; thou shall also reign with him in glory![249] This is very clear from John Wesley's thinking that he is proposing a religion of the heart that is a renewed heart by the blood of Jesus or regenerated person who is justified by the grace of God.

---

[248] Kenneth. J. Collins and Jason E. Vickers, eds., *The Sermon of John Wesley: A Collection for the Christian,* "Upon our Lord's Sermon on the Mount-2," 488.

[249] Kenneth. J. Collins and Jason E. Vickers, eds., *The Sermon of John Wesley: A Collection for the Christian,* "Upon our Lord's Sermon on the Mount-13," 407.

4.9.2 Christian Responsibilities

John Wesley in sermon, "On Living without God," says that, "*we may clearly perceive the wide difference there is between Christianity and morality. Indeed nothing can be surer than that true Christianity cannot exist without both the inward experience and outward practice of justice, mercy, and truth; and this alone is given in morality. But it is equally certain that all morality, all the justice, mercy, and truth which can possibly exist without Christianity, profited nothing at all, is of no value in the sight of God, to those that are under the Christian dispensation. Let it be observed, I purposely add, "to those that are under the Christian dispensation," because I have no authority from the Word of God "to judge those that are without." Nor do I conceive that any man living has a right to sentence all the heathen and Mahometan world to damnation. It is far better to leave them to him that made them, and who is "the Father of the spirits of all flesh;" who is the God of the Heathens as well as the Christians, and who hates nothing that he hath made. But meantime this is nothing to those that name the name of Christ: -- all those, being under the law, the Christian law, shall undoubtedly be judged thereby; and, of consequence, unless those is so changed as was the animal above mentioned, unless they have new senses, ideas, passions, tempers, they are no Christians. However just, true, or merciful they may be, they are but Atheists still!*[250]

Every person who is caught up with some kind of disease needs to make efforts to find it out and look for the remedy of it. The cure of spiritual, as of bodily diseases, must be as various as are the causes of them. The first thing, therefore, is to find out the cause; and this will naturally point out the cure. For instance: Is it sin which occasions darkness? What sin is it outward sign of any kind? Does your conscience accuse you of committing any sin, whereby you grieve the Holy Spirit of God? Is it on this account that he is departed from you, and that joy and peace are departed with him. How can you expect they should return, till you put away the accursed thing? "Let the wicked forsake his way;" "cleanse your hands, ye sinners;" "put away the evil of your doings;" so shall your "light break out of obscurity;" the Lord will return and "abundantly pardon." If darkness be occasioned by manifold and heavy and unexpected temptations, the best way of removing and preventing this is, to teach believers always to expect temptation, seeing they dwell in an evil world, among wicked, subtle, malicious spirits, and have an heart capable of all evil. Convince them that the whole work of sanctification is not, as they imagined, wrought at once; that when they first believe they are but as new-born babes, who are gradually to grow up, and may expect many storms before they come to the full stature of Christ. Above all, let them be instructed, when the storm is upon them, not to reason with the

[250] Robert W. Burtner & Robert E. Chiles, eds., *John Wesley's Theology*, 228.

devil, but to pray; to pour out their souls before God, and show him of their trouble.[251]

But what is **self-denial** wherein are we to deny ourselves and whence does the necessity of this arise I answer, the will of God is the supreme, unalterable rule for every intelligent creature; equally binding every angel in heaven, and every man upon earth. Nor can it be otherwise: This is the natural, necessary result of the relation between creatures and their Creator. But if the will of God be our one rule of action in everything, great and small, it follows, by undeniable consequence that we are not to do our own will in anything. Here, therefore, we see at once the nature, with the ground and reason, of self-denial. We see the nature of self-denial: It is the denying or refusing to follow our own will, from a conviction that the will of God is the only rule of action to us. And we see the reason thereof, because we are creatures; because "it is he that hath made us, and not we ourselves."[252]

John Wesley clearly points that our responsibility as Christian is as of Good **steward**. He says, "In what respects we are now God's stewards. We are now indebted to Him for all we have; but although a debtor is obliged to return what he has received, yet until the time of payment comes, he is at liberty to use it as *he* pleases. It is not so with a steward; he is not at liberty to use what is lodged in his hands as he pleases, but as his master pleases. He has no right to dispose of anything which is in his hands, but according to the will of his lord. For he is not the proprietor of any of these things, but barely entrusted with them by another; and entrusted on this express condition, -- that he shall dispose of all as his master orders. Now, this is exactly the case of every man, with relation to God."[253] John Wesley says that God has entrusted to us with many things to which we have to take care and use it for the glory of God. God has entrusted us with our soul, an immortal spirit, made in the image of God; entrusted us with our bodies (those exquisitely wrought machines, so "fearfully and wonderfully made,") with all the powers and members thereof. He has entrusted us with the organs of sense; of sight, hearing, and the rest: But none of these are given us as our own, to be employed according to our own will. With a portion of worldly goods; with food to eat, raiment to put on, and a place where to lay our head; with not only the necessaries. Are we using all of these with the sense of stewardship or with the sense of ownership?

In his sermon **"The Good Steward,"** John Wesley affirms two things; affirm first, is the immortality of the souls and the concept of one judgment in contrast

---

[251] Kenneth. J. Collins and Jason E. Vickers, eds., *The Sermon of John Wesley: A Collection for the Christian,* "The Wilderness State," 447, 451.

[252] Kenneth. J. Collins and Jason E. Vickers, eds., *The Sermon of John Wesley: A Collection for the Christian,* "The Self Denial," 340.

[253] Kenneth. J. Collins and Jason E. Vickers, eds., *The Sermon of John Wesley: A Collection for the Christian,* "The Good Steward," 326.

to the teaching of Roman Catholic Church that there are two judgments. He ends the sermon with talking about the sufficiency of God's grace. A Good steward is to use what God has given and in accordance with the will of God. So we are stewards of our soul, bodies, goods and talents together. Everything what we have is of the Lords and we need to be accountable to him. We need to be steward of our speech and keep the tongue tamed. It is also the stewardship of our bodies which are god's temple and thus we need to be keeping them holy. I think we are also steward of money what he has given to us and therefore, we need to use them wisely. Wesley talks about that we need to be sound in our learning also because we are steward of the learning and love both. It is our responsibility to be more clear in our learning and do not get astray from faith. Wesley clearly points out that whatever we have on earth is of the lord's and it should be clearly used for the glory of the lord. There is no room to build our own empire which people normally do. Wesley clearly brings about the sense of accountability which would be there on the judgment day. He challenges to us to put on the armor of God so that we are not in difficult state of mind. The ultimate goal of all is to glorify God and bring honor to his name. Our words and works are accountable to God and hence, we need a clear picture of all things.

John Wesley had been very clear in his thought. When he talks about the **use of money** we could find his basic concepts run into three line of thinking- E**arn** all you can- **Save** all you can and **Give** all you can. He calls that God himself calls for wise use of money. The first thought is gain all you can but not at the cost of life. We should be gaining this but should not hurt our hearts or body. It should neither be at the cost of other people or neighbors which are done often. One thing which is very clearly pointed out that we should not play with the life of others which could lead us away from God. It is more of equal distribution of the money and rightly gaining it. We don't try to take others share but give properly to them. Secondly we should be thinking of saving the money and not wasting the money just for worldly things and self pleasure. It is very interesting to see that Wesley talked about that we should not go for the worldly type of expensive clothing or ornaments which drifts us away from God and holy life. We have to have the spirit of contentment and use it more carefully.

"**Gain all you can**." Here, we may speak like the children of the world: We meet them on their own ground. And it is our bounden duty to do this: We ought to gain all we can gain, without buying gold too dear, without paying more for it than it is worth. But this is certain we ought not to do; we ought not to gain money at the expense of life, or (which is in effect the same thing) at the expense of our health. To gain all we can without hurting our mind any more than, to gain all we can without hurting our neighbor should be our aim. "**Save all you can.**" Do not throw the precious talent into the sea: Leave that folly to heathen philosophers. Do not throw it away in idle expenses, which is just the same as throwing it into the sea. Spend no part of it merely to gratify the desire of the flesh, the desire of the eye, or the pride of life. And why should you throw away money upon your children, any more than upon yourself, in delicate food, in gay or costly apparel, in superfluities of any kind? Why should you purchase for them more pride or lust, more vanity, or foolish and hurtful desires? They do not want any more; they have enough already; nature has made ample provision for them: Why should you be at farther expense to increase their temptations and snares, and to pierce them through with more sorrows? First, provide things needful for yourself; food to eat, raiment to put on, whatever nature moderately requires for preserving the body in health and strength. Secondly, provide these for your wife, your children, your servants, or any others who pertain to your household. If when this is done there be an over plus left, then "do good to them that are of the household of faith." If there be an over plus still, "as you have opportunity, do well unto all men." In so doing, you give all you can.[254] He is also against the accumulation of the money which would be used for worldly things. He also brings s the concept of stewardship not the lordship. Very much applicable to the Indian Christianity set up where people want to accumulate money. He also sees that we need to be responsible person to take care of our family and kids. It is our responsibility and should not depend upon others for this. It is great teaching in the area of saving money and resources both for the cause of ministry. This should be taught to be great Wesleyan heritage.

Riches, either desired or possessed, naturally lead to some or other of these foolish and hurtful desires; and by affording the means of gratifying them all, naturally tend to increase them. And there is a near connection between unholy desires, and every other unholy passion and temper. We easily pass from these to pride, anger, bitterness, envy, malice, and revengefulness; to a head-strong, unadvisable, unreprovable spirit: Indeed, to every temper that is earthly, sensual, or devilish. All these desire or possession of riches naturally tends to create, strengthen, and increase. And by so doing, in the same proportion as they prevail, they "pierce men through with many sorrows;" sorrows from remorse, from a guilty conscience; sorrows flowing from all the evil tempers which they inspire or increase; sorrows inseparable from those desires themselves, as every unholy desire is an uneasy desire; and sorrows from the contrariety of those desires to each other, whence it is impossible to gratify them all. And, in the end, "they drown" the body in pain, disease, "destruction," and the soul in everlasting "perdition."[255]

John Wesley continued to talk about the perils of money in Armenian magazine and wrote article about it. Riches are something which are more than necessity and need. He was more concerned with the Methodist that they become rich and later would become just nominal Christian fold. Wesley had stressed on

[254] Kenneth. J. Collins and Jason E. Vickers, eds., *The Sermon of John Wesley: A Collection for the Christian,* "The Use of Money," 305, 308, 310.

[255] Kenneth. J. Collins and Jason E. Vickers, eds., *The Sermon of John Wesley: A Collection for the Christian,* "The The Danger of Riches," 318.

giving and he himself gave more than 30000 pounds in his life time which was quite much in his time and would be a sacrificial giving which he gave in his time. He defines by this sermon the concept of being rich. He says it is something which is more than what is needed to live with or more than our daily requirement. The rich are accumulating the wealth on earth. I think he is against the concept of capitalism. It is doing with desire to have more at the cost of others. It is snatching the share of others for our greed. They often succumb to temptation and fall. The pride of life and flesh leads for more accumulating and thus they end up in crisis. The best thing to be happy is to give to others and so that there would be shared wealth and joy could be increased. John Wesley maintained that Christians are both salt and light their witness should be there outside the four walls of the church. He said a secret and unobserved religion cannot be a religion of Jesus Christ. In this context Wesley clearly says, "let your light shine to people." Thus, Christian life is hidden or concealed. It has to reach to people and be a peacemaking tool. Christian faith should be related to the present context of society and be an example for the world. Christians are to shine and let people get rid of the darkness. In other words, Christianity is to dispel the blindness of the world and proclaim the love of Christ.

4.10 John Wesley and Eschatology

It is very clear that John Wesley's understanding of eschatology has great relevance for the Christian lives at present which calls for a holy living in this world. In John Wesley's thinking there is emphasis on the final goal/objective where there is also focus on the life of the final kingdom which is available to human even at present. Both John and Charles Wesley's use of a form of realized eschatology was consistent with their emphasis on the present experience of the believer. Through the hymns, as they were sung and heard, the eschaton came to life. It was no longer a far-off promise, but a part of present reality. This was true because the doctrine "was no longer contained in abstract and prosy definitions, unintelligible to the great majority; it lived in simple inspired phrases so unforgettable that the singers became thinkers who presently made truth their own." John Wesley's personal interest in "vital Piety" and "social holiness" is well known. John Wesley was, in a real sense, a man of this world. For Wesley, Christian commitment naturally includes an active concern for one's society; that is, an intense interest in its betterment and an energetic pursuit of those means that will make it more nearly akin to the kingdom of God. Thus, it is no surprise to see John Wesley involved in matters pertaining to education, prison reform, politics, and health improvement.[256]

However, it is of particular interest to this study to note that Wesley's concern for the living of this life is heavily colored by his view of man's ultimate existence.

[256] Jerry L. Mercer, "The Destiny of man in John Wesley's Eschatology," *Wesleyan Theological Journal*, 2/1 (January-May, 1967), 56.

In his sermon, "Satan's Devices," John Wesley warns his listeners to keep clear their understanding of the relation between this world and world to come. "*Our eye may be insensibly turned aside from that crown which the righteous Judge hath promised to give at that day "to all that love is appearing;" and we may be drawn away from the view of that incorruptible inheritance which is reserved in heaven for us. But this also would be a loss to our souls, and an obstruction to our holiness. For to walk in the continual sight of our goal, is a needful help in our running the race that is set before us.*"[257]

For Wesley, a proper concept of life after death serves not only as a continual remedial to present Christian commitment, but also as an encouragement for the sinner to turn to Christ and experience justification. John Wesley does not have eschatology, when one considers such a subject in the light of the results of systematic theology. John Wesley does emphasize much on those subjects usually connected with a serious consideration of eschatology, i. e., death, the intermediate state of the soul, the resurrection, the second coming of Christ, the judgment, the end of the world, heaven, and hell.

There had been some discussions that John Wesley is not bothered about the eschatological events nor he has dealt much of it. It is not to mean that John Wesley is uninterested or unconcerned about eschatological or "end-time" events. It must be remembered that Wesley, like eighteenth century Anglicanism, is more concerned with a practical application of Biblical teaching than with its systematic formulation. There had been also some observations that John Wesley's eschatology is some sought of realized eschatology. John C. Bomer opines that John Wesley's theology of the Lord's Supper stresses the basic idea of realized eschatology.[258] Colin W. Williams sees in Wesley a type of realized eschatology, particularly in his concept of the kingdom of God and the doctrine of sanctification. Colin Williams, finds emphasis on realized eschatology in his view of sanctification under three primary headings in line with Henry Carter, (1) the new way of life—inward holiness reaching out to produce social holiness; (2) inward religion—as an eschatological foretaste of perfection; and (3) social religion—the present realization in part of the ultimate kingdom of God.[259]

In John Wesley's views, Kingdom of Heaven and Kingdom of God are two phrases for one thing. They mean barely a future happy state of heaven, but a state to be enjoyed on earth. In view of now and not yet John Wesley sees the Christian life as pilgrim way with this present time as the time of preparation for final life of the kingdom. This decision can be made because kingdom is already present

---

[257] Kenneth. J. Collins and Jason E. Vickers, eds., *The Sermon of John Wesley: A Collection for the Christian,* "Satan's Device," 468.

[258] John C. Borner, *The Sacrament of the Lord's Supper in Early Methodism* (Westminster: Dacre Press, 1951), 184.

[259] Colin W. Williams, *John Wesley's Theology Today: A Study of the Wesleyan Tradition in the Light of Current Theological Dialogue*, 194-195.

to us and we are invited to enter. It is termed "the kingdom of God," because it is the immediate fruit of God's reigning in the soul. As soon as ever he takes unto himself his mighty power, and sets up his throne in our hearts, they are instantly filled with this "righteousness, and peace, and joy in the Holy Ghost." It is called "the kingdom of heaven" because it is (in a degree) heaven opened in the soul. For whosoever they are that experience this, they can aver before angels and men, Everlasting life is won, Glory is on earth begun.[260]

4.10.1 Eschatology (Eternal Life)

We can locate that John Wesley emphasized on the reality of the gift of kingdom of God to us now. In John Wesley's view men came to the world to prepare for the eternity and live a life which is worthy of him. The one perfect Good shall be your one ultimate end. One thing shall ye desire for its own sake, -- the fruition of Him that is All in All. "One happiness shall ye propose to your souls, even a union with Him that made them; the having "fellowship with the Father and the Son;" the being joined to the Lord in one Spirit. One design you are to pursue to the end of time, -- the enjoyment of God in time and in eternity. Desire other things, so far as they tend to this. Love the creature as it leads to the Creator. But in every step you take, be this glorious point that terminates your view. Let every affection, and thought, and word, and work, be subordinate to this. Whatever ye desire or fear, whatever ye seek or shun, whatever ye think, speak, or do, be it in order to your happiness in God, the sole End, us well as Source, of your being."[261] In talking about the human destiny John Wesley is much clear and in his sermons he tries to bring some clarity. Every possession in this world is relative and his life is hidden in Christ and he will share the riches of glory in the life to come. "*How truly wise is this man! He knows himself; -- an everlasting spirit, which came forth from God, and was sent down into an house of clay, not to do his own will, but the will of Him that sent him. He knows the world; -- the place in which he is to pass a few days or years, not as an inhabitant, but as a stranger and sojourner, in his way to the everlasting habitations; and accordingly he uses the world as not abusing it, and as knowing the fashion of it passes away. He knows God; -- his Father and his Friend, the parent of all good, the centre of the spirits of all flesh, the sole happiness of all intelligent beings. He sees, clearer than the light of the noon-day sun, that this is the end of man, to glorify Him who made him for himself, and to love and enjoy him forever. And with equal clearness he sees the means to that end, to the enjoyment of God in glory; even now to know, to love, to imitate God, and to believe in Jesus Christ whom he hath sent.*"[262]

[260] Albert C. Outler & Richard P. Heitzenrater, eds., *John Wesley's Sermons: An Anthology*, "The Way To the Kingdom," 127.

[261] Albert C. Outler & Richard P. Heitzenrater, eds., *John Wesley's Sermons: An Anthology*, "The Circumcision of the Heart," 28.

[262] Kenneth. J. Collins and Jason E. Vickers, eds., *The Sermon of John Wesley: A Collection for the Christian*, "Upon Our Lord's Sermon On the Mount-13," 404.

John Wesley had viewed that man was created to love him, serve him on earth and enjoy him of all eternity. Man was not created to please himself or gain money, or get praises from men or to seek happiness in any created things. We need to be reminded that we are pressing towards goal and that is heaven.[263] God hath joined from the beginning pardon, holiness, heaven. And why should man put them asunder O beware of this! Let not one link of the golden chain be broken. "God, for Christ's sake hath forgiven me. He is now renewing me in his own image. Shortly he will make me meet for him, and take me to stand before his face. I, whom he hath justified through the blood of his Son, being thoroughly sanctified by his Spirit, shall quickly ascend to the `New Jerusalem, the city of the living God.' Yet a little while, and I shall `come to the general assembly and church of the first-born, and to God the Judge of all, and to Jesus the Mediator of the New Covenant.' How soon will these shadows flee away, and the day of eternity dawn upon me! How soon shall I drink of `the river of the water of life, going out of the throne of God and of the Lamb? There all his servants shall praise him, and shall see his face and his name shall be upon their foreheads. And no night shall be there; and they have no need of a candle or the light of the sun. For the Lord God enlightened them, and they shall reign forever and ever.[264]

John Wesley had cleared the thought by asserting that **resurrection** requires that the self-same body that died should rise again. Nothing can be said to be raised again, but that very body that died. If God give to our souls at the last day a new body, this cannot be called the resurrection of our body; because that word plainly implies the fresh production of what was before. "*The body that we shall have at the resurrection shall be immortal and incorruptible: "For this corruptible must put on incorruption, and this mortal must put on immortality." Now, these words, immortal and incorruptible, not only signify that we shall die no more, (for in that sense the damned are immortal and incorruptible,) but that we shall be perfectly free from all the bodily evils which sin brought into the world; that our bodies shall not be subject to sickness, or pain, or any other inconveniences we are daily exposed to. This Scripture calls "the redemption of our bodies," -- the freeing them from all their maladies. Were we to receive them again, subject to all the frailties and miseries which we are forced to wrestle with, I much doubt whether a wise man, were he left to his choice, would willingly take his again; -- whether he would not choose to let his still lie rotting in the grave, rather than to be again chained to such a cumbersome clod of earth. Such a resurrection would be, as a wise Heathen calls it, "a resurrection to*

[263] Colin W. Williams, *John Wesley's Theology Today: A Study of the Wesleyan Tradition in the Light of Current Theological Dialogue*, 194.

[264] Kenneth. J. Collins and Jason E. Vickers, eds., *The Sermon of John Wesley: A Collection for the Christian,* "Satan's Device," 471.

another sheep." It would look more like redemption to death again, than a resurrection to life. Our bodies shall he raised in glory."[265]

4.10.2 Eschatology (Changed Things/Judgment)

John Wesley was of the strong opinion that if true religion need to develop then there should be a great ethical and social transformation carrying on. All people of God are called to be a witness to our redemption and live a life which is worthy of him and prepare for the glory to come. "*The most glorious of all will be the change which then will take place on the poor, sinful, miserable children of men. These had fallen in many respects, as from a greater height, so into a lower depth, than any other part of the creation. But they shall "hear a great voice out of heaven, saying, Behold, the tabernacle of God is with men: And he will dwell with them, and they shall be his people, and God himself shall be their God." (Rev. 21:3, 4.) Hence will arise an unmixed state of holiness and happiness far superior to that which Adam enjoyed in Paradise. In how beautiful a manner is this described by the Apostle: "God shall wipe away all tears from their eyes; and there shall be no more death, neither sorrow, nor crying, neither shall there be any more pain: For the former things are done away!" As there will be no more death, and no more pain or sickness preparatory thereto; as there will be no more grieving for, or parting with, friends; so there will be no more sorrow or crying. Nay, but there will be a greater deliverance than all this; for there will be no more sin. And, to crown all, there will be a deep, an intimate, an uninterrupted union with God; a constant communion with the Father and his Son Jesus Christ, through the Spirit; a continual enjoyment of the Three-One God, and of all the creatures in him!*"[266]

But will "the creature," will even the brute creation, always remain in this deplorable condition God forbid that we should affirm this; yea, or even entertain such a thought! While "the whole creation groaned together," (whether men attend or not,) their groans are not dispersed in idle air, but enter into the ears of Him that made them. While his creatures "travail together in pain," he knows all their pain, and is bringing them nearer and nearer to the birth, which shall be accomplished in its season. He sees "the earnest expectation" wherewith the whole animated creation "waited for" that final "manifestation of the sons of God;" in which "they themselves also shall be delivered" (not by annihilation; annihilation is not deliverance) "from the" present "bondage of corruption, into" a measure of "the glorious liberty of the children of God." Nothing can be more express: Away with vulgar prejudices, and let the plain word of God take place. They "shall be

---

[265] John Wesley, "On the Resurrection of The Dead," http://wesley.nnu.edu/john-wesley/the-sermons-of-john-wesley-1872-edition/sermon-137-on-the-resurrection-of-the-dead/ (accessed on 08/10/16).

[266] Albert C. Outler & Richard P. Heitzenrater, eds., *John Wesley's Sermons: An Anthology*, "The New Creation," 499-500.

delivered from the bondage of corruption, into glorious liberty," -- even a measure, according as they are capable, -- of "the liberty of the children of God."[267]

The person by whom God will judge the world, is His only-begotten Son, whose "goings forth are from everlasting;" "who is God over all, blessed forever." Unto him, being "the out beaming of his Father's glory, the express image of his person" (Heb. 1:3), the Father "hath committed all judgment, because he is the Son of Man" (John 5:22, 27); because, though he was "in the form of God, and thought it not robbery to be equal with God, yet he emptied himself, taking upon him the form of a servant, being made in the likeness of men" (Phil. 2:6, 7); yea, because, "being found in fashion as a man, he humbled himself" yet farther, "becoming obedient unto death, even the death of the cross. Wherefore God hath highly exalted him," even in his human nature, and "ordained him," as Man, to try the children of men, "to be the Judge both of the quick and the dead;" both of those who shall be found alive at his coming, and of those who were before gathered to their fathers.

The time, termed by the prophet, "the great and the terrible day," is usually, in Scripture, styled the day of the Lord. The space from the creation of man upon the earth, to the end of all things, is the day of the sons of men; the time that is now passing over us is properly our day; when this is ended, the day of the Lord will begin. But who can say how long it will continue "With the Lord one day is as a thousand years, and a thousand years as one day" (2 Pet. 3:8). And from this very expression, some of the ancient fathers drew that inference, that, what is commonly called the Day of Judgment would be indeed a thousand years: and it seems they did not go beyond the truth; nay, probably they did not come up to it. For, if we consider the number of persons who are to be judged, and of actions which are to be inquired into, it does not appear that a thousand years will suffice for the transactions of that day; so that it may not improbably comprise several thousand years. But God shall reveal this also in its season.

He will bring to light, not the hidden works of darkness only, but the very thoughts and intents of the heart. And what marvel for he "searches the reins, and understands all our thoughts." "All things are naked and open to the eyes of him with whom we have to do." "Hell and destruction are before him without a covering. How much more the hearts of the children of men!." And in that day shall be discovered every inward working of every human soul; every appetite, passion, inclination, affection, with the various combinations of them, with every temper and disposition that constitute the whole complex character of each individual. So shall it be clearly and infallibly seen, who was righteous, and who unrighteous; and in what degree every action, or person, or character was either good or evil. The wicked, meantime, shall be turned into hell, even all the people that forget God. They will be "punished with everlasting destruction from the

---

[267] Kenneth. J. Collins and Jason E. Vickers, eds., *The Sermon of John Wesley: A Collection for the Christian,* "The General Deliverance," 631.

presence of the Lord, and from the glory of his power." They will be "cast into the lake of fire burning with brimstone," originally "prepared for the devil and his angels;" where they will gnaw their tongues for anguish and pain; they will curse God and look upward.[268] John Wesley's picture of hell is really literal presentation of the New Testament language. In spite of all this he never used this picture for threatening people in this world. His theology is more optimistic in nature which talks about the change in present context.

[268] Albert C. Outler & Richard P. Heitzenrater, eds., *John Wesley's Sermons: An Anthology*, "The Great Assize," 314, 318.

Chapter 5

Wesleyan Theology
Nineteenth and Twentieth Centuries

The Nineteenth-Century Holiness Movement began in the North during the 1830s with two major streams: The Tuesday Meetings of the Palmers in New York City and the Ministry of Charles G. Finney (1792-1875) in Oberlin College. National Camp Meeting Association for the Promotion of Holiness first met in 1867 (in Vineland, New Jersey). This was a further experience of testimony and revival, similar to the camp meetings. Radical Holiness Movement where people were not content with the Methodist way of doing holiness, and some within the Methodist church were not happy about the Holiness movement. In the 1870s and 1880s a number of State Holiness Associations arose to provide interdenominational fellowship and to even offer ministerial credentials. The only essential was a statement that a person had experienced sanctification; Methodist church membership was no longer required. John Wesley famously proclaimed a form of Christian perfectionism. He predicted that personal holiness would strengthen society, deepen the commitment of Christians, and even establish Christ's kingdom on earth.

Wesleyan/Holiness denominations began to develop during 1840s. The important part of Wesleyan/Holiness Missions is the role of women in establishing supporting, and serving in mission.[269] By end of the nineteenth century, Methodist theologians in both England and North America were interacting more with currents in their culture. They turned attention to the new theological trends being championed in Germany. This resulted, by the turn of the century, in a stream of "modernist" or "liberal" Methodist theologies. In the mid-twentieth century, the optimism of liberal theology was subject to critique by the movement

[269] David Bundy, "Wesleyan/Holiness mission" *Evangelical Dictionary of World Missions,* edited by Harold Netland and Charles Van Engen (Michigan: Baker Books, 2003), 1011.

known as Neo-orthodoxy. The evangelical Revival within the angelical church, a result of the Methodist revival, was to transform the upper class of England and to help England become the great leader of nations and the keeper of the world peace during the 19th century. Whitefield was the prophet, John Wesley the organizer, and Charles the songster of the Methodist revival.[270]

The Development of Wesleyan Thought

The emphasis on justification by faith as the foundation and sanctification as the building upon it kept the Methodist people moving perpetually toward God. Even entire sanctification as an instantaneous experience was never cause to sleep. These distinctives of the Wesleyan tradition were powerful tools for the perpetuation of the Evangelical Revival.[271] Originally Wesley championed the fight against injustices like slavery and the lack of prison reform many followed in his footsteps. The cry of the early Holiness movement (which carried the banner of the Wesleyan tradition throughout the nineteenth century) was, "Repent, believe, and become an abolitionist." At turn of the century, the Wesleyan tradition then deeply embedded within the Holiness movement, splintered. The principles of scriptural holiness still have meaning and contain much that is yet, precious and important for our contemporary world.[272]

Wesleyan/Holiness Missions are those missions that took place initially on the revivalist edges of the Methodist Episcopal church and within the contexts of the denominations that grew out of that church with "personal and social Holiness" as major themes articulated by Wesley; many groups became Pentecostal after 1906. And more known as Wesleyan, Holiness, or "sanctified" Pentecostal churches. There are three primary methods of mission works: 1. Mission Based on the itinerancy model of John Wesley. 2. The "Board" methods of mission modelled on the *American Board of Commissioners of the Foreign Mission* (ABCFM); and 3, "Self-Supporting mission" on the basic of ideas developed by William Taylor.[273]

Wesleyan/Holiness denominations began to develop from 1840s. The important part of Wesleyan/Holiness Missions is the role of women in establishing supporting, and serving in mission. The end of the nineteenth century, Methodist theologians in both England and North America were interacting more with currents in their culture. They turned attention to the new theological trends being championed in Germany. This resulted, by the turn of the century, in a stream of "modernist" or "liberal" Methodist theologies. In the mid-twentieth

[270] Earle E. Cairns, *Christianity through the Centuries* (Michigan: Zondervan Publishing House, 1981), 383-384.

[271] R. G. Tuttle Jr., "Wesleyan Tradition" *Evangelical Dictionary of Theology,* edited by Walter A. Elwell, (Michigan: Baker Academic, 2003), 1269.

[272] R. G. Tuttle Jr., "Wesleyan Tradition" *Evangelical Dictionary of Theology,* 1270.

[273] David Bundy, "Wesleyan/Holiness mission" *Evangelical Dictionary of World Missions,* edited by Harold Netland and Charles Van Engen (Michigan: Baker Books, 2003), 1011.

century, the optimism of liberal theology was subject to critique by the movement known as Neo-orthodoxy.[274]

5.1 Francis Asbury (1745-1816)

The name of Francis Asbury stands for American Methodism just as surely as that of John Wesley represents the British origins of the movement. Wesley, of course, appointed Asbury, sending him (among others) to America as a traveling preacher.[275] Francis Asbury was born at Hamstead Bridge, Staffordshire, England on August 20 or 21, 1745, to Elizabeth and Joseph Asbury. His parents converted under the ministry of John Wesley about the time of their son's birth and were fervent Christians. His father was poor and illiterate. He was converted at the age of 13. By the age of 18, he was called by Wesley to preach. He began rising ***at 4 a.m.*** to pray and read Scripture. He continued this practice the rest of his life.[276] Under his parents' faithful teaching and example, Asbury matured. English-born Francis Asbury certainly had the numbers: during his 45-year ministry in America, he traveled on horseback or in carriage an estimated 300,000 miles, delivering some 16,500 sermons.[277] Asbury became a local lay preacher for Methodist meetings at the age of 18. At the age of 22, John Wesley appointed him as a traveling preacher. During the first year, he was Wesley's assistant and preached in ***25*** different settlements. Without asking Boardman's permission, he borrowed a horse and rode into the countryside, thus making his first circuit in America by going to several New York communities.[278]

The family moved to a cottage at Great Barr, Sandwell, His mother wanted him to become the Archbishop of Canterbury, so she read the Bible to him, sang him hymns, and prayed over him.[279] His mother exerted great influence over Francis. She taught him to read the Bible before he was 6 years old and instilled in him a strong fear of sin. A shy, introspective boy who was intimidated by bullying classmates and a harsh schoolmaster, he had only 6 years of formal education. Asbury had a religious awakening at the age of 14, after which he began to attend meetings of the Methodist Society. He soon became an exhorter and later a preacher. At the Bristol Conference of the Methodists in 1771, he volunteered to

---

[274] Earle E. Cairns, *Christianity through the Centuries* (Michigan: Zondervan Publishing House, 1981), 383-384.

[275] Robert F. Lay, "American saint: Francis Asbury and the Methodists," *Wesleyan Theological Journal*, 45/2 (September-December, 2010), 295.

[276] William P. Farley, Francis Asbury: Spartan Apostle of Early America http://enrichmentjournal.ag.org/200603/200603_116_francis_asbury.cfm (accessed on 17/11/16).

[277] Francis Asbury: Methodist on horseback www.christianity today.com/history/people/denomination alfounders/francis-asbury.html (accessed on 12/07/16).

[278] Wesley.nnn.edu/other-theologian/francis-asbury (accessed on 12/07/16).

[279] Herbert Asbury, *A Methodist Saint: The Life of Bishop Asbury* (New York: Alfred A. Knopf, Inc., 1927), 1.

go to America as a missionary. He arrived in Philadelphia on Oct. 27, 1771, and went to New York to work under Richard Boardman, one of the first missionaries sent to America by the Methodist Society. Francis Asbury found church discipline lax and the city sinful. Without asking Boardman's permission, he borrowed a horse and rode into the countryside, thus making his first circuit in America by going to several New York communities.[280] Those living outside the big cities were disbursed across large areas and had little contact with other Christians. Asbury saw an opportunity and, like most entrepreneurs, capitalized aggressively. Using Wesley's methods, Asbury formed preaching circuits in rural areas. He recruited and ordained young men to preach to congregations that formed near each circuit (circuit riders).[281] They preached wherever hearers would gather: in barns, fields, living rooms, or later, at camp meetings. Congregations often numbered only 10 to 25 people.[282] In Asbury's day, there were few hotels in the backwoods of America. When nightfall came, Asbury and his traveling companion would seek shelter by knocking on the closest door. They were seldom refused, but the accommodations were not great. Often they slept in drafty cabins, a piece of buckskin separating them from the cold, dirt floor. Flea-and lice-plague-ridden animals often bedded a few feet away. Dry bread and hemlock (not good) tea were served for breakfast.

On September 4, 1771, at the age of 26, Francis Asbury began his journey to Philadelphia from Pill near Bristol. "It cost him much to leave home and kindred, as is witnessed by his affectionate letters and sacrificial remittances home: but the call of God was not to be denied." Before he left, he wrote a letter to his family. "I wonder sometimes how anyone will sit to hear me, but the Lord covers my weakness with his power. I trust you will be easy and quieter. As for me, I know what I am called to. It is to give up all, and to have my hands and heart in the work, yea, the nearest and dearest friends. Let others condemn me as being without natural affection, disobedient to parents, or say what they please. I love my parents and friends, but I love my God better and his service. And though' I have

---

[280] Francis Asbury Facts, http://biography.yourdictionary.com/francis-asbury (accessed on 16/11/16).

[281] Circuit riders had to be young, in good health, and single (since marriage and a family forced preachers to settle in one area and leave the traveling ministry). Unlike their counterparts in other denominations, Methodist circuit riders did not have to have a formal education. Leaders of the new church wanted educated, trained circuit riders, but they wanted even more to spread their ministry to people on the frontier who needed Christian guidance. Circuit riders had a simple plan of evangelism. They went where the people lived, and they ministered to their needs. Often, one of the first visitors to a family who had just arrived on the frontier was a Methodist circuit rider. During the day, he might help out with chores or assist with teaching the children. In the evening, after dinner, he would offer religious instruction to the family and to any neighbors who wished to join them.

[282] William P. Farley, Francis Asbury: Spartan Apostle of Early America http://enrichmentjournal.ag.org/200603/200603_116_francis_asbury.cfm (accessed on 17/11/16).

given up all; I do not repent, for I have found all.[283] A miserable and sober man, Asbury constantly subjected himself to spiritual and physical problems. A variety of physical problems plagued him during the 45 years in which he traveled the American continent; in spite of this he rode at least 5,000 miles a year, preaching and exhorting at every opportunity. Asbury's prestige grew as his circuit widened. He preached first in Pennsylvania, Maryland, Delaware, and Virginia and later in the South and the West.[284]

Asbury's power of perseverance and his single-minded devotion to Christ's cause were exemplary. Nothing but significant health problems deterred him from his arduous schedule. He continued in spite of violent and persistent headaches, constant hemorrhoids (a significant problem for a man on horseback), intensity of depression, dissensions in leadership, and criticism. His self-denial and willingness to suffer to reach the lost made him stand out among his peers. Passionate love for those without Christ drove him. Like Paul he could boast, "Death is at work in us, but life is at work in you" (2 Corinthians 4:12). And, like Paul, the amazing resurrection life that followed Asbury's ministry was in direct proportion to his death. He was zealous for personal holiness. Like most Methodists, he believed in the possibility of sinless perfection through instant sanctification by a supernatural work of the Holy Spirit.[285] Francis Asbury confronted the church that was tolerant of the evil of slavery and appealed to governmental leaders for intervention and change. He also prayed for slavery to completely end and looked forward of a change within the society.[286] He was a prophet of social change who voiced against the liquor and asked to denounce it as well he also had challenged to denounce slavery a century before the abolition took place. He lived in voluntary poverty, dressing cheaply, even buying the cheapest saddles despite the huge amount of time he spent on horseback. He gave away almost all the money that ever came his way.[287]

In 1789, Asbury was instrumental in starting a publishing house which today is the world's largest religious publisher. In the same year, he started a periodical which under different names and with some lapses, has continued until this day. At once books and papers began to pour from the presses in a stream which has been constantly increasing in volume for more than a century and a half and is

---

283 Frank Baker, *From Wesley to Asbury: Studies in Early American Methodism* (Durham, NC: Duke University Press, 1976), 113-115.

284 Charles Ludwig, *Francis Asbury: God's Circuit Rider* (Milford, Michigan: Mott Media, 1984), 5-7.

285 Darius Salter, *America's Bishop* (Nappanee, Ind.: Evangel, 2003), 145-147.

286 Matt Lockett, "7 Ways Circuit Rider Francis Asbury Showed Us How to Contend Against Injustice." http://bound4life.com/blog/2015/04/06/7-ways-circuit-rider-francis-asbury-modeled-how-to-contend-against-injustice/ (accessed on 16/11/16).

287 Chris R. Armstrong, "Indelible marker: Methodist Francis Asbury left his fingerprints all over American Christianity," *Christianity Today,* 53/12 (December, 2009): 65.

today far greater than it has ever been. He may almost be said to deserve the title of American Publisher Number One. In 1814, his health started to fail and he became ill. In 1816, he started to regain strength and continued his preaching journey. He "preached his last Sermon in Richmond, Virginia" on March 24, "and died at the home of George Arnold near Fredericksburg." Asbury had times when he tended to have gloomy thoughts and opinions. He believed himself to be "a true prophet of evil tidings, as it suits my cast of mind." Although he was pessimistic, those who knew him considered him an extremely sensitive person. In his journal he recorded more failures and misgivings than success in his ministry. He loved simplicity and had "frequent spells of morbid depression."[288]

In his unparalleled career, he preached about 16,500 sermons, or at least once a day, and traveled about 270,000 miles, or 6,000 a year, presiding in no less than 224 annual conferences, and ordaining more than 4,000 preachers. When he came to America the Methodists numbered 10 preachers and 600 members; when he died, after forty-five years of work, they had 695 preachers and 214,235 members.[289] He lived in voluntary poverty, dressing cheaply, even buying the cheapest saddles despite the huge amount of time he spent on horseback. He gave away almost all the money that ever came his way.

5.2 William Carey (1761-1834)

The eighteenth-century English missionary William Carey (1761-1834) is remembered for his outstanding missiological significance. His life has been the topic of no fewer than fifty biographical profiles, most focusing centrally on his missionary endeavors and their present significance.[290] His boyhood playmates called him Columbus and an elderly colleague called him a "miserable enthusiast.[291] Christopher Smith opines that "A scholarly quest for the 'historical Carey' is long overdue. In spite of the fact that scores of biographies have been written about him, layers of popular mythology still remain to be cut through before the actual contours of his career as a pre-Victorian mission leader will be uncovered."[292] Some missionary historians and biographers such as Robert Glover, Basil Miller and

---

[288] William Larkin Duren, *Francis Asbury, Founder of American Methodism and Unofficial Minister of State* (New York: The Macmillan Company, 1928), 75-77.

[289] "Francis Asbury: Father of American Methodism", http://www.tlogical.net/bioasbury.htm (accessed on 17/11/16).

[290] Timothy George, *Faithful Witness: The Life and Mission of William Carey* (Birmingham, AL: New Hope, 1991), 5.

[291] Mary Drewery, *William Carey: A Biography* (Grand Rapids: Zondervan Publishing House, 1979), 12, 31.

[292] A. Christopher Smith, "William Carey, 1761-1834, Protestant Pioneer of the Modern Mission Era," in *Mission Legacies: Biographical Studies of Leaders of the Modern Missionary Movement,* eds., Gerald H. Anderson, Robert T. Coote, Norman A. Horner, and James M. Phillips (Maryknoll, N.Y.: Orbis Books, 1994), 245.

others address him with the title "Father of Modern Missions" who really changed the thinking of mission and challenged the traditional understandings.[293]

William Carey, the Baptist missionary, stands out as the pioneer and the great symbolic figure of the beginning of the modern Protestant missionary movement. Carey was born into a Church of England home on August 17, 1761, the eldest of Edmund and Elizabeth Carey's five children. His father was a weaver but later became a teacher and a parish clerk. Carey was unfit to work outdoors, as he suffered from a skin disease that made it painful for him to go out in the bright sun.[294] While he was a student, Carey worked with his uncle as a gardener till he turned 14. Although, William was a poor country boy, living in a landlocked province far from London and the sea, he *was* able to count his blessings. These he turned to good use by applying himself to acquiring knowledge during spare time. This developed into a lifelong passion for botany and agriculture. Later, to earn living he worked as a shoemaker till he was 28. He was, therefore, apprenticed to Clarke Nichols, a shoemaker at Hakleton, who died two years later.

William Carey lived during a time of great change, when Europe's Enlightenment was beginning to make itself felt in English church and society. While a teenager, newspapers and mass-produced literature periodically came his way as a young Midlands man, he became vividly aware of the outside world through reading about the American revolution and Captain Cook's voyages of discovery in the Pacific. Six years (1787-1793) were spent pastoring Particular Baptist churches in Northamptonshire that was when he became aware of early Protestant missionary work in North America during the past 150 years.[295]

Due to this background, some officers of the East India Company used to look down upon him even after Carey was ordained as a priest of the Baptist mission. He had studied Greek, Hebrew, and Latin. This study encouraged him to learn various languages and thus, he became a linguist. Carey left England on June 13, 1793 with the intention of preaching the gospel in India. He arrived in Kolkata five months later; on November 11, 1793 the East India Company had established its political control over most of the Indian Territory by then. Even though the officers of the East India Company were Christians, unlike the Portuguese, they avoided mixing up political governance and missionary work.[296] In 1793, after a five-month voyage, he arrived in India, where he lived the remaining forty years of his life. Never returning home, he died in Serampore in

---

[293] Robert Glover, *The Progress of World Wide Missions* (New York: Harper, 1960), 59. See also Basil W. Miller, *William Carey* (Grand Rapids: Zondervan Publication, 1952), 5.

[294] Mary Drewery, *William Carey, Shoemaker and Missionary* (London: Hodderand Stoughton, 19?8), 13.

[295] A. Christopher Smith, "The legacy of William Carey," *International Bulletin of Missionary Research,* 16/1 (January, 1992), 3.

[296] Camil Parkhe, *Contribution of Christian Mission In India* (Gujarat: Gujarat Sahity Prakash, 2007), 114.

1834. Despite only a very modest formal education, Carey was driven by a thirst for knowledge throughout his life. His uncle was a gardener, and Carey developed a lifelong interest in botany. He taught himself first the classical language, then several modern European languages. He eventually undertook Bible translations in twenty-five Indian languages and dialects and served as a professor of Indian languages for thirty years at Fort William College in Calcutta.[297] His first employment was as an apprentice shoemaker. But in 1779 this nominal Anglican experienced an evangelical conversion and four years later joined the Baptists. His remaining time in England was spent cobbling, teaching school, and serving as pastor of small Baptist congregations. His first years in India, until 1800, were difficult. In addition to preaching; he worked as superintendent of an indigo factory and translated the New Testament into Bengali.

Fully convinced of the need for foreign missionary work, and after study of what both Roman Catholics and Protestants had already done, Carey published a small book in 1792. The contents are summarized in its full title: *An Enquiry into the Obligations of Christians to Use Means for the Conversion of the Heathens, in which the Religious State of the Different Nations of the World, the Success of Former Un*dertaking, *and the Practicability of Further Undertakings, are Considered.* In May 1792, Carey was the preacher for a meeting of Baptist ministers at Nottingham. His sermon was a stirring challenge to accept Christ's commission to preach the Gospel to all nations. At their next meeting, in October in Kettering, the ministers responded by creating the Particular Baptist Society for Propagating the Gospel among the Heathen. It was this society that accepted Carey's offer of himself as a missionary and that sponsored him in his work in India.[298]

5.2.1 William Carey and Moravians Impact

Carey's first writing mentions about Moravians is seen in his 1792 Enquiry. He begins by arguing that Christ's command to preach to all is still valid and that only the impossibility of doing it would excuse us. But it is not impossible to do. "Have not the popish missionaries surmounted all those difficulties which we have generally thought to be insuperable? Have not the missionaries of the *Unitas Fratrum,* or Moravian Brethren, encountered the scorching heat of Abyssinia, and the frozen climes of Greenland, and Labrador, their difficult languages, and savage manners?"[299] Next comes a survey of the efforts to expand the church,

[297] David A. Schattschneider, "William Carey, Modern Missions, and Moravian Influence", *International Bulletin of Missionary Research,* 22/1 (January, 1998): 9.

[298] David A. Schattschneider, "William Carey, Modern Missions, and Moravian Influence", 9.

[299] David A. Schattschneider, "William Carey, Modern Missions, and Moravian Influence", 10. See also William Carey, *An Enquiry into the Obligations of Christians, to Use Means for the Conversion of the Heathens, in which the Religious State of the Different Nations of the World, the Success of Former Undertakings, and the Practicability of Further Undertakings, are Considered* (Leicester, England, 1792; facsimile ed. with introduction, London: Carey Kingsgate Press, 1961), 11.

beginning with Pentecost and continuing up to his own time. "But none of the moderns have equaled the Moravian Brethren in this good work; they have sent missions to Greenland, Labrador, and several of the West-Indian Islands, which have been blessed for good. They have likewise sent to Abyssinia, in Africa, but what success they have had I cannot tell.[300]

Joseph Hutton writes that Carey "flung down on the parlor table some numbers of a missionary magazine entitled *Periodical Accounts,* and . . . exclaimed: 'See what these Moravians have done!'[301] Mission communities which was developed by William Carey shows that this was adopted from Moravian missionaries. When William Carey and the other missionaries (six families in all) established themselves in the Danish colonial port of Serampore in 1800, the Moravian influence was once again evident in Carey's plan. The group was organized into an deliberate community at Carey's direction. Though each family had modest quarters, meals were taken together, everyone's earnings were put into a common treasury, decisions were decided by majority vote, and responsibilities ranging from housekeeping duties to leading devotional exercises were rotated on a monthly basis. A weekly meeting, on Saturday evening, was held to allow any member of this extended family to air grievances that might have arisen against another during the week. This arrangement, though not eliminating all interpersonal frictions, would effectively serve the needs of the original missionary group.[302]

But another views, which is brought forth by Mary Drewery, in her recent biography of Carey, shows that maybe he was not at the meeting at all, since "his name does not appear among the list of subscribers to the projected Mission. If he was there," she continues, "no doubt he would have pointed to the successful work of the Moravians in Africa and the West Indies."[303] From the beginnings of their activity the Moravians had favored communal living arrangements for their missionaries. These arrangements had been described in detail by Augustus Gottlieb Spangenberg, their leader after the death of Zinzendorf in 1760. By 1788 several of Spangenberg's German writings about the missions had appeared in English translation, including his *Instructions for the Members of the Unitas Fratrum, who Minister in the Gospel Among the Heathen.* Chapter 7 is entitled, "Relations of the Missionaries to Each Other—Joint Housekeeping and Trades—

---

[300] David A. Schattschneider, "William Carey, Modern Missions, and Moravian Influence", 37.

[301] Joseph E. Hutton, *A History of Moravian Missions* (London: Moravian Publication Office, 1923), 3. Cited by David A. Schattschneider, in "William Carey, Modern Missions, and Moravian Influence", 10.

[302] David A. Schattschneider, "William Carey, Modern Missions, and Moravian Influence", 10.

[303] Mary Drewery, *William Carey, Shoemaker and Missionary* (London: Hodder & Stoughton, 1978), 41.

Household Churches—Conferences." Here was the description of missionary life that Carey adapted for his community in Serampore.[304]

A final point of contact in this network was realized by Carey only after he and his friends began their work in Serampore. They were establishing themselves on the very site where there had previously been a Moravian mission. In the early decades of Moravian activity the Brethren established many mission stations, and if there was no response after a few years, the effort was closed out and the personnel assigned elsewhere. Karl Friedrich Schmidt, a preacher, and Johannes Grassman, a physician, were sent by the Moravians and arrived in Serampore in 1777. They learned the Bengali language and began a translation of the Bible. But since they had to earn their own living, they had little time for traditional missionary activities. The caste system kept them from coming into close contact with the Indians. Although under the flag of Protestant Denmark, there were very few Protestants in town, and the Moravian presence was opposed by Roman Catholic and Armenian Orthodox citizens. In 1792, after fifteen years, the Moravian mission was abandoned.[305] Perhaps, even though this Moravian effort was not entirely without result. In December 1800, Carey baptized his first Indian convert, Krishna Pal, a Hindu carpenter who is said to have first heard about Christianity from Grassman while doing carpentry work for him. William Carey and the Moravians seem to be worked as part of a single network. They all labored at crucial turning points in the development of Protestant missions, and their stories shows as great moments in missionary history who have put a mark in the history of the Church.

5.2.2 William Carey and Personal Life

William Carey was married three times. Before he reached the age of twenty, he married Dorothy Plackett—sister-in-law of his employer, six years his senior, unlettered, provincial, unimaginative—who never shared his dream. There is no evidence as to whether the marriage was a love-match. One of Carey's biographers commented, "Never had minister, missionary or scholar a less sympathetic mate, due largely to...latent mental disease...and a reproachful tongue.[306] Reluctantly, Dorothy followed Carey to India where she suffered from the heat, the humidity, the constant fevers, the dysentery, and the constant danger to her little children. She soon sank into deep depression caused by culture shock and spent the last

---

[304] Augustus G. Spangenberg, *Instructions for Missionaries of the Church of the Unitas Fratrum, or United Brethren,* trans., 2nd rev. & enl. ed. (London: Brethren's Society for the Furtherance of the Gospel Among the Heathen, 1840), pp. iv-v, 56. Cited by David A. Schattschneider, in "William Carey, Modern Missions, and Moravian Influence", 12.

[305] Joseph E. Hutton, *A History of Moravian Missions* (London: Moravian Publication Office, 1923), 165. Cited by David A. Schattschneider, in "William Carey, Modern Missions, and Moravian Influence", 12.

[306] Mary Drewery, *William Carey: A Biography* (Grand Rapids: Zondervan Publishing House, 1979), 21.

thirteen years of her life with the door locked and the walls padded. Dorothy vented wild accusations about Carey and tried on several occasions to kill him, but Carey insisted on caring for her personally. She died of a fever in 1807. He married Shalom, six months after the death of Dorothy. With this linguistically gifted, Danish lady-of-means, whom he baptized in the Danish enclave in 1802, he enjoyed thirteen years of marital bliss. During the final years of their married life, Charlotte was a complete invalid. When she died in 1821 at the age of 60, Carey was heartbroken.[307] Another gracious helpmeet came along two years later in the person of a British widow. Grace Hughes had been part of colonial Bengal for many years. She cared for Carey during his remaining years, nursing him through illness and bereavement. She lived to survive him.[308]

In Serampore, each family had a spacious property, separate apartments, but they shared a common table and a common library. Each family had a personal allowance, but all other earnings went into a common fund, from which all expenses were met. Each had his personal hobby—Ward, his presses; Marshman, his book; and Carey, his botanical garden. It is almost miraculous that they were able to avoid serious interpersonal conflicts which are the curse of so many missionary relationships. Probably their subtle humor and friendly rivalry helped glue them together. Ward, the youngest, died in 1823; Marshman and Carey labored together until 1834.[309]

5.2.3 William Carey: The Mission Model

Even though, Carey lived two hundred years before, he still serves as a prototype for the effective cross-cultural missionary—even when measured by contemporary criteria in the present conditions. William Carey engrossed himself in the language and culture of the Indian people. Due to the limitations imposed on him by his own colonial government, for five years Carey and his young family disappeared into the tiger-infested interior where he supported himself by agriculture and the management of an indigo factory while mastering Bengali. He knew it would be necessary to encourage and train Indian missionaries. By taking secular employment he emulated the method of the Apostle Paul and anticipated the modern method of the "tentmaker missionary" so popular today. His "wilderness experience" improved his indigenous philosophy.

William Carey modeled the typical bi-vocational, agricultural missionary. Like Paul, he sometimes used his botanical, agricultural, and scientific skills to support his family and his mission; at other times, these skills served as a ministry and a satisfying hobby, which not only fed hungry people, but also opened doors

307 Timothy George, *Faithful Witness: The Life and Mission of William Care* (Birmingham, AL: New Hope, 1991), 161.

308 A. Christopher Smith, "The Legacy of William Carey," *International Bulletin of Missionary Research,* Vol. 16/1 (January, 1992): 4.

309 Leon McBeth, *Men Who Made Missions* (Nashville: Broadman Press, 1968), 92.

for evangelism and made a bridge between people. Carey also pioneered Bible translation which has led to the work of the Bible Societies. His self-acquired language skills helped him become an amazing translator, especially when we consider the limitations under which he worked. He and his colleagues, with the help of Indian pundits, translated the Bible into thirty-seven languages. Besides, in order to better understand the Hindu religion, they translated a number of the Hindu classics. These accomplishments brought recognition to Carey as a linguist, scientist, anthropologist, amazing for a man who never had a formal education.[310]

William Carey and his companions had a deep social consciousness. The Baptist Missionary Society missionaries who followed Carey were largely responsible for the abolition of slavery in the British Empire. They also were instrumental in abolishing inhuman practices in India such as the burning of widows with their deceased husbands[311] (Sati). Carey's early motto, "Expect great things from God; attempt great things for God," became the pattern of his life and career. Christopher Smith opines that the Serampore mission leaders constituted a remarkable team of highly motivated, hard-working, mutually supportive, closely collaborating... (Workers) ... who stuck together through thick and thin for several decades. That in itself was no mean achievement.[312]

5.3 Nathan Bangs (1778-1862)

He was the son of Lemuel Bangs and Rebecca Keeler; who married Mary Bolton of Edwardsburgh Township, Upper Canada, and they had 11 children. Nathan Bangs was an American Christian theologian in the Methodist tradition. Lemuel Bangs, himself, was an honest, intelligent, stalwart blacksmith, and a staunch Churchman, with the Puritan traditions of his family. He was born in Stratford, Connecticut, who had limited education, taught in school, and in 1799 went to Upper Canada in search of work as either a teacher or a land-surveyor. He was converted to Methodism in 1800 and worked for eight years as a wandering preacher in the wilderness of the Canadian provinces, serving communities in the areas of Kingston, York, London, Niagara, and Montreal. He married Canadian Mary Bolton and, after a brief stint in Lower Canada, was transferred back to the United States in 1808, first in Albany and then New York in 1810. In 1812, Bangs was made the Presiding Elder of the Lower Canada District, also riding the Montreal Circuit. Bangs was esteemed within the church.[313] As publisher, journalist, historian, and ecclesiastical statesman Bangs helped to shape directly

---

310 Justice C. Anderson, "William Carey: A bi-centennial Tribute," *Southwestern Journal of Theology*, 35/1 (September-December, 1992): 43.

311 Stephen Neill, *A History of Christian Missions* (New York: Penguin Books, 1980), 264.

312 Christopher Smith, "A Tale of Many Models: The Missiological Significance of the Serampore Trio." *Missiology*, 20/4 (1992): 494.

313 Nathan Bangs, https://en.wikipedia.org/wiki/Nathan_Bangs (accessed on 20/11/16).

and indirectly the development of Methodism in Upper Canada. His presence and advice helped William Case, Thomas Madden, and others to establish the autonomous Upper Canadian conference of the American church. In 1828, he was involved with John and William Ryerson, James Richardson, and Philander Smith in the formation of the independent Methodist Episcopal Church of Canada. His services were recognized by the offer of appointment as its first general superintendent or bishop, which he declined.

Nathan Bangs was not only a public but a representative man, in the Methodist Episcopal Church, for more than half a century. During nearly sixty years he appeared almost constantly in its pulpits. He was the founder of its periodical literature, and of its "Conference course" of ministerial study, and one of the founders of its present system of educational institutions.

Nathan Bangs was a respected elder statesman of Methodism at the time when Phoebe Palmer and the Holiness movement were rising to prominence. He had had a long career as a pioneering evangelist, pastor, editor, mission's promoter (he founded the Methodist Missionary Society),[314] educator, historian, and apologetic for Methodism (especially in opposing the people who held the idea of predestination. Experiencing entire sanctification early in his Christian life, Bangs became a life-long advocate of a holiness emphasis and was closely associated with Mrs. Phoebe Palmer's Tuesday Meeting.[315] He had known her since she was a child and had given hearty support for her holiness promotion. Nathan Bangs had published more material on eschatology than Phoebe Palmer. He was always very optimistic about the future, the prospects of the Methodist Church, and the Christian cause generally.[316]

The impression is that Bangs was much more concerned about the unity, spirituality, and numerical prosperity of the church than the moral tragedy of slavery. He could affirm that the disputes between the North and the South were "a deleterious influence upon the interests of true religion" and not utter a word in this context about the evil influence of slavery on the "interests of true religion." Social reform was clearly not very high on his priority list. The benevolent fruition of sanctification did not necessarily include strong moral opposition to social evil in its systemic manifestations. For Bangs, there were great millennial events in the imminent offing, but the path to this dream society was through the workings of the Lord for personal regeneration that would somehow bear fruit for the rule of Christ on the earth. It was a very activist mode, but a personal Salvationist mode, not a collective, political one in its ultimate thrust.

---

[314] Nolan B. Harmon, ed. *Encyclopedia of World Methodism,* Vol. 1 (Nashville: The Methodist Publishing House, 1974), 214.

[315] Abel Stevens, *Life and Times of Nathan Bangs* (New York: Carlton and Porter, 1883), 345.

[316] Abel Stevens, *Life and Times of Nathan Bangs.* 345.

5.3.1 Nathan Bangs' Contribution towards Writings

Nathan Bangs, first as leader of the Methodist Book Concern in New York City and later as the founder of the Christian Advocate newspaper, broadcast Methodist ideas and concerns through published media. John Wesley shared his ideas by publishing sermons, hymnals, a magazine, and various books to provide his followers with current material on the world and Methodism. Bangs institutionalized this by creating the first uniquely Methodist printing press, publishing multiple books and pamphlets, many of which formed the core of Methodist Sunday Schools.[317] Moreover, he was the first missionary secretary appointed by its General Conference, the first clerical editor of its General Conference newspaper press, the first editor of its Quarterly Review, and, for many years, the chief editor of its Monthly Magazine and its book publications. He may be pronounced the principal founder of the American literature of Methodism; a literature now remarkable for its extent, and of no inconsiderable intrinsic value. Besides his innumerable miscellaneous writings for its periodicals, he wrote more volumes in defense or illustration of his denomination than any other man. Bangs also wrote A History of the Methodist Episcopal Church from its Origin in 1776 to the General Conference in 1840, an exhaustive four volume work that remains the most extensive scholarly treatment of early Methodism in America.[318]

5.3.2 Nathan Bang's Concept of Christian Perfection and Holiness

A mind so profoundly imbibed with religious earnestness as that of young Bangs, could not fail to seize on a truth like this. "From reading the holy Scriptures," he writes, "Mr. Wesley's Plain Account of Christian Perfection, and Mr. Fletcher's writings on the subject, I clearly saw the necessity of a deeper piety than I had yet attained; of being sanctified throughout, soul, body, and spirit. Formerly I was condemned as a guilty sinner, and hardly dared to look up to God for mercy; now I felt reconciled to him, could pray in faith, and enjoyed peace, while a sweet compunction weighed me down at the footstool of divine mercy. I hated sin with a perfect hatred, and consequently felt an utter aversion to all its pleasures. Such confidence had I in the Christian purity and influence of Mr. Warner, who professed the blessing of sanctification, and, I doubt not, enjoyed it, that I loved his very presence."[319]

Bangs fully believe that we are both justified and sanctified by grace, through faith in the Lord Jesus Christ, and that when so justified or sanctified the holy Spirit sets his seal upon our hearts, and gives us an evidence that the work is done. All those Scriptures, therefore, which speak of the necessity of having faith in

---

[317] Abel Stevens, *Life and Times of Nathan Bangs,* 38.

[318] Nathan Bangs, "Telling our Stories," http://www.nyac.com/ files/archives/250anniversary/ biography bulletin inserts/bulletin-insert-bangs (accessed on 20/11/2016).

[319] Abel Stevens, *Life and Times of Nathan Bangs,* 38.

God, of believing in the Lord Jesus Christ, etc., I need hardly say I fully embrace, and urge upon others as necessary conditions of justification and sanctification. "But this faith is always accompanied by works. Even the penitent sinner, seeking the pardon of his sins, must repent and 'do works meet for repentance; he must 'cease to do evil, and learn to do well,' according to his light and opportunity." It not only gave it life and energy, by inspiring its congregations with devout and transforming aspirations, but it was the precise sentiment needed as the basis of its ministry. Nothing short of entire self-sacrifice could consist with the duties and privations of that ministry; and, according to their doctrine of perfection, entire consecration was the preliminary of entire sanctification. These holy men, then, in making an entire public sacrifice of themselves, did so as a part of an entire consecration to God, for the purpose of their own entire personal sanctification, as well as their usefulness to others.[320]

Bangs was quite forthright in expressing the relationship between his views on the dynamics of sanctification and the inspiration to benevolent and missionary efforts. Sanctification not only gives a proper sense of priorities about truth, but for the believer these "essential truths" penetrate "the depths of his soul, burn within him like 'fire shut up in his bones,'" and "he is impelled forward in the grand work of conquering the world to Jesus Christ." The sum total of Bangs' concept is that the "conquering of the world to Jesus Christ" is largely a matter of personal conversion to Christ, rather than primarily the subjection of the social order to Christian ideals.[321] Bangs defended Armenian thought against the Calvinistic thinking of his day. He was a strong believer of prevenient grace but not at the expense of total depravity. He argued that because of grace, humankind does have the ability to respond to God. For Nathan Bangs, the millennium would be a spiritual rule of Christ on the earth which will be brought on through the agency of the Church (inspired and empowered by the Holy Spirit), not a visible and literal bodily presence of Christ on the earth. This millennial period would then be followed by the literal and visible appearing of Christ at the "great white throne" judgment to put down all final opposition to His rule.[322]

5.4 Phoebe Worrall Palmer (1807-1874)

Phoebe Palmer was born in New York City in 1807 and died there in 1874. Her father had been converted in England under John Wesley's preaching and set up a staunch Methodist home when he immigrated to America. Phoebe

---

[320] Abel Stevens, *Life and Times of Nathan Bangs*, 36.

[321] Nathan Bangs, *The Present State, Prospects, and Responsibilities of the Methodist Episcopal Church* (New York: Lane and Scott, 1850), 231, 241, 271. Cited by Woodrow W. Whidden, in "Eschatology, Soteriology and Social Activism in Four Mid-Nineteenth Century Holiness Methodists," Wesleyan Theological Journal, 29/1-2 (March-December, 1994): 98-99.

[322] Nathan Bangs, *The Present State, Prospects, and Responsibilities of the Methodist Episcopal Church*, 99.

embraced her parents' Methodist faith as a child and remained true to it all her life.[323] Besides her contributions as a theologian, she also significantly influenced the course of American religion as a revivalist, feminist, and humanitarian. As a theologian she provided the link between John Wesley and the Pentecostals by modifying his theology of Christian perfection.[324] Palmer grew up in a religious culture heavily influenced by Wesleyanism. The Methodism of her time drew deeply from biographies of ministers who believed that the Holy Spirit was the only thing needed to help one interpret the Bible.[325] In 1827, she married Walter Palmer, who was at that time training in the medical profession. He supported her so that she could participate in evangelistic efforts full time. She also had six children but only three of them survived.[326] She resolved the tension in her life by consciously deciding to dedicate herself first to God and then to her family. The result was an immediate peace and freedom. Her thinking was shaped by these tragedies and her decision as well as by her upbringing and personal study of Scripture and Wesleyan writings. Palmer's zeal and energy as an evangelist after 1837 carried implications for the Christian tradition was well as for the role of women in society.[327]

Harold E. Raser concludes that "in filling the traditional expositions of holiness with very specific meaning, Palmer created something new."[328] Phoebe Palmer was a leading figure in the holiness movement that shaped American Methodism in the 1840's and 1850's. Active in Sunday school teaching, mission work, prolific writing, and a wide range of benevolent activities—including a prison ministry and a unique mission, for that day, among the urban poor.[329] Thomas Oden writes, "Phoebe Palmer, after having been one of the most widely

---

[323] Charles Edward White, The beauty of holiness: the career of Phoebe Palmer," *Fides et historia,* 19/1 (February, 1987): 22-23.

[324] Charles Edward White, "Phoebe Palmer and the Development of Pentecostal Pneumatology" *Wesleyan Theological Journal,* 23/1-2 (January-December, 1988): 198. See also Charles Edward White, *The Beauty of Holiness: Phoebe Palmer as Theologian, Revivalist, Feminist, and Humanitarian* (Grand Rapids: Zondervan, 1986), 45.

[325] Jennifer A. Miskov, "Missing Links: Phoebe Palmer, Carrie Judd Montgomery, and Holiness Roots within Pentecostalism", *Penteco Studies,* 10/1 (2011): 9.

[326] N. A. Hardesty, "Your Daughters Shall Prophesy", *Chicago Studies in the History of American Religion,* J. C. Brauer and M. E. Marty, eds., (Brooklyn, NY: Carson Publishing Inc. 1991): 54-55.

[327] Karen B. Coffing, "Character & Personality: Phoebe Palmer and Aimee Semple McPherson as Mirrors of American Culture," *Fides et historia,* 28/1 (December-June, 1996): 50.

[328] Harold E. Raser, *Phoebe Palmer: Her Life and Thought* (Lewiston, NY: Edwin Mellen, 1987), 155.

[329] George De Vries, Jr. "Phoebe Palmer and spiritual independence", *Reformed Journal,* 37/8 (August, 1987): 3.

known women of her time in England and America, has remained virtually unknown during the past hundred years."[330]

Palmer's sanctification experience in 1837, at the age of 29 was the significant factor that led to her public evangelism and journalism. Palmer regularly worked to evangelize New York by going into prisons, conducting meetings, serving the poor, and speaking at camp and revival meetings. In 1864, the Palmers bought a publishing house as well as the popular holiness magazine entitled *The Guide to Holiness*, which she edited until her death. Her Tuesday holiness and prayer meetings became a template for Wesleyan holiness revivalism throughout the nineteenth century.[331] Palmer also was involved in The New York Female Assistance Society for the Relief and Religious instruction of the Poor as well as helping meetings. Palmer believed that the gift of salvation carried an obligation to spread the gospel. She urged holy living, a life so dedicated to God that it was a consuming passion. Every activity of every day should be arranged to further the Kingdom of God. Phoebe viewed child-rearing, domestic chores, and church-related activities with the same devotion and goal-orientation. Her dress and lifestyle were plain, due to her conviction that Christians had no time for extravagances. Jewelry and ornamentation cost money that could be used in missions rather than in bringing attention to a woman in an unfavorable way.[332]

5.4.1 Phoebe Palmer and Revivalism

The turning point in Mrs. Palmer's life came at nine o'clock, on the evening of July 26, 1837, when she experienced "entire sanctification." Three of her children had died in infancy. As she grieved over her loss, Phoebe Palmer became convinced that God had taken her children because she had loved them too much and because she was spending too much time on them. She resolved to resign everything she held dear to God, promising that she would never murmur at any step of obedience he required. She also resolved that the time she would have spent with her children would, henceforth, be dedicated to the Lord's service. She thought of her commitment as the "living sacrifice" God required, and became convinced that God had accepted her offering.[333]

D.W. Dayton starts his discussion of the American Holiness movement by recounting the story of two sisters, Sarah Lankford and Phoebe Palmer. They organized a prayer meeting in the 1830s called the "**Tuesday Meeting**" which became a "center of revival within Methodism" for spreading the doctrine

[330] Diane Leclerc, "Wesleyan Holiness Feminist Hermeneutics: An Historical Rendering with Contemporary Considerations," *Wesleyan Theological Journal*, 36/2 (September-December, 2001): 111.

[331] Melvin E. Dieter, *The Holiness Revival of the Nineteenth Century* (Metuchen, NJ: The Scarecrow Press. 1980), 82.

[332] Karen B. Coffing, "Character & Personality: Phoebe Palmer and Aimee Semple McPherson as Mirrors of American Culture," 57.

[333] Charles Edward White, The beauty of holiness: the career of Phoebe Palmer," 23.

of sanctification.[334] Palmer conducted these meetings "for the Promotion of Holiness" in New York City, from 1835-1874; the emphasis being on living a holy life that was set free from sins power. While the original meetings were actually started by her sister Sarah, it was Palmer who emerged as the main leader. By 1839, the meetings were also opened to men. The Tuesday meetings transcended denominational barriers and were open to include Baptists, Quakers, Congregationalists, Episcopalians, Mennonites, and others.[335] Many professed entire sanctification, and some established similar "Tuesday Meetings" in 238 places, some as far away as England, India, and New Zealand. Besides leading the Tuesday Meeting, Phoebe Palmer also spoke at camp-meetings and revival services.[336] Phoebe Palmer's emphasis on lay ministry was new to revivalism. Mrs. Palmer was the first to organize their labors effectively. Phoebe Palmer did not just mention house-to-house visitation as one of a number of tasks to help the minister. Rather, she gave it priority in her message, and also organized the church members into bands to see that it was done. Her emphasis on the role of the laity helped to transform revivalism.[337]

One of the reasons for their great success in these meetings that took place outside of the church is because there was the start of a decline among Methodist class meetings and these Tuesday meetings modeled similar characteristics of those classes and were in some sense a recovery of Wesley's original intentions. Sarah, although not as well-known as her younger sister Palmer, did a lot to encourage her sister. She worked among the poor in New York City and was a main influence in leading Palmer to obtain the sanctification of the times. Sarah broke through the barriers of private and public that were prevalent in her time by welcoming into her home those whom she taught.[338] In spite of chronic health problems, she continued the camp meeting visits until her death some thirty-five years later. She spent four years promoting holiness in the British Isles through revival services. Of her numerous publications, her books *The Way of Holiness, Faith and Its Effects,* and *Promise of the Father* (which argues for the legitimacy of women in ministry) are perhaps the most notable.

---

[334] D. W. Dayton, *Theological Roots of Pentecostalism (*Metuchen, New Jersey: Scarecrow Press, 1987), 9.

[335] C. E. Jones, "Holiness Movement," in *The New International Dictionary of Pentecostal and Charismatic Movements: Revised and Expanded Version.* S. M. Burgess, ed. (Grand Rapids, MI: Zondervan, 2002), 727.

[336] Charles Edward White, The beauty of holiness: the career of Phoebe Palmer," 27.

[337] Ibid., 28.

[338] Jennifer A. Miskov, "Missing Links: Phoebe Palmer, Carrie Judd Montgomery, and Holiness Roots within Pentecostalism", 10.

5.4.2 Phoebe Palmer's Theological Method

Palmer Palmer never published an analysis of how she arrived at theological formulations, but scattered through her writings are many comments about the various ways to discover God's truth. From these occasional remarks, one may induce the method of her theology. Not surprisingly for one who imbibed Methodism with her mother's milk, her method turns out to be the Wesleyan quadrilateral of Scripture, reason, experience, and tradition.[339] **Scripture:** Phoebe Palmer's theology began with the Bible. She was convinced that "the Bible is the living voice of the living God." Phoebe was fond of repeating, "The voice of the Scriptures is the voice of the Holy Ghost." Mrs. Palmer thought the voice of the Holy Spirit in the Scriptures wag even more reliable than a heavenly voice. She pointed out that Peter heard the heavenly voice at the Transfiguration, and yet called the Scripture "the more sure word of prophecy" (2 Peter 1:17- 19).[340] **Reason:** After the Scripture itself, the second focus of theological authority for Phoebe Palmer was human reason. She taught that the proper way to learn how to think and act was first to ask the Holy Spirit to teach through the Scripture, and then to urge rational hermeneutical rules to interpret that Scripture.[341] **Experience:** The irony of Mrs. Palmer's position about experience is that experience taught her that Scripture is superior to experience. She seems to be trapped in the logical cul-de-sac of arguing on the basis of experience that experience may not always be valid. Phoebe Palmer's position is not absurd, however. True, experience did lead her to Scripture, but her reliance on Scripture was not dependent on her experience.

5.4.3 Phoebe Palmer's Understanding of Sanctification

At first glance, it does not seem that Palmer was teaching a doctrine of entire sanctification (i.e., Christian perfection) different from that of Wesley, for she generally agrees with his theological construal. With Wesley, she asserts that Christian perfection is not a state of absolute perfection, neither is it angelic perfection or Academic perfection (i.e., the created human state before the fall). Instead, Christian perfection is a relative state of perfection. It might be best characterized as a moral perfection within the limits of human reason.[342] While agreeing with Wesley about sanctification as a second work of grace, Palmer

[339] Charles Edward White, "What the Holy Spirit Can and Cannot Do: The Ambiguities of Phoebe Palmer's Theology of Experience" *Wesleyan Theological Journal,* Volume 20/1 (March-June, 1985): 5.

[340] Charles Edward White, "What the Holy Spirit Can and Cannot Do: The Ambiguities of Phoebe Palmer's Theology of Experience."

[341] Charles Edward White, "What the Holy Spirit Can and Cannot Do: The Ambiguities of Phoebe Palmer's Theology of Experience" 7.

[342] Kevin T. Lowery, "A Folk in the Wesleyan road: Phoebe Palmer and the appropriation of Christian Perfection," *Wesleyan Theological Journal,* 36/2 (September-December, 2001): 189.

specifically simplified and modified his doctrine to make it more accessible to everyone. She agreed with John Fletcher's connection of the baptism of the Holy Spirit with entire sanctification and built upon Adam Clarke's ideas to connect holiness with power. She additionally emphasized immediate sanctification more than a gradual process. From Clarke, she drew on the concept that entire sanctification was not the end goal but the beginning of the Christian life. She made famous her "altar theology," which made sanctification accessible in a three stages which included entire consecration, faith, and sharing one's testimony. Lastly, she advocated that the truth in the Bible alone could be the proof for entire sanctification.[343] Palmer was more based on Scripture and the writing of John Wesley in her discussions. John Wesley taught that sanctification was the end result of a life of holy living, but Phoebe Palmer adapted his message to a doctrine of perfectibility as an immediate possibility from the time of a "second blessing," or an additional encounter with God after the initial salvation experience.

In place of believing in instantaneous entire sanctification, and waiting for it by practicing Wesley's generalized Christian discipline, Phoebe Palmer substituted a "shorter way" to holiness. All one needed to do was follow this simple three-step process for being sanctified: (1) entire consecration, (2) faith, and (3) testimony.[344] The first step to entire sanctification is entire consecration, "a perfect and entire yielding up of all to Christ, an entire trust in Christ, and a continuous reliance on Christ, for all needed grace under all diversity of circumstance or experience." It is a once-and-for-all surrender of "body, soul, and spirit; time, talents, and influence; and also of the dearest ties of nature, which must be reaffirmed daily. It is a determination that "we give ourselves at *once* wholly and forever away to [God's] service," in order that we may be unto him a peculiar people, zealous of good works, not living to ourselves. The second step to entire sanctification is to exercise faith. According to Mrs. Palmer, in 2 Corinthians 6:16—7:1 God promises to receive the offering of those who separate themselves from all evil through entire consecration. If believers entirely consecrate themselves to the Lord, they have God's word that He sanctifies them. Whether or not one feels any difference after devoting every area of one's life to the Lord, one must not question whether God has sanctified the heart. To doubt that one is entirely sanctified is to doubt God's word. One must not trust feelings; one must trust the written word of God.

The third step in the sanctification process is testimony. The work has already occurred, but it must be ratified as believers publicly bear witness to what, on the basis of the Scripture, they know God has done in the heart. While John Wesley had opined that those who received the blessing should tell other

343 Charles Edward White, "What the Holy Spirit Can and Cannot Do: The Ambiguities of Phoebe Palmer's Theology of Experience", 12.

344 Charles Edward White, "Phoebe Palmer and the Development of Pentecostal Pneumatology", 205.

believers, Phoebe Palmer asserted the "binding nature of the obligation to profess the blessing. Mrs. Palmer taught that Romans 10:9-10, which speak of believing in the heart and confessing with the mouth, requires public profession as well as heart faith for God's work to be effective. Not to tell others is to withhold the honor due to Christ; in addition, simple gratitude requires the Christian to acknowledge what the Lord has done in the heart.[345] R. D. Gooden opines that John Wesley taught that "Christian perfection, synonymous with holiness, entire sanctification, and perfect love" was a second work of grace that was separate from salvation.[346] For Phoebe Palmer "entire sanctification" meant utterly giving over to God everything she was, everything she had, all her relationships, dreams, hopes, and especially her will. It meant putting herself on the altar of Jesus to be a living sacrifice, an "eternal surrender of life, reputation, and friends dearer than life." The life of surrender was, for Palmer, "the way of holiness."[347]

As Palmer's theology began to develop, the Bible began to take precedent over all other human words. She proclaimed that "Christian Perfection, or 'holiness, was based entirely on Scripture: 'Not Wesley, not Fletcher, not Finney, not Mahan, not Upham, but the Bible, the holy Bible, is the first and the last. Palmer also believed that "the Bible is the standard, the groundwork, the platform, the creed." M. A. Noll opines that this trend of thinking came at a time when America was passionate about liberty when he says, "A principal reason that so many denominations sprang to life in America between the War of Independence and the Civil War...was the new opportunity for unfettered interpretation of Scripture. Americans in the early nineteenth century transformed their battle cry of the Reformation, 'the Bible alone' into a distinctly American appeal- 'no creed but the Bible![348] Phoebe Palmer promoted the cause of women's rights in two ways: by example and by argument. In an age when many thought it improper for a woman to speak in public, she addressed thousands in camp-meetings and revivals. In a day when most considered it unfitting for a woman to teach men, pastors and professors came every Tuesday to sit at her feet.[349]

Palmer's influence was awesome in addition to her evangelical efforts, in which more than 20,000 professed to be saved or sanctified (including B. T. Roberts, founder of the Free Methodists, Frances Willard, leader of the WCTU, and the Englishwoman Catherine Booth, wife of William Booth, founder of the

---

[345] Ibid., 205-206.

[346] R. D. Gooden, *Introduction to Faith Cures, and Answers to Prayer*, by Mrs. Edward Mix. (New York, NY: Syracuse University Press, 2002), xix.

[347] Elaine A. Heath, "The Via Negative in the life and Writing of Phoebe Palmer," *Wesleyan Theological Journal*, 41/2 (September-December, 2006), 89.

[348] Jennifer A. Miskov, "Missing Links: Phoebe Palmer, Carrie Judd Montgomery, and Holiness Roots within Pentecostalism", 20. See also M. A. Noll, *History of Christianity in the United States and Canada.* (Grand Rapids, MI: William B. Eerdmans Publishing Company, 1992), 151.

[349] Charles Edward White, *The Beauty of Holiness: The Career of Phoebe Palmer*, 28.

Salvation Army), Palmer wrote seventeen books and edited the widely circulated "Guide to Holiness" She was cofounder and director of the Five Points Mission in New York City (a precursor of the later settlement houses for the urban poor), served as secretary of the Female Assistance Society, and was a promoter of Methodist missions to China and Palestine.[350] Phoebe Palmer's success was in a large measure due to her clarity in the method of obtaining the experience, and in the fact that she made Scripture the basic evidence. Palmer's theology contains a strong call for women to live out their new spiritual potential. Palmer's religious vision provided nineteenth-century holiness women with a new confidence, not only to know them as fully devoted to God, but also to be fully themselves. Palmer's burning utterances changed history—not only the religious history of the nineteenth-century, but also the individual histories of women who walk in Palmer's footsteps. She not only gave them an example, she gave them theologically-based requisites that demanded that they refuse to keep silent in the churches and in the world.[351]

5.5 Daneil Steele (1824-1914)

Daniel Steele was born in Windham, New York, attended Wesleyan University, where he received a Bachelor of Arts (1848), a Master of Arts (1851), and a Doctor of Divinity degree (1868). He began his career in education as the Professor of Ancient Languages and Literature at Genesee College in Lima, New York. In 1869, after several years of teaching, Steele became the acting president of Genesee College until 1871. Steele decided to join Syracuse University, where he was appointed as the Professor of Mental and Moral Philosophy, one of only five faculty positions in the College of the University (later called the College of Liberal Arts).[352] In 1872 he retired from the university, and returned to pastoral work in the New England Conference of the Methodist Episcopal Church. It was in this period of time that Steele began to publish his theological books and writings that would establish him as a prominent figure in the Holiness Movement. In 1886, Steele returned to academia once more, becoming the Professor of Doctrinal Theology at Boston University. He was a great Bible scholar and theologian associated with the Methodist Holiness movement. He had a varied career as a pastor, college professor, and college administrator.

He had written many books which shows his caliber and personality as a great theologian such as Love Enthroned in 1875 which talked about the doctrine of entire sanctification includes the author's personal testimony to the experience. This was the first of Steele's "holiness books." Another book was Milestone Papers

---

[350] George De Vries, Jr. "Phoebe Palmer and Spiritual Independence", 4.

[351] Diane Leclerc, "Wesleyan Holiness Feminist Hermeneutics: An Historical Rendering With Contemporary Considerations," 126.

[352] Garrison, S. Olin. "The Life and Writings and Daniel Steele," http:/www.criagladams.com/ /boston forty witnesses (accessed on 11/09/2016).

in 1878 which was a collection of essays on entire sanctification. Another book was *A Substitute for Holiness, or Antinomianism* in 1887. This book is Steele's refutation of Dispensationalist. This is his only book on end-times teachings. His primary concern is the way that Dispensational teaching undermines the call to Christian holiness. Another book was Old Testament Commentaries in 1891. A Defense of Christian Perfection in 1896 was a defense to refute Dr. James Mudge's book *Growth in Holiness toward Perfection*.[353]

5.5.1 Daneil Steele's Concept of Christian Perfection/Holiness

Daneil Steele in his book "A defense of Christian Perfection" clearly states that Christian perfection is not found in the articles of faith because they don't talk about the basic doctrines of the Christian faith. It is also not just located in the ideals but it needs the full surrender to God in will and practice both. Then ideal perfection will come forth in the beauty of faultlessness.[354] Holiness is that condition of human nature wherein the love of God rules. In Daneil Steele views holiness in man must be the same as holiness in God, else there is no significance in the command of Peter to "obedient children" of God: "Become ye yourselves also holy... for I am holy" (I Peter i, 14-16). The moral attributes of God cannot be fully different from human being.

The term "holy" points to our privilege and obligation to live lives free from sin and wholly devoted to Christ, who died that we might not live unto self. In every pulpit and prayer meeting the fact should be constantly rung out that all who have taken upon themselves the name of Christ are called to be saints, holy ones.

Holiness begins when the principle of purity, namely, love to God, is shed abroad in the heart in the new birth. But entire sanctification is that act of the Holy Ghost whereby the justified soul is made holy. This instantaneous work of the Sanctifier is usually preceded and followed by a gradual growth in grace. The Spirit certifies this purification. It is the incoming of the abiding Comforter into the consciousness of the believer bringing his own light. We do not need a lantern to see the sunrise. Its chief inferential evidences are oneness with Christ, easy victory over sin, rejoicing nevermore, praying without ceasing, and in everything giving thanks. Purity is to be distinguished from maturity. When inbred sin is destroyed there can be no increase of purity, but there may be an eternal increase in love and in all the fruits of the Spirit. Sanctification is not the same with justification. Justification is a change of our state from guilt to pardon; sanctification is a change of nature from sin to holiness.[355]

---

[353] http://www.craigladams.com/Steele/ (accessed on 13/09/16).

[354] Daniel Steele, *A Defense of Christian Perfection* (New York: Hunt & Easton, 1896). http:/hollypg.com/ebooks/holiness/Steele/ a defense of Christian perfection (15/09/2016).

[355] Amos Binney & Daniel Steele, *Binney's Theological Compend*, http://www.imarc.cc/br/binney's.html (accessed on 19/09/16).

So the believer's complete development is realized only by a supreme act of self-crucifixion, followed by a life of total self-abnegation; in the words of Wesley, "naked, following a naked Christ," whose holiness as the "Son of man was evinced in his coming into the world, "not to be ministered unto, but to minister, and to give his life a ransom for many. Regeneration is a great and glorious change. It is the beginning of the new life. The regenerate man is a new creature in Christ Jesus. To him all things have become new. New heavens are above, and a new earth is beneath. He has been translated out of darkness into a marvelous light.[356]

5.6 Charles Elmer Cowman (1868-1924)

Charles Elmer Cowman was a missionary evangelist in Japan. He was also one of the cofounders of the Oriental Missionary Society (now One Mission Society; formerly OMS International). Charles Cowman was born on March 13, 1868,[357] in Toulon, Illinois, to David and Mary Cowman. While he was only two weeks old his parents dedicated him to God's service and his lullabies were old fashioned hymns. David and Mary Cowman expected to make training of their children the supreme business of their lives and prayed for the divine guidance.[358]

He grew up in the Methodist Episcopal Church. Charles' parents, David and Mary Cowman, were of pioneer stock. They moved from Illinois to Iowa in 1870, brought a farm and established a home. The Cowman homestead became a favorite stopping place for the roving circuit riders and religion was administered in healthy does by father Cowman and a man described as "the very soul of honor and one who expected as much from everybody else." The daily readings from the thumb-worn family Bible left an indelible impression upon the mind of the boy. Charles Cowman priceless was quiet courage and a genuine love for hard work.[359] Sunday was the Lord's Day in the Cowman home and was treated seriously. Even sub-zero weather was no excuse for not attending the small Methodist chapel where family was part of it. Religious training in the home was given first place and nothing was allowed to compromise with that. In the family Bible was read daily at home which had really kept a great impact on Charles where he remembered many portions of the Bible. Another important rule they had in their home was never go into debt.[360]

Charles was an intelligent hard working youth who at the age of 15 accepted a summer job working as a telegraph operator. He did so well that he chose not

[356] Daneil Steele, *Love Enthroned: Essays on Evangelical Perfection* (New York: Eaton and Mains, 1908), 35.

[357] Lettie B. Cowman, *Missionary Warrior: Charles E. Cowman*, New Condensed Edition (Indiana: OMS International, Inc., 1989), 5.

[358] Ibid.

[359] Edward and Esther Erny, *No Guarantee But God: The Story of the Founders of OMS International* (Indiana: OMS International, 1986), 2.

[360] Lettie B. Cowman, *Missionary Warrior: Charles E. Cowman*, 8.

to return to school. With quick advancements, Charles was able to marry his childhood friend, Lettie Burd in 1889. When Lettie was very ill, Charles had prayed to God for her healing but when she became well, he forgot his vow to serve God but God did not. During their first year of marriage, they moved to the Rocky Mountains in order to escape city life. When the high altitude caused Lettie to become very sick though, they returned to Chicago for the next 10 years. In 1893, Lettie experienced conversion and one month later Charles was profoundly converted. This conversion changed, transformed him to a vibrant witness for God and even a better worker. Serving Jesus was a first priority of his thoughts, words and life.

5.6.1 Telegraphs Mission Board

Within a short period of time 75 people had come to Jesus in the Telegraph office. (The first one was Ernest A Kilbourne whom we will look at in a future devotional and was a co-founder of OMS.) These converted co-workers formed The Telegraphers' Mission Band which sent letters explaining the Gospel to telegraphers all over the United States, Great Britain and Australia.[361] The Cowmans' were originally connected with the Methodist Board of Missions, but came in contact with The International Apostolic Holiness Union in 1900 and became lifelong members of the Union from then. The Union had been established by Martin W Knapp, at Cincinnati, Ohio in 1897 to promote camp meetings and evangelism, with the key Bible doctrines of the Healing of the Sick, the Return of our Lord, and the Evangelization of the The Cowmans went to Japan and established the OMS in 1901 on the same lines as The International Apostolic Holiness Union, after ordination by them back in the USA that same year. It was seen as the Missionary arm of the IAH Union and in time became regarded as "the child of the whole holiness movement."[362]

5.6.2 The Oriental Missionary Society (OMS)

In the late 1890s, Charles met and befriended Juji Nakaka at his church, Grace Methodist Episcopal Church. Charles Cowman and E. A. Kilbourne were students with Juji at Moody Bible Institute. When Juji returned to Japan the Telegraphers' Mission Band financially supporting him. Experiencing a clear call from God, Charles and Lettie left America on February 1, 1901, to serve as missionaries in Japan. They worked with Nakada and shared a mutual dream of starting a Bible training institute. "The aim of the institute would not be to produce classical scholars, but young men and women who could handle their mother tongue with effect, who was steeped in the Bible and who could so proclaim it as to arrest and influence all classes of people."[363] Within a few months God brought the dream

---

[361] Lettie B. Cowman, *Missionary Warrior: Charles E. Cowman*, 2-3.

[362] http://chrisfieldblog.com/2009/02/13/charles-elmer-cowman (accessed on 10/10/16).

[363] Lettie B. Cowman, *Missionary Warrior: Charles E. Cowman*, 52.

to reality when they were able to open a mission hall where Nakada preached in the evening and leaders were trained in the daytime. This was the beginning of the Oriental Missionary Society. In 1902, E. A. Kilbourne joined Cowman and Nakada to assist in their growing ministry which witnessed moving into larger facilities in Tokyo in 1903.

No stranger to technology or the importance of communication, Charles quickly established a monthly periodical now called OMS Outreach. He had a vision to share Jesus with the unreached people of Japan; He believed that two missionaries and ten Japanese could visit the homes of the entire province in six months of time. So every person (6 crore) in Japan might hear the Gospel in the next five years."[364] The Great Village Campaign started in 1913 and was completed in early 1918. Teams of missionaries visited every town, village and home throughout Japan, proclaiming the Gospel and distributing Bibles (30 lakhs Bibles in Tokyo alone) this campaign took a toll on Charles' health and he and Lettie returned to the States in 1917. Despite frequent heart attacks, Charles is described by Lettie as "Although broken in body, he kept an oversight of the home office and every department of work on the field, dictating letters by the hundreds."[365]

5.6.3 Bible Colleges Initiatives

In Tokyo Having outgrown their original building, a need for a larger building for the Bible Training Institute arose in early 1903. By the end of 1903, a new school had opened in Tokyo, providing ample room to grow. The larger space not only accommodated more students, but also provided for great conventions and hundreds of guests. In Korea in 1904, three Koreans went to Japan to attend the Tokyo Bible Training Institute. Through these students, OMS began to make connections with Korea. By 1910, they were able to send two missionaries from England, John and Emily Thomas, to Korea. Shortly after their arrival, another Bible Training Institute opened, just outside Seoul. Similar to Japan's school, the Seoul Bible Training Institute fostered much growth and transformation of the surrounding region.

Charles Cowman was a skilled winner of souls. What he lacked in training he made up for in compelling love and sympathetic understanding that broke down all resistance. In less than six months he personally led 75 people to the Lord. He was always buying the opportunities and redeeming the time. He was a good sales man. He did not leave the case with closed doors but always looked for the answer.[366] For a week in advance he prepared for the message. Many hours he spent on his knees before the open word. He preached his first sermon in the

---

[364] Ibid., 125.

[365] Ibid., 142.

[366] Edward and Esther Erny, *No Guarantee But God: The Story of the Founders of OMS International,* 5.

Little Hell Mission Hall. This inspired him to open mission of his own and many youth came to know the Lord through him.[367]

Even in his retirement time he had passion for the mission and he began to form the plan for the work in China. A map of China was hung in his study room and he was praying for it day and night. He had committed himself and his all into God's hands and was both an advocate and an illustration of Holiness which was practical and demonstrable. He was delighted in developing men, while he stayed in the background. He practiced habitual self-denial. He also tried to exercise prayer as the main weapon in fighting Satan and his wiles. Most of his life he lived to do the "will of God" as the highest form of faith, and its spiritual success as its crowning point - "Not my will, but thine be done." Charles Cowman believed and practiced that before the soul can be beautified with spiritual graces, it must first be stripped of worldly ornaments and trifling loves that leave the heart divided against itself. It is said that everywhere he went he carried a great map of Japan and Korea. Slowly the candle of life was burning low. He was stricken with severe heart attack and was unable to proceed, because doctor advised that he must stop his public work at once. Charles Cowman's faith was to be put to test because Charles underwent for almost six years in great suffering. He was confined to his room but that sick room became a sanctuary of prayer.[368]

5.6.4 Lettie Burd Cowman (1870-1960)

Lettie Burd Cowman also known as L. B. Cowman, was an American writer and author of the devotional books *Streams in the Desert* and *Springs in the Valley.* Cowman published her books under the author name *Mrs. Charles E. Cowman.* She was also one of the cofounders of The Oriental Missionary Society (later known as OMS International, and eventually One Mission Society). Edward and Esther Erny states that "she was a missionary executive, an internationally known speaker, the organizer of the gospel distribution missions and she would be remembered most of an apostle of consolation."[369] The life of Mrs. Lettie Cowman will remain a great standard of faith and forever an illustration of the sufficiency of divine grace in the midst of suffering. Lettie Burd Cowman was born to Isaac and Margaret Burd in Afton, Iowa in 1870. Lettie was soon surrounded with art, literature and music. She had a life of abundance and few demands. In 1889 she got married to Charles Cowman and their first home was in Colorado in the midst of Rocky Mountains.[370]

---

[367] Ibid., 6-7.

[368] Lettie B. Cowman, *Missionary Warrior: Charles E. Cowman*, 20.

[369] Edward and Esther Erny, *No Guarantee But God: The Story of the Founders of OMS International,* 63.

[370] Edward and Esther Erny, *No Guarantee But God: The Story of the Founders of OMS International,* 66.

After the Cowmans returned to the United States in January 1918, Charles' health continued to decline. As he suffered in pain, Lettie suffered, watching her husband slowly fade away. During this time, her best-selling devotional book, *Streams in the Desert*, was conceived. Lettie wrote a daily devotional based on her hardships and her experiences of fellowship with God. Each daily section contains a Bible passage and a quote from another author. The title of the book comes from Isaiah 35:6, "Then will the lame leap like a deer, and the mute tongue shout for joy." Water will gush forth in the wilderness and streams in the desert. No one expected *Streams* to be as successful as it was. Cowman was not seeking success during the time she wrote it. When the book was being printed, her publisher was certain they would never publish more than the original printing of 3,000. Yet, many readers found they could connect with *Streams* because it "spoke to those who had difficulty relating their own sufferings to the noble and eternal purposes of a loving and all-wise God. Cowman often stated, "I did not write *Streams*. God gave me *Streams*."[371] In the midst of her new writing career, Lettie continued serving as President of OMS as her first priority. She was determined to carry out the Every Creature Crusade (now known as Every Community for Christ), which Charles started in Japan as the Great Village Campaign. She began speaking at camp meetings and conventions. Just as Charles felt such a strong calling to proclaim the Gospel to every individual in Japan, Lettie felt a similar call to distribute the Gospel to all the nations.

5.7 Ernest A. Kilbourne (1865-1928)

He was a missionary who worked as evangelist in Japan. He is best known for being a cofounder of the Oriental Missionary Society (now One Mission Society; formerly OMS International). He was a remarkable personality, chosen by God to share with Charles Cowman the burden of leadership in OMS. He was great writer, administrator and missionary pioneer. Ernest A. Kilbourne was born on March 13, 1865, in Niagara Falls, Ontario, Canada. Two years after his birth, his family moved to the villages of Conestogo and Winterbourne in Ontario. His father established a general store, which contained a district telegraph and post office. The Kilbourne family attended the red brick Methodist church. By the age of 14, Kilbourne was employed in a telegraphy job, and while still in his teens, he left Ontario to work with the Western Union in the United States.[372]

One day; Cowman, who had recently become a passionate Christian, approached Kilbourne at work and shared with him his thoughts for a half an hour. Kilbourne remained silent through Cowman's message, and his lack of response led Cowman to believe he had failed in one of his first endeavors to share

---

371 Edward and Esther Erny, *No Guarantee But God: The Story of the Founders of OMS International*, 77.

372 Edward and Esther Erny, *No Guarantee But God: The Story of the Founders of OMS International*, 48.

about Christ. However, much to Charles' surprise, Ernest entered the workplace the following day and announced, "I went home last night after our conversation and did just what you told me. It is all settled and I gave myself to Christ." Kilbourne joined the Grace Methodist Church and also began night classes at the Moody Bible Institute. He began to witness for friends and coworkers, and he and Cowman would even place tracts in mailboxes on their walks home from work. A pivotal moment for Kilbourne and Cowman occurred when the two men attended a missionary convention where they heard founder of the Christian and Missionary Alliance, A. B. Simpson, speak. Simpson's message about missions gave the men the opportunity to have their minds and hearts opened to missionary work.

At the age of 21, Kilbourne was determined to become a writer and to see the world. He set out from New York on a trip around the world. He went to Europe, South Africa, Australia, New Zealand, and the Hawaiian Islands. Once back in the U.S., he began working as a telegraph operator in Virginia City, Nevada, where he met and fell in love with Julia Pittinger. A Roman Catholic girl, Julia Pittinger, was born in Virginia City and was one of 17 children. They were married by the Reverend Laurence Ridgely of St. Paul's Episcopal Church in 1888. After marrying, Kilbourne requested a transfer to the thriving city of Chicago, where he had hope of becoming a successful telegrapher. He was transferred and, in a short time, became divisional chief along with a man named Charles Cowman under whom almost 1000 operators worked.[373]

He was about 30 years old when his fellow telegrapher, Charles Cowman led him to a personal saving knowledge of the Lord Jesus Christ. From that day onward their hearts were knit together, and Charles Cowman and Ernest Kilbourne began a lifelong friendship and Christian partnership.[374] With a new vision came a dramatic and distinct call to go to the East Asia as the faith missionary. At this time Kilborune he received a unusual revelation which was not very clear. *He saw a great highway bridge which spanned the distance from North America across the Pacific Ocean to Japan. From Japan, a span of bridge reached Korea, and from Korea a third touched China. From China, the great highway seemed to extend directly to heaven.*[375] After having this vision he kept on praying for the East Asia and in doing so he got a big map and laid his hands on Asia and prayed for the unreached people who were still waiting for the Good news.

Ernest recognized this as part of God's call on his life. However, before he launched out to fulfil this great vision, he worked an extra year in the Chicago

373 Edward and Esther Erny, *No Guarantee But God: The Story of the Founders of OMS International,* 49.

374 Bill Vermillion, Living Water periodical on the title of "People Who Lived for Holiness: The Life and Ministry of Ernest Albert Kilbourne", KEHC (Seoul: Seoul Theological University), 1.

375 Edward and Esther Erny, *No Guarantee But God: The Story of the Founders of OMS International,* 50.

telegraph office to repay a debt he felt he owed to the telegraph company. Soon afterwards he left for Japan in 1902 to join his former friend and coworker, Charles Cowman.[376] Kilbourne was 38 when he first arrived in Japan. He fit in well with the Japanese culture, reputed to be a man of quiet, deep, and intense faith, with a reverent mood. Retiring reserved, and self-disciplined as a leader, he worked tirelessly behind the scenes, but faithfully alongside the more fiery and flamboyant Juji Nakada and Cowman, lending his steady hand and heart. He served in a multifunctional capacity as communications director and editor, public relations and fund raiser, and chief financial officer. Kilbourne had always been passionate for journalism, so after he arrived in Japan, he began a newsletter, Electric Messages, in November 1902 with the purpose of sharing reports of the work in Japan with telegraphers, friends and supporters back home. The magazine contained inspirational stories of God's power and was filled with jargon that the telegraphers would be familiar with. In 1914, it was renamed The Oriental Missionary Society, based on Jeremiah 50:2, "*Declare ye among the nations and publish and set ye up a standard.*"[377]

He had a great heart for the native mission and also believed that this is the only solution for the mission work. He believed that we belong to God and everything what belongs to us belongs to God as well. He had exchanged his expensive gold watch for a cheap one a clear example of abandoning things for the cause of God.[378] He persuaded his wife to sacrifice her wedding ring for the cause of missions. Even generous life insurance policy was dropped and withdrew him from costly expenses. He was a man of self denial. During the week he wore suit unbuttoned, and on Sundays he buttoned it to bring a change.[379] OMS Co-founder Ernest A. Kilbourne's commitment and convictions as a pioneer of today's OMS continue to be characterized in his work *The Great Commission*. He wrote with passion: *Each generation of (Jesus' disciples) has a debt to pay to its generation of unsaved people of whatever nation or color; and while failure to accomplish its mission has marked each successive generation since the days of the early church, our individual responsibility has not lessened in the slightest degree, for the Great Commission has not been withdrawn or cancelled, but comes thundering down the corridors of time to this enlightened age and generation. Yes, it is human to shrink and shirk and shift, and to manufacture excuses, but this yoke is upon every child of God; and our efforts to throw*

---

[376] Bill Vermillion, Living Water periodical on the title of "People Who Lived for Holiness: The Life and Ministry of Ernest Albert Kilbourne", 2.

[377] Ernest A. Kilbourne, https://en.wikipedia.org/wiki/Ernest_A._Kilbourne (accessed on 25/11/16).

[378] Edward and Esther Erny, *No Guarantee But God: The Story of the Founders of OMS International,* 54.

[379] Ibid., 55.

it off only increase the condemnation which will fall upon all who fail to multiply the talent which God has given.[380]

There's something about the spiritual tone and tenor, commitment and dedication of our spiritual forefathers that drive us to our knees in recognition of our own weaknesses, frailties, and foibles. Our own motivation and drive is brought into clear contrast and dark definition. There should be a self check whether we are doing with our life and calling to which we have been called? Have we spent ourselves in complete abandonment compared to those upon whose shoulders we stand? Have we used our time and talents wisely and without any reserve?[381] Or is it time to repent and renew our commitment and dedication, asking God to fill us anew with His Spirit and passion that characterized those who went before us. Ernest Kilbourne lives on the testimonies of the faithful Christians who bear the name of Jesus Christ in Japan, Korea and China.

5.8 Wesley L. Duewel (1916-2016)

He was born June 3, 1916, in St. Charles, MO, to the late Louis and Ida Luelf Duewel who were God-honoring parents. His father was an evangelical pastor, Bible college president, and radio preacher. His mother was a godly woman with a deep and meaningful prayer life. According to his mother's testimony, Wesley made his first profession of faith as a child, and soon thereafter testified to his sense of call to serve as a missionary to India. Throughout his life, he based life-changing decisions on the increasing spiritual maturity. Wesley relied primarily on prayer and a sanctified sense of God's guidance as he met and married his first wife, Betty Raisch, in 1939. He discovered she had also claimed his life verse, Isaiah 54:2-3a "*Enlarge the place of your tent; stretch your tent curtains wide, do not hold back; lengthen your cords, strengthen your stakes. For you will spread out to the right and to the left.*" This promise served as a predictor of his eventual worldwide ministry.[382] Wesley Duewel gave himself to world missions for 75 years. After ministry in India for nearly 25 years, he was president of One Mission Society (1969-1982). He was a member of the Wabash Conference of the Free Methodist Church for 48 years. From early childhood, Dr. Duewel had a deep love for the Word of God. His writings and poems on the Holy Spirit, revival, and soul

---

380 Bill Vermillion, Living Water periodical on the title of "People Who Lived for Holiness: The Life and Ministry of Ernest Albert Kilbourne", 2. Quoted from Bridge Across The Century, p. xii.

381 Bill Vermillion, Living Water periodical on the title of "People Who Lived for Holiness: The Life and Ministry of Ernest Albert Kilbourne", 2. Quoted from Bridge Across The Century, p. xii.

382 Bill Vermillion, Living Water periodical on the title of "People Who Lived for Holiness: The Life and Ministry of Wesley L. Duewel", KEHC, (Seoul: Seoul Theological University), 1.

winning call God's people back to prayer, the source of all power for ministry and express his hunger and passion.[383]

During Bible college studies, Wesley prayed earnestly for "an effectual door" to open for him to serve in India. By 1940, Wesley and Betty Duewel were among the first group of seven OMS missionaries who sailed for India. For 25 years Wesley and Betty carried a special burden for a praying spirit-filled church in India. Every ministry activity was earmarked with faithfulness in the harvest and earnest prayer. After a quarter of a century, there was one church for every year they labored in love, with about 60 members each, and three small Bible schools (Allahabad Bible Seminary, Allahabad, Madras Theological College, Chennai and Calcutta Bible Seminary, Kolkata) in three states of India. Returning for an OMS Board meeting in 1964, somewhere over the Pacific, between Honolulu and Los Angeles, Wesley prayed again: "*Oh Lord, give us 1,000 people who will commit themselves to pray for 15 minutes a day for at least one year, specifically praying for our OMS India work.*" God honored that prayer with 1,500 people from 30 nations who prayed over the next twelve months. It was a "*spiritual jump start*" which broke down barriers and opened the way for the Gospel to advance like never before.

Recognized as an authority on missions, Dr. Duewel served for 16 years on board of directors of Missio Nexus (formerly Evangelical Fellowship of Mission Agencies), as president 1969-1972, 19 years on North American Board of World Evangelical Fellowship, 20 years on board of National Association of Evangelicals, and a life trustee of Asbury Theological Seminary. In 2007, Missio Nexus honored him by presenting it's first-ever Lifetime of Service Award. In 2009, Evangelical Fellowship of India presented him the "Lifetime Service Award in recognition of his servant leadership exemplified to the Body of Christ and faithful contribution to the Church and Mission in India." He was prominent in leadership of North India Christian Literature Society, and Bible Society of India. He helped spearhead Evangelical Fellowship of India and was its president until he was transferred from India.[384]

In 1969, Dr. Duewel was elected as the fifth president of OMS. Known as a great man of prayer, Dr. Duewel concluded his 13 year organizational leadership tenure in 1982 with a mission-wide emphasis called, "*Decade of Harvest.*" Following his presidency, Dr. Duewel was led to expand his writing ministry. His first major book has become a modern-day classic entitled, **Touch the World through Prayer**. He stated that, "*You can stand beside the great evangelists of our day; accompany any missionary to the remote reaches of the earth; contribute to the ministry of any pastor or evangelist in the world; or mediate the healing of Jesus Christ to the sick, ill, or faint of heart anywhere on the globe. Prayer is not the only thing*

---

[383] http://ghherrmann.com/memsol.cgi?user_id=1758493 (accessed on 11/11/16).

[384] http://ghherrmann.com/memsol.cgi?user_id=1758493 (accessed on 11/11/16).

you must do. It is the greatest thing you can do."[385] Dr. Duewel held the degrees of Doctor of Education from University of Cincinnati and Doctor of Divinity from Taylor University. His articles appeared in many publications and for 12 years he edited *Revival Magazine*, published in 12 languages. He ministered in 45 countries. For years, Dr. Duewel taught a senior adult Sunday school class. He enjoyed sharing his testimony to God's faithfulness, with a deep concern for un-evangelized millions and a constant emphasis upon prayer as key to harvest and revival.[386]

Dr. Wesley Duewel's writings on the Holy Spirit, revival, and soul winning call God's people back to prayer, the source of all power and passion for ministry. His hundreds of poems and all of his books express his hunger and passion. His opinion vies about prayers are marvelous and challenging which calls the church of God to be prayer warrior. Many Christians are so spiritually frail, sickly, and lacking in spiritual vitality that they cannot stick to prayer for more than a few minutes at a time. No form of Christian service is both so universally open to all and so high in Christ's priority for all Christians as prevailing prayer. Nothing is more calculated to begat a spirit of prayer than to unite in social prayer with one who has the Spirit himself. Prayer has mighty power to move mountains because the Holy Spirit is ready both to encourage our praying and to remove the mountains hindering us. Prayer has the power to change mountains into highways. Prayer is God's ordained way to bring His miracle power to bear in human need. Prayer is the master strategy that God gives for the defeat and rout of Satan. Prayer is the only adequate way to multiply our efforts fast enough to reap the harvest God desires. Prayer is the supreme way to be workers together with God. Prayer is your way, often the only way, to water the harvest. There is no easier sin to commit than the sin of prayerlessness. It is a sin against God and against Man. We have been so busy depending on our own natural strengths, our good training and our busyness that we don't have time for God that is why we are near to spiritual bankruptcy.[387]

5.9 Billy Graham (1918-)

Billy Graham's father, William Graham (1888-1962), six feet two, like his son, only lankier, was born and raised on his father's prosperous dairy farm on the outskirts of Charlotte. Frank Graham's religious raising was Methodist, and in a Methodist revival in his youth he was "soundly converted." Billy Graham's mother was Morrow Coffey (1892-1981), she was Presbyterian, well-grounded at an early age in the Shorter Catechism, given to memorizing Scripture passages, and, from

---

[385] Wesley L. Duewel, *Touch the World through Prayer* (Michigan: Francis Asbury Press, 1986), 11.

[386] http://www.legacy.com/obituaries/indystar/obituary.aspx?pid=178004970 (accessed on 11/11/16).

[387] http://prayer-coach.com/2010/05/24/prayer-quote-wesley-duewel/ (accessed on 11/12/16). Also see Wesley L. Duewel, *Touch the World through Prayer* (Michigan: Francis Asbury Press, 1986).

own girlhood experiences, a believer in a God who "gives direct answers to prayer. It should be said that because of Billy Graham's early Presbyterian inculcation from his mother, the finer points of Christian nurture were left to his mother. It is a reasonable assumption that some measure of Billy Graham's authoritative no "ifs," "buts," or maybes" kind preaching derives from the authoritative answers, Billy's mother also encouraged him to take part beginning with a "sentence prayer" rehearsed in advance in the family's daily devotions and to memorize Scripture verses. Billy Graham was the oldest of four children: two boys and two girls. The Graham home was a place in which from the standpoint of both industry and religion little was left to hence.[388] In 1927, when he was eight years old, the family moved from their white frame house to a newly built red brick home. He was raised in the Associate Reformed Presbyterian Church by his parents and is of Scottish and Irish descent. Before this, in 1924, when Graham was only five, he focused on the outdoors. At the same time, he started as a student at the Sharon Grammar School.[389] Starting to read books from an early age, Graham loved to read novels for boys, especially *Tarzan*. Like Tarzan, he would hang on the trees, and gave the popular Tarzan yell, scaring both horses and drivers. According to his father, that yelling had led him to become a minister.

5.9.1 Billy Graham's Turning Point

While Graham's parents were strict Calvinists, it would be an unfamiliar traveling evangelist who would set Graham on a profound spiritual path. At the age of 16, Graham attended a series of revival meetings run by evangelist Mordecai Ham. Despite the fact that Graham was a well-behaved adolescent, Ham's sermons on sin spoke to young Graham. And Billy went to the revival with one of the farmers, Albert McMakin. While preaching his sermon Doctor Ham pointed his figure to Billy "you are a sinner" and finally Billy responded the alter call and accepted Christ as his personal saviour. Billy began to preaching to the younger children on the farm, inspired by Mordecai Ham. All summer long, Billy sold brushes and evangelized South Carolina. Billy Graham in 1940 graduated from the Florida Bible Institute he won a certificate as a Bible trained student. When he got back to Charlotte, invitations from a number of communities to conduct revivals were waiting for him. One of them, to York, Pennsylvania, he accepted in the summer of 1940, he conducted with moderate success. A greatest urge was for more education or, rather, for education in something more than the Bible.

He enrolled at Wheaton College, a coeducational school located twenty five miles west of Chicago in Wheaton, Illinois. Wheaton College was founded in 1853 by Wesleyan Methodists. Full of prayerful atmosphere and evangelistic activities and Campus revivals, Billy Graham was honoured to be the president of the Christian Council in his senior year at Wheaton College. To earn his living

---

[388] John Pollock, *Billy Graham* (Great Britain: St. Paul's House, 1966), 16-18.

[389] James E. Kilgore, *Billy Graham, The Preacher* (New York: Exposition Press, 1968), 15.

expenses he drove a truck, did work for the jobs around town.[390] Here he would meet his future wife, Ruth McCue Bell. Ruth was the daughter of a missionary, and lived with her family in China until she turned 17. After graduating with a bachelor's in anthropology, Graham and Bell were married on August 13, 1943.[391]

5.9.2 Billy Graham's Evangelistic Endeavour

The beginning of Billy's evangelistic success occurred in Venice, sixty miles south of Tampa. One hundred people were in the congregation to listen to him preach, thirty two people responded to his alter call. Once Torrey Johnson Called him to preach to the soldiers which was one of Billy's few dark moments, one of those moments of crippling chest tightening, dry mouth, lip quivering doubt, but he accepted the invitation to preach. When his talk was over forty two soldiers came to Christ. The youth for Christ movement was a national phenomenon by early 1946. Billy was relieved to hear President Truman praised it. Time magazine ran a story on it. The newspaper empire of William Randolph Hearst assigned one reporter to it. Advance planning was a very big part now, and that was Billy's job.[392] He established a routine for Bible reading that he hoped would stay with him forever. Every day he read five Psalms and enough of Proverbs so that he would read each book completely every month. Proverbs instructed him how to deal with his fellow men. Psalms inspired him to talk to God. In addition he read enough of the rest of Scripture each day to get completely through the Bible once each year.[393] In 1950, Graham founded theBilly Graham Evangelistic Association (BGEA) with its headquarters in Minneapolis. The association relocated to Charlotte, North Carolina in 1999. BGEA ministries involve in Hour of Decision, a weekly radio program broadcast around the world for more than 50 years. A syndicated newspaper column, *My Answer*, carried by newspaper across the United States and distributed by Tribune Media Services. Christianity Today was started in 1956 with Carl F. H. Henry as its first editor. World Wide Pictures, which has produced and distributed more than 130 films.[394]

The friendship between Graham and John Stott led to a further partnership in the Lausanne Movement, of which Graham was founder. It built on Graham's 1966 World Congress on Evangelism in Berlin. Along with Christianity Today, Billy Graham convened what *TIME* magazine described as "a formidable forum, possibly the widest–ranging meeting of Christians ever held with 2,700

[390] John Pollock, *Billy Graham,* 95-96.

[391] Billy Graham Biography, http://www.biography.com/people/billy-graham-9317669#synopsis (accessed on 20/11/16).

[392] Sam Wellman, *Billy Graham* (Secunderabad: OM Books, 2003), 110.

[393] Stanley High, *Billy Graham* (USA: McGraw-Hill Book Company, 1956), 16-18.

[394] William Franklin "Billy" Graham, Jr., https://en.wikipedia.org/wiki/Billy_Graham (accessed on 15/11/16).

participants from 150 nations gathering for the International Congress on Word Evangelization. This took place in Lausanne, Switzerland (July 16–25, 1974), and the movement which ensued took its name from the host city. Its purpose was to strengthen the global church for world evangelization, and to engage ideological and sociological trends which bore on this. Graham invited Stott to be chief architect of the Lausanne Covenant, which issued from the Congress and which, according to Graham, "helped challenge and unite evangelical Christians in the great task of world evangelization." The movement remains a significant fruit of Graham's legacy, with a presence in nearly every nation.[395] 10,000 delegates that met in Amsterdam in 2000 encompassed a plethora of denominations from all over the world. Baptists, Lutherans, Methodists, Presbyterians, Pentecostals, Bible church leaders, and even Roman Catholics and Eastern Orthodox participated in these meetings. These evangelism conferences have been some of the most ecumenical or interdenominational world congresses ever held. Behind all of them, Graham was the motivating force. These world congresses of evangelism literally changed the face of world Christianity.[396]

5.9.3 Black and White Liberative Discussion

In March, 1953, at his Chattanooga crusade, Billy could not deny the truth of the Gospel any longer. He was angry when he saw ushers putting up ropes to separate blacks and whites. He strode back and ripped down the ropes himself. He announced publicly, "Jesus Christ belongs neither to the coloured nor the white races; there are no colour line with Christ, as he repeatedly said that God looks upon the heart. Billy went about it, He phoned the governors of North Caroline in Tennessee to urge them to address the racial problems from a spiritual point of view and promote justice.[397] He had been a bold personality which has invaded millions of hearts and come to know the real liberator Jesus Christ. He was also against communism and began relentlessly to hammer away at the threat of Communism. Billy knew the Russians had forced their godless way of life on all the countries of Eastern Europe. Communism was dreary and hopeless, deliberately separated from God.[398] Graham's faith led to the maturing view of race and segregation; he believed that integration was necessary for religious reasons: "there is no scriptural basis for segregation, Graham argued, the ground

---

[395] William Franklin "Billy" Graham, Jr., https://en.wikipedia.org/wiki/Billy_Graham (accessed on 15/11/16).

[396] Denton Lotz, "Billy Graham: An Appreciation", *Baptist History and Heritage*, 41/3 (June-December, 2006), 53.

[397] Billy Graham, *A Bible Standard for Evangelists* (USA: Worldwide Publications, 1984), 2-3.

[398] Sam Wellman, *Billy Graham*, 124.

at the foot of the cross is level, and it touches my heart when I see whites standing shoulder to shoulder with blacks at the cross.[399]

Billy Graham moved ahead to build bridges to the Jewish and Roman Catholic worlds. The American Jewish Committee bestowed its first "National Interreligious Award" upon Graham for his support of Israel and for "strengthening mutual respect and understanding between the evangelical and Jewish communities," some Catholic priests and bishops even began encouraging their people to attend his crusades.[400] Billy graham had viewed that, "*We are concerned with Christian faith; not Catholic or Protestant faith. There is only one Christ. There is one God. Whether you're Roman Catholic or Protestant, Jesus said to Nicodemus, "You need to be born again." That's what I'm asking everyone to do. How they find their way and settle their lives afterward is up them and God and the Church, or other believers.*"[401]

5.9.4 Billy Graham and Mass Media

On January 1, 1944 Billy welcomed listener of Songs in the Night from "the friendly church in the pleasant community of Western Springs." The radio experience helped his preaching. Billy also launched a weekly television show called Hour of Decision. The show aired stirring clips of his crusades. Other times, the show had Billy sitting in the comfortable chair as if in the home library and delivering a calm, reasoned, low key questions. He personally did not believe such a low key approach was very effective, but maybe he could persuade some listeners who were turned off by the stronger approach of his personal appearances and his radio program. He had no intention of giving up the television show either.[402] In 1951, Billy got talked into sponsoring Christian films. He formed worldwide pictures, which made two movies called Mr. Texas and Oilton. He even had a premiere for Mr. Texas in Hollywood with Cecil B. De Mille in the audience. In spite of stinging criticism of the film as hopelessly amateurish, Billy just shrugged and prayed their efforts would get better. In 1975 another picture was launched, "the hiding place."[403]

In order to expand and maintain a professional ministry, Graham and his colleagues eventually incorporated the Billy Graham Evangelistic Association (BGEA). Graham began broadcasting his sermons over the radio during a Christian show called ***Songs in the Night***. Once a week he also hosted a program called ***The Hour of Decision***, a program ABC initially transmitted to 150 stations before reaching its peak of 1,200 stations across America. Eventually this program

[399] William Martin, *Prophet with Honor: The Bitty Graham Story* (New York: William Morrow, 1991), 170-71.

[400] Richard V. Pierard, "From Evangelical Exclusivism to Ecumenical Openness: Billy Graham and Sociopolitical Issues," *Journal of Ecumenical Studies*, 20/3 (June-September, 1983), 427.

[401] Billy Graham, "Man for all People," *Christian Life*, 44 (July, 1982), 28-29.

[402] Billy Graham, *A Bible Standard for Evangelists*, 16-20.

[403] Sam Wellman, *Billy Graham*, 121.

was converted into a television show which ran for three years. The success of Graham's radio and television programs speak to his role as a Christian media visionary. Graham used the media as a means for spreading the gospel of Christ, allowing him to access millions of people around the globe.[404] He had an open mind and was willing to grow and change. In his closing address at the 2000 Amsterdam Conference, Graham challenged Christian leaders worldwide saying, "*I do not believe we should spend our time cursing the darkness. I do not believe we should spend our time in useless controversy, trying to root out the tares while harming the wheat. I do not believe we should give in to the force of evil and violence and indifference. Instead, let us light a fire.*"[405]

Billy Graham has been acceptable to all denominations and traditions because he has not sought to proselytize, but rather in a humble way, to comfort grieving people and offer hope. Such humility is a lesson for us all.

5.10 Evangelical Church of India

Evangelical Church of India (ECI) was founded in the mid 50's, initially by the Oriental Missionary Society now renamed as One Mission Society- founded by Charles E. Cowman and E. A. Kilbourne[406] commenced OMS ministry in the year 1901 in Japan.[407] The object of the OMS was to train and equip indigenous leaders and plant Churches in the countries where they operate. Dr. Donald McGavran made following observation in relation to Evangelical Church of India, "No movement in the Indian church history can be compared to the uniqueness of Evangelical Church of India, especially in its area of being a model of hope and in the area of transformation."[408]

The arrival of Oriental Mission Society missionaries (Now One Mission Society) in 1939 could be the beginning of the Evangelical Church in India along with the missionaries such as Rev. Bud Kilborne and his wife was the landmark. 7 missionaries came as a team to start the work in 1941. Dr. & Mrs. Wesley Duewell, Miss Ella Taylor, Rev. & Mrs. Roy Davis and Rev. & Mrs. J. T. Semonds. Two weeks later Dr. & Mrs. Eugene Erny joined the team. Rev. & Mrs. Roy Davis and Rev. & Mrs. J. T. Semonds were sent to Mysore to start the work.[409] Robert Wood

---

[404] Billy Graham Biography, http://www.biography.com/people/billy-graham-9317669#synopsis (accessed on 20/11/16).

[405] Billy Graham, *Amsterdam 2000* (Minneapolis: World Wide Publications, 2001), 112.

[406] M. Ezra Sargunam, *Multiplying Churches in Modern India* (Chennai: Federation of Evangelical Churches of India, 1974), 55.

[407] http://www.ecionline.org/index.php?option=com_content&view=article&id=71&Itemid=517 (accessed on 17/12/16).

[408] M. Ezra Sargunam, ed., *Mission Mandate II* (Ayanavaram, Chennai: Mission Educational Books, 2006), 424.

[409] M. Ezra Sargunam, *Multiplying Churches in Modern India* (Madras: Federation of Evangelical Churches in India, 1974), 60-61.

opined that OMS work in India began in 1941 at Allahabad and in July 1942 Allahabad Bible Seminary began with the Holiness convention with 16 students along with one student from Trinadad and one from British Guiana.[410]

An English Missionary society had owned this place as a refuge for women. The place had contained attractive dormitories, missionaries and workers residence, class room and chapel. The London based Zenanah Bible and Medical mission had build this compound in memory of wife of Lord Muir, a 19th century Governor of Oudh Province and named it as, "The Lady Muir Memorial compound."[411] Later the property was purchased by OMS. While referring the OMS Work in Japan J. Herbert Kane had opined that the OMS concentrated on Church planting and Bible school work. It emphasized four truths: a new life, sanctification, divine healing and second coming of Christ.[412] But it is also seen that OMS had some major objectives such as to train national leaders, Evangelism which is soul winning and to establish indigenous churches.[413] In 1943 in the month of July Karnataka Bible Seminary began in Gadag in a rented house with 4 students. It was closed in 1972. In 1949, Mar Thoma church Bishop invited OMS to start the work in Madras (presently known as Chennai) Rev. D. Samuel was appointed as the pastor in Tamil Nadu.[414]

Till 1969 there were 20 churches only and in 1972 it grew up to 30 churches. The first church was planted somewhere in 1952 and till 1967-68 the OMS field Executive committee was in charge of the administration of the church through their appointed national and missionary leaders, but after 1969-70 amendments, ECI became fully autonomous and elected its own leaders and OMS withdrew their administrative control. In 1954 the first Annual conference was held. The constitution was approved and the church was registered under society act under the name Evangelical Christian Church (ECC) of India and later in 1976 it came to be known as Evangelical church of India.[415] In 1969, Rev. G. C. Khanna was elected as the first President of the ECCI. Later it was handed over to Rev. Aslam Abraham. In 1974, Rev. M. Ezra Sargunam (Father Bishop of ECI) took over the mantle of the church leadership. The un-wavered vision of Father Bishop

---

[410] Robert D. Wood, *In these Mortal Hands: The Story of the Oriental Missionary Society: The First 50 Years* (Greenwood: OMS International, INC, 1983), 269.

[411] Robert D. Wood, *In these Mortal Hands: The Story of the Oriental Missionary Society: The First 50 Years,* 268.

[412] J. H. Kane, *A Global View of Christian Missions: From Pentecost to the Present* (Michigan: Baker Book House, 1971), 250.

[413] K. Abraham, "An Evaluation of the Church Planting Ministry of Evangelical Church of India in Selected Districts in North India" (M,Th. Thesis, Senate of Serampore College, 1994), 44-45.

[414] K. Abraham, "An Evaluation of the Church Planting Ministry of Evangelical Church of India in Selected Districts in North India" 52.

[415] K. Abraham, "An Evaluation of the Church Planting Ministry of Evangelical Church of India in Selected Districts in North India", 2.

Ezra Sargunam enabled the church to set a goal to make use as a church planting movement.

5.10.1 The Growth of Evangelical Church of India

ECI had a goal to have 1000 churches by the year 2000, but it reached that objective by 1998 and since then they target towards 2000 churches by 2005. To say after several years of deliberation ECI has adopted Episcopalian form of church where Rev. Dr. Ezra Sargunam was elected as the first bishop of the Evangelical Church of India, and was concentrated on February 13th 1993. Further, it had a vision to formulate five dioceses with their head quarters at Madras, Delhi, Bombay, Calcutta and Hyderabad with five bishops with the All India Administrative Office in Madras with the registered office in Allahabad under one All India Conference and One board of Governors and there is hope that the Christian groups will integrate within the framework of the ECI. The Evangelical Church of India is registered at the All India Conference level under the Societies Registration Act XXI of 1860, at Lucknow, U.P., the registration number being 449 of 1958-59. The Board of Governors of the AIC is the Governing Body and the Trustees of the Society. Prior to 1976, the Society was called the Evangelical Christian Church and also came to be known as the Evangelical Christian Church of India and was officially changed to assume the present name Evangelical Church of India.[416]

The Strong National Leadership with a sense of clear vision, mission and passion to reach the unreached for Christ had really led the growth. The concept of Every Community for Christ (ECC) and its team ministries paved the way for ECI's Church Planting Ministry in various parts of India, more specifically in South India. The Indian Missionary Moment (IMM) the national missionary arm of the church has set in motion a great movement among the laity with a big leap forward in reaching many unreached people groups especially in North India. Regional and Linguistic Seminaries to train evangelists, pastors and leaders for the church at regional and national level. The focus of ECI's ministry had been on the oppressed and suppressed, the socially marginalized like the Dalits and Tribals who had been always very receptive to the Gospel.

5.10.2 Bishop Dr. M. Ezra Sargunam (1938-)

Bishop Sargunam is certainly one of the leading pioneer church planters in India today. As the head of the Evangelical Church of India (ECI), Bishop Sargunam is the visionary behind the movement to evangelize and plant churches among all of the people groups of India.[417] Bishop Ezra Sargunam is a second generation Christian. His father was a little boy when he and his parents came to Christ from

---

[416] K. Abraham, "An Evaluation of the Church Planting Ministry of Evangelical Church of India in Selected Districts in North India", 64.

[417] Bishop Ezra Sargunam - Chennai, India, http://www.jlwilliams.org/partners/profile/asia_india_-_ezra_sargunam (accessed on 15/01/17).

other faith. Later in life, his father came under the influence of great missionaries like Amy Carmichael and Rev. T. Thomas Walker. Bishop Ezra Sargunam was born on July 19, 1938 in Pannaeilai village in the State of Tamil Nadu, South India. He was given name "Ezra" because his father happened to read about the life and ministry of the scribe Ezra (Nehemiah 8), during his morning devotion several hours before his birth. At the age of 18, he accepted Jesus Christ and had the assurance of salvation at a Billy Graham crusade in Madras (now Chennai). He did his graduate and post-graduate studies in Theology in Madras, Allahabad and at the Serampore University as well as in California, USA and was conferred the "Doctor of Divinity" (*honoris causa*) degree for his dissertation on *International Development and Church Growth*. He became a Pastor in 1957 at the age of 19. He was married to Mangalam, a wonderful woman of prayer, in the year 1962, who remained a great support to him in the ministry, until she went to be with the Lord on 29th February 2008. He has two married daughters and four grandchildren.

Bishop Sargunam received the initial vision and passion for church planting quite early in life at the age of 19, while he was an evangelist at a village called Porur on the outskirts of Madras, where the first ECI church was planted during 1957-58. It is from this village the ECI church planting movement spread throughout the length and breadth of India. The Porur Church is now one of the largest congregations of ECI with a membership of over 2000. Almost 90 percent of them are first generation Christians. When Bishop Ezra Sargunam was a student in the Allahabad Bible Seminary during 1961-62, he and his fellow students had once gone to distribute tracts to the pilgrims gathered on the banks of the Ganges for the *Kumba Mela.* This angered the Hindu zealots, who beat them up and chased them away. In the ensuing stampede, Bishop Sargunam was pushed to the ground and trampled upon. With physical injuries, he had to walk all the way back to the Seminary (about 15 miles) because the bus that was arranged to take them back to the Seminary left without him in the haste to escape the ire of the Hindu militants. Later that evening, he went to the seminary library and his eyes fell on a large Bible kept on a specially made desk. A Christian Sadhu had gifted this Bible to the seminary. As he opened the first page of the Bible, he saw Paul's exhortation to the Ephesians elders from Acts 20:24 written on it. He read it over and over again and it sort of became his life text. *But none of these things move me; nor do I count my life dear to myself, so that I may finish my race with joy, and the ministry which I received from the Lord Jesus, to testify to the gospel of grace of God.'* It was in 1972 when Bishop Sargunam was a Pastor of the Church at Kilpauk that he prayerfully set the goal of the first 100 ECI churches. After the completion of the first 200 churches in the Eighties, in a step of faith, ECI set a goal of a 1000 ECI churches by 2000 AD.

Then God gave Bishop Sargunam the vision for another 1000 churches before AD 2005, which we have been able to achieve through the grace of God. But this has not quenched the thirst of this aggressive church-planter. His ultimate goal in life is to realise the God-given vision of planting one church among every responsive people group of India.[418] In 2005, he has provided relief to thousands of tsunami-hit families. Bishop Sargunam has authored, co-authored and edited a number of books, including *Multiplying Churches in Modern India, Mission Mandate, Religious Toleration and Social Harmony, Perayar Nirubangal* (Tamil), and has written various articles on theological, social and political issues. As the Executive Vice President of the United Minorities Forum, Tamil Nadu-Pondicherry, and as a member of various inter-religious, cultural and social organisations, Bishop Sargunam has played a key role in promoting religious and social harmony among various peoples of India, especially in the South. As a social and political activist, Bishop Sargunam has participated in various demonstrations in support of human rights and the rights of the Dalits (former untouchables), minorities and the oppressed people of India. Recognising Bishop Sargunam's service towards religious and social harmony, the Government of Tamil Nadu appointed him as the Chairman of the State Minorities Commission in 1996, a position he held for four years. Bishop Ezra Sargunam has paved a way to be the role model for evangelism, church planting, baptism, raising voice for the voiceless, accomplishing justice, administration, so on and so forth. We are indeed privileged to be part of this great church planting movement "Evangelical Church of India."

5.10.3 Evangelical Church of India and Social Activities

Evangelical Church of India has been involved in relief efforts in most parts of our country. ECI's relief efforts have brought comfort to several victims. ECI's response to the catastrophes is spontaneous through the ECI's relief team. Pastors, Seminary Students and Volunteers from ECI Congregations rush to the affected places and areas at any time with relief materials. The disaster of 26 December 2004 Tsunami left nearly thousands people dead and millions homeless across South Asia. Along the Southern Coast of India and in the Andaman and Nicobar Island alone, 10,000 people were killed. All of sudden, over 300 thousand people from thousands of fisher families were on the streets. Tsunami caused extensive damage to human life and property, in a matter of few minutes, many lives were lost was more to the people living nearer to the coastline, specially the fisher folk. The fisher folk who were the devotee of the sea god became helpless as they were put into chaos by the sea. They were left without hope and lost the direction in their life. On hearing the news Bishop Dr. Ezra Sargunam, president Bishop of ECI visited and swung in to action, on the spot and arranged for feeding the stranded people. Apart from feeding the people ECI systematically made plans to help the Tsunami victim. Beginning with feeding ECI with the help of various partners helped the victims to go back to their fishing with hope in Christ.

---

[418] Evangelical Church of India-History, http://www.ecionline.org/index.php?option=com_content&view=article&id=71&Itemid=517 (accessed on 15/01/17).

Relief & Development Department is functioning as a social service wing of ECI. Under the leadership of our Bishop-President and under the administrative control of our Bishop, Chennai Diocese ECI renders service for the downtrodden and underprivileged segment of the society, through this department. There are following wings which help to cater the needs of the society such as: ECI- Happy Homes, Medical Centers, Sewing Training Centers, Good Samaritan Water Supply, and Jesus Well ministry, help in natural disaster and other activities which are of great help to elevate people.[419] There are also health care and community development programs. the health care and community development project was launched in the year 1991 as a part of the Relief and Development Department. During the initial years it provided medical care to the poorest of the poor in the slums. Health Care and Community Development Department evolved as a separate department in the year 2013. The aim of this department is to encourage people to be healthy, to know how to stay healthy, to do what they can individually and collectively to maintain health and to seek help when needed.[420] There are many rehabilitative programs running and also training programs which brings awareness about the health and hygiene. Thus, Evangelical Church of India is catering overall development of the society and allowing people to become more self based and health conscious. The grace learning centre has been another hallmark of Evangelical Church of India where almost 1500 children who are orphan/ abandoned or marginalized are being trained and given opportunities to develop and grow. Activities like feeding, tutoring and counseling the children started receiving great responses from the different communities.

5.11 Relevance of John Wesley's Theology

John Wesley was a man called by God at a particular time in history to revive and renew a church desperately out of touch with the lower and middle classes of England. His courage and persistence in seeing the task though to the end is best seen within the discussion of Elsie Houghton who opines that "after his conversion experience, it is said his future course was sealed and for more than fifty years he labored, through evil report and good report, to spread the everlasting gospel, travelling more miles, preaching more sermons, publishing more books and making more converts than anyone man of his day or perhaps of any day, and dying at last, in harness, at the patriarchal age of eighty-eight years."[421]

John Wesley, as other reformers and revolutionaries in Christian history, aimed to restore "primitive Christianity" – recapturing the vitality of the New

[419] Relief & Development, http://www.ecionline.org/index.php?option=com_content&view=article&id=78&Itemid=506 (accesed on 15/01/17).

[420] Health care, http://www.ecionline.org/index.php?option=com_content&view=article&id=79&Itemid=507 (accessed on 15/01/17).

[421] Elsie Houghton, *Christian Hymn-Writers* (Mid Glamorgan: Evangelical Press of Wales, 1982), 80.

Testament communities in his day. Wesley was unusually willing to cooperate and dialogue with Christians of other traditions. Wesley looked forward to the return of Christ as a living hope. In the meantime, he anticipated "providential increases" in kingdom influence as people were converted, walked in community and lived out the Sermon of the Mount in the power of the Spirit. This balance of hope and practical action energized the call to holiness and social change without utopian fantasies or dystopian fatalism. Wesley was a powerful preacher and called his audiences to repentance and faith, to personal trust in the grace of Jesus Christ. Wesley believed that God's prevenient grace was working in unbelievers, softening hearts and preparing them to accept the message. Personal conversion through justifying grace begins the believer's life in the kingdom. Sanctification is the pilgrimage to Christian perfection and real progress is possible.

John Wesley always respected ecclesial authority and structure, even as he transformed it. Education and maturation of thought were a vital part of his efforts. Wesley taught that every regenerated believer has a new disposition and thus, the potential for holy love and personal discipline. Wesley opposed slavery with all his being and the Methodist movement condemned the practice in the late 18th century, assisting Wilberforce and others in eliminating this social evil. Wesley worked tirelessly for justice in all domains, including education, sanitation ("cleanliness is next to godliness" meant clean water and housing. 21st century advocacy for justice must integrate personal responsibility with social policy, spiritual transformation with institutional change.[422]

Wesley's economic teaching declared property rights and protection for poor and needy. He believed in productive work, but not at the expense of health and family. Giving includes church and foreign missions…and alleviating poverty. He excoriated the over-emphasis on luxury goods at the expense of basics for the working class. At the same time he opposed high taxation and favoritism for some enterprises at the expense of others. In short, Wesley affirmed the dignity of the person, the rule of law and private property while affirming that a spiritual legacy is worth so much more than a bank account. While it is true that his message was at variance with the largest part of eighteenth-century Anglican preaching, it also is true that his preaching brought Revival to England. Wesley's doctrine sanctification demands unconditional love. Today's post-modern individualized community demands a relation explanation of the Wesleyan doctrine of sanctification. And this is because friendship demands a relationship, which consequently awakens the individualized post-modern mind and heart to the necessity of one. Friendship also requires love as a condition for acceptance, understanding, and development. Friendship is not to be taken for granted, just as Christian perfection-one need to maintain it.

---

[422] Charles Self, "Why John Wesley Matters for 21st Century Mission" http://www.missioalliance.org/why-john-wesley-matters-for-21st-century-mission/ (accessed on 17/01/17) .

As we know that John Wesley was a man of eighteenth century. There is no doubt that although Wesley was a man of his time and his religion was strongly associated with his culture, his theological response to class distinction and slavery has its serious implication to the bonded labor system in India.[423] In a context when Orthodox Hinduism does not believe that god created all alike or that all Hindus have equal rights and duties.[424] Wesley's theology of man being made in the image of God and therefore, God's love, free grace and atonement offered equally to all. Wesley belief of men/ women being as equal before God comes from all human beings created in His image, the redemptive processes are available to all without distinctions of anything. John Wesley challenged us to regard and respect all people rich or poor/ white or black all are created in the image of God to be treated equally. There was no distinction or inequality in God's purpose as far as creating human being was concerned.

John Wesley clearly recognized the necessity and urgency of justice, mercy and truth. He also emphasized that such principles have to be reflected in one's own life in order to please God. In holding to the principle of justice, every Indian should express his/her primary concern about who are also created by God with equal rights to live with freedom. John Wesley's understanding on holiness, sanctification and Christian Perfection played a crucial role in the eighteenth century as well as on the twenty first century it keeps an realistic impact. Frank Whaling had viewed that John Wesley was the greatest Christina of the Modern age of the Church.[425] It is clear from his endeavor that John Wesley worked hard to live a holy life and practiced what he believed. John Wesley had become instrumental to bring the spiritual and also the social awakening in the Eighteenth century. Thus, John Wesley poses a new dimension of sovereign merit of goodness, a new standard of honesty and a new way of accepting the duties of life cheerfully towards other people in the society.[426] C. E. Vulliamy had opined that, "He was a great light, rising in a vital time of darkness and confusion, and showing men that a vital religion was the one thing which could give them happiness, security and peace."[427] John Wesley was very strong in opposing the slavery system which implies that he stood for equality and justice. His efforts were to bring the equality and justice in the society and thus needs to practice and partake in these efforts of the people so that the kingdom of God could be established on earth.

---

[423] Joseph Basappa Suray, *Towards a Theology of Universality: John Wesley's Socio-Economic, Political and Moral Insights on British Class and Indian Caste Distinction*, 401.

[424] J. E. Sanjana, *Caste and Outcaste* (Bombay: Thacker & Co. Ltd., 1946), 248.

[425] Frank Whaling, ed., *John and Charles Wesley* (London: SPCK, 1981), xix.

[426] Frank Whaling (ed.) *John and Charles Wesley*, xix.

[427] C. E. Vulliamy, John Wesley (London: Geoffrey Bles, 1933), 359.

Bibliography

Abraham, K. "An Evaluation of the Church Planting Ministry of Evangelical Church of India in Selected Districts in North India." M.Th. Thesis, Senate of Serampore College, 1994.

Abraham,William J. "John Wesley's Conception and Use of Scripture," *Wesleyan Theological Journal,* 33/1 (Spring, 1998): 7-8.

Albert C. Outler & Richard P. Heitzenrater, eds., *John Wesley's Sermons: An Anthology.* Nashville: Abingdon Press, 1991.

Anderson, Justice C. "William Carey: A bi-centennial Tribute," *Southwestern Journal of Theology*, 35/1 (September–December, 1992): 40-44.

Armstrong, Chris R. "Indelible Marker: Methodist Francis Asbury left his fingerprints all over American Christianity", *Christianity Today,* 53/12 (December, 2009): 65.

Ashton, T. S. *The Industrial Revolution, 1760-183*0. New York: A Galaxy Book, 1964.

Baker, Frank, ed., *The Works of John Wesley, Letters,* vol. 26. Oxford: Clarendon Press, 1982.

Baker, Frank and Richard P. Heitzenrater, eds., *The Bicentennial Edition of the Works of John Wesley,* Volumes-7 Nashville: Abingdon Press, 1984.

Baker, Frank. *From Wesley to Asbury: Studies in Early American Methodism.* Durham, NC: Duke University Press, 1976.

Black, Jeremy. *The Politics of Britain.* United Kingdom: Manchester University Press, 1993.

Borner, John C. *The Sacrament of the Lord's Supper in Early Methodism.* Westminster: Dacre Press, 1951.

Bowmer, John C. *The Sacrament of the Lord's Supper in Early Methodism*. London: Dacre Press, 1951.

Brockwell, Charles W. Jr., "John Wesley's Doctrine of Justification," *Wesleyan Theological Journal,* 18/2 (September–December, 1983): 18-32.

Bundy, David. "Wesleyan/Holiness Mission" *Evangelical Dictionary of World Missions,* edited by Harold Netland and Charles Van Engen. Michigan: Baker Books, 2003.

Cairns, Earle E. *Christianity through the Centuries.* Michigan: Zondervan Publishing House, 1981.

Cannon, William R. "John Wesley's Doctrine of Sanctification and Perfection," *The Mennonite Quarterly Review,* 35/2 (April, 1961): 91-95.

Cannon,W. R. *The Theology of John Wesley: With Special Reference to the Doctrine of Justifi*cation. New York: Abingdon-Cokesbury, 1956.

Carter E. H. and R. A. F. Mears. *A History of Britain.* Oxford: Clarendon Press, 1957.

Crawford, Michael. *Seasons of Grace: Colonial New England's Revival Tradition in Its British Context.* New York and Oxford: Oxford University Press, 1991.

Crockett,William. *Eucharist: Symbol of Transformation.* New York: Pueblo Publishing, 1989.

Crump, David. "The Preaching of George Whitefeild and his use of the Mathew Henry's Commentary," *Crux,* 25/3 (September, 1989): 19-28.

Christensen, Michael J. "Theosis and Sanctification: John Wesley's Reformulation of a Patristic Doctrine," *Wesleyan Theological Journal,* 31/2 (March-May, 1996): 71-94.

Clements Heather A. & Cassandra S. Sequivel, "John Wesley, First Peoples of North America and Christian Perfection," *Wesleyan Theological Journal,* 46/2 (March-May, 2011): 150-167.

Clifford, Alan C. *Atonement and Justification, English Evangelical Theology, 1640-1790.* Oxford: Clarendon Press, 1990.

Coffing, Karen B. "Character & Personality: Phoebe Palmer and Aimee Semple McPherson as Mirrors of American Culture," *Fides et historia,* 28/1 (December-June, 1996): 48-67.

Collins, Kenneth J. & Jason E. Vickers, eds., *The Sermons of John Wesley: A Collection for Christian Journey,* The New Birth. Nashville: Abingdon Press, 2013.

Collins, Kenneth J. *The Scripture Way Salvation.* Nashville: Abingdon, 1997.

Cowman, Lettie B. *Missionary Warrior: Charles E. Cowman,* New Condensed Edition. Indiana: OMS International, Inc., 1989.

Cubie, David L. "Placing Aldersgate in John Wesley order of Salvation," *Wesleyan Theological Journal,* 24 (1989): 32-53.

Dallimore, Arnold. *George Whitefield: The Life and Times of the Great Evangelist of the Eighteenth-Century Revival,* Vol. 2.Westchester, Illinois: Cornerstone Books, 1979.

Dayton, D. W. *Theological Roots of Pentecostalism.* Metuchen, New Jersey: Scarecrow Press, 1987.

Dieter, Melvin E. *The Holiness Revival of the Nineteenth Century.* Metuchen, NJ: The Scarecrow Press. 1980.

Dorman, Ted M. "Forgiveness of Past Sins: John Wesley on Justification," *Pro Ecclesia,* 10/3 (June, 2001): 275-294.

Doughty, W. L. *John Wesley Preacher*. London: Epworth Press, 1955.

Drewery, Mary. *William Carey: A Biography.* Grand Rapids: Zondervan Publishing House, 1979.

Drewery, Mary. *William Carey, Shoemaker and Missionary.* London: Hodderand Stoughton, Books Ltd., 1966.

Dreyer, Frederick A.*The Genesis of Methodism.* Pennsylvania: Lehigh University Press, 1999.

Duewel, Wesley L. *Touch the World through Prayer.* Michigan: Francis Asbury Press, 1986.

Duren, William Larkin. *Francis Asbury, Founder of American Methodism and Unofficial Minister of State.* New York: The Macmillan Company, 1928.

Eavey, C. B. *History of Christian Education.* Chicago: Moody Press, 1966.

Eayrs, George. *John Wesley: Christian Philosopher and Church Founder.* London: The Epworth Press, 1926.

Erny, Edward and Esther. *No Guarantee But God: The Story of the Founders of OMS International.* Indiana: OMS International, 1986.

Fitchett, W. H. *Wesley and His Century*. Cincinnati: Jennings and Graham, 1966.

George, Timothy. *Faithful Witness: The Life and Mission of William Carey.* Birmingham, AL: New Hope, 1991.

George, Timothy. *Faithful Witness: The Life and Mission of William Care.* Birmingham, AL: New Hope, 1991.

Glover, Robert. *The Progress of World Wide Missions.* New York: Harper, 1960.

Graham, Billy. *A Bible Standard for Evangelists.* USA: Worldwide Publications, 1984.

Graham, Billy. *Amsterdam 2000.* Minneapolis: World Wide Publications, 2001.

Green, V. H. H. *John Wesley*. London: Thomas Nelson and Sons Ltd., 1964.

Green, V. H. H. *The Young Mr. Wesley*. London: Edward Arnold Ltd., 1961.

Hampton, David. *Methodism and Politics in British Society*. London: Hutchinson, 1985.

Harmon, Nolan B. ed., *Encyclopedia of World Methodism,* vol. 1. Nashville: The Methodist Publishing House, 1974.

Haykin, Michael A. G. ed., *The Revived Puritan: The Spirituality of George Whitefield.* Dundas, Ontario: Joshua Press, 2000.

Heitzenrater, Richard P. *Wesley & the People Called Methodists.* USA: Abingdon Press, 1995.

Herbert Asbury, *A Methodist Saint: The Life of Bishop Asbury.* New York: Alfred A. Knopf, Inc., 1927.

Higgins, P. L. *John Wesley, Spiritual Witness.* Minneapolis: T. Denison and Co., 1960.

High, Stanley. *Billy Graham.* USA: McGraw-Hill Book Company, 1956.

Hoskins, Steven T. "Eucharist and Eschatology in the Writings of the Wesleys," *Wesleyan Theological Journal,* 29/1-2 (August-January, 1994): 64-80.

Houghton, Elsie. *Christian Hymn-Writers.* Mid Glamorgan: Evangelical Press of Wales, 1982.

Hutton, Joseph E. *A History of Moravian Missions.* London: Moravian Publication Office, 1923.

Hynson, Leon O. *To Reform the Nation.* Michigan: Francis Asbury Press, 1984.

Irwin Reist, "John Wesley's view of the Sacraments: A Study in the Historical Development of a Doctrine," *Wesleyan Theological Journal,* 6/1 (1971): 41-54.

Jones, C. E. "Holiness Movement," in *The New International Dictionary of Pentecostal and Charismatic Movements: Revised and Expanded Version.* S. M. Burgess, ed., Grand Rapids, MI: Zondervan, 2002.

Jones, Scott J. *John Wesley's Conception and Use of Scripture.* Nashville: Abingdon Press, 1995.

Junker, Tercio Bretanha "Sacramental Spirituality: A Reflection on Wesleyan and Brazilian Methodist Eucharist Context," *Apuntes,* 33/4 (December, 2013): 124-148.

Kane, J. H. *A Global View of Christian Missions: From Pentecost to the Present.* Michigan: Baker Book House, 1971.

Keefer, Luke L. "John Wesley: Disciple of Early Christianity," *Wesleyan Theological Journal,* 19/1 (April-May, 1984): 23-32.

Kilgore, James E. *Billy Graham, The Preacher.* New York: Exposition Press, 1968.

Kisker, Scott Thomas. "Justified but Unregenerate? The Relationship of Assurance to Justification and Regeneration in the thought of John Wesley." *Wesleyan Theological Journal,* 28/1 (March-May, 1993): 45-58.

Latourette, Kenneth Scott. *A History of Christianity.* London: Eyre and Spottiswoode Ltd, 1955.

Lay, Robert F. "American Saint: Francis Asbury and the Methodists," *Wesleyan Theological Journal,* 45/2 (September-December, 2010): 295-298.

Leclerc, Diane "Wesleyan Holiness Feminist Hermeneutics: An Historical Rendering with Contemporary Considerations," *Wesleyan Theological Journal,* 36/2 (September-December, 2001): 105-132.

Lloyd, Alan. *The Wickedest Age: The Life and Times of George III.* United Kingdom: Brydone, 1971.

Loane, M. L. *Oxford and the Evangelical Succession.* London: Butterworth, 1950.

Logan, J. C. *Theology of Evangelism in Wesleyan Heritage.* USA: Abingdon Press, 1994.

Long, D. Stephen. *John Wesley's Moral Theology.* Nashville: Kingswood Books, 2005.

Ludwig, Charles. *Francis Asbury: God's Circuit Rider.* Milford, Michigan: Mott Media, 1984.

Maddox, Randy "The Rule of Christian Faith, Practice, and Hope: John Wesley on the Bible," *Methodist Review,* 3 (2011): 1–35.

Mahaffey, Jerome Dean "George Whitefield homiletic art: neo-sophism in the Great Awakening," *Homiletic,* 31/1 (April-May, 2006): 11-22.

Marsden, George. *Jonathan Edwards: A Life.* New Haven: Yale University Press, 2003.

McBeth, Leon. *Men Who Made Missions.* Nashville: Broadman Press, 1968.

Merritt, John G. "Dialogue within a Tradition: John Wesley and Gregory of Nyssa Discuss Christian Perfection," *Wesleyan Theological Journal,* 22/2 (March-May, 1987): 92-116.

Mickey, Paul A. *Essentials of Wesleyan Theology.* Michigan: Zondervan Publications, 1980.

Miller, Basil W. *William Carey.* Grand Rapids: Zondervan Publication, 1952.

Miskov, Jennifer A. "Missing Links: Phoebe Palmer, Carrie Judd Montgomery, and Holiness Roots within Pentecostalism," *PentecoStudies,* 10/1 (2011): 8-28.

Mithra, H. G. *Wesley's Philosophy of Education for Socio-Spiritual Change.* New Delhi: Christian World Imprints, 2016.

Neill, Stephen. *A History of Christian Missions.* New York: Penguin Books, 1980.

Newton, John A. *Susanna Wesley and Puritan Tradition in Methodism.* London: Epworth Press, 1969.

Nicholson, Roy S. "John Wesley and Ecumenicity," *Wesleyan Theological Journal,* 2/1 (April-May, 1967): 75-76.

Noll, M. A. History *of Christianity in the United States and Canada.* Grand Rapids, MI: William B. Eerdmans Publishing Company, 1992. Morrow, 1991.

Noll, Mark. *The Old Religion in a New World: The History of North American Christianity.* Grand Rapids: Eerdmans, 2002.

Oden, Thomas C. *John Wesley's Scriptural Christianity: A Plain Exposition of his Teaching on Christian Doctrine.* Michigan: Zondervan Publishing House, 1994.

Olson, Mark K. eds., *The John Wesley Reader on Christian Perfection: Developments in Doctrine and Theological System.* Fenwick, MI: Truth in Heart, 2008.

Outler, Albert C. "John Wesley: Folk-Theologian," *Theology Today,* 34/2 (July, 1977): 150-160.

Outler, Albert C. ed., *John Wesley*. New York: Oxford University, 1964.

Outler, Albert C. ed., *The Works of John Wesley: Sermons,* vol. 1. Nashville: Abingdon Press, 1984.

Parkhe, Camil. *Contribution of Christian Mission in India.* Gujrat: Gujarat Sahity Prakash, 2007.

Plumb, J. H. *England In the Eighteenth Century (1714-1815*). United Kingdom: Penguins, 1978.

Pollock, J. *George Whitefield and the Great Awakening.* New York: Doubleday, 1972.

Pollock, John. *Billy Graham.* Great Britain: St. Paul's House, 1966.

Rack, Henry. *Reasonable Enthusiast.* London: Epworth Press, 1989.

Randy L. Maddox and Paul W. Chilcote, *A Plain Account of Christian Perfection.* Kansas: Beacon Hill Press, 2015.

Raser, Harold E. *Phoebe Palmer: Her Life and Thought.* Lewiston, NY: Edwin Mellen, 1987.

Reuteler, James T. *The Essentials of Methodism*. Colorado: Bible Studies Aurora, 2013.

Reuteler, James T. *The Essentials of Methodism*. Colorado: Bible Studies Aurora, 2013.

Salter, Darius. *America's Bishop*. Nappanee, Ind.: Evangel, 2003.

Sanjana, J. E. *Caste and Outcaste*. Bombay: Thacker & Co. Ltd., 1946.

Sargunam, M. Ezra. *Multiplying Churches in Modern India.* Chennai: Federation of Evangelical Churches of India, 1974.

Sargunam, M. Ezra, ed., *Mission Mandate II.* Ayanavaram, Chennai: Mission Educational Books, 2006.

Schattschneider, David A. "William Carey, Modern Missions, and Moravian Influence", *International Bulletin of Missionary Research*, 22/1 (January, 1998): 8-12.

Scott, Thomas Kisker, "Justified but Unregenerate? The Relationship of Assurance to Justification and Regeneration in the thought of John Wesley." *Wesleyan Theological Journal,* 28/1. March-May, 1993.

Shepherd, Victor. "That We May Perfectly Love Thee: John Wesley and Sanctification," *Touchstone,* 6/2 (May, 1988): 27-37.

Shelley, Bruce L. *Church History in Plain Language*. Dallas: Word Publishing, 1995.

Sigsworth, John Wilkins. *World Changer: Karl Marx and John Wesley*. Canada: Easingwold Publications, 1982.

Simon, John S. *John Wesley and the Methodist Societies.* London: Epworth Press, 1952.

Smith, Harmon L. "Wesley's Doctrine of Justification: Beginning and Process," *Duke Divinity School Bulletin*, 28/2 (May, 1963): 88-98.

Smith, Timothy L. "George Whitefield and Wesleyan Perfectionism," *Wesleyan Theological Journal*, 19/1 (March-April, 1984): 63-85.

Smith, A. Christopher. "The legacy of William Carey," *International Bulletin of Missionary Research,* 16/1 (January, 1992): 2-8.

Smith, A. Christopher. "A Tale of Many Models: The Missiological Significance of the Serampore Trio." *Missiology,* 20/4 (1992): 494.

Snyder, Howard A. *The Radical Wesley*. USA: InterVarsity Press, 1980.

Steele, Daniel. *A Defense of Christian Perfection*. New York: Hunt & Easton, 1896.

Steele, Daneil. *Love Enthroned: Essays on Evangelical Perfection*. New York: Eaton and Mains, 1908.

Stevens, Abel. *Life and Times of Nathan Bangs.* New York: Carlton and Porter, 1883.

Stout, Harry S. *The Divine Dramatist: George Whitfield and the Rise of Modern Evangelicalism.* Grand Rapids: Eerdmans, 1991.

Suray, Joseph Basappa. *Towards a Theology of Universality: John Wesley's Socio-Economic, Political & Moral Insights on British Class & Indian Caste Distinctions*. New Delhi: Christian World Imprints, 2015.

Telford, John. *The Life of John Wesley*. London: Charles H. Kelly, 1900.

Thomas, Sunil. "Wesleyan Tradition on Holiness and its Significance," *Bethany Journal of Theology,* 6/2 (September, 2014): 67-71.

Thompson, Bard. *Liturgies of the Western Church.* Philadelphia: Fortress Press, 1980.

Thorsen, Donald A. D. *The Wesleyan Quadrilateral: Scripture, Tradition, Reason & Experience as a Model of Evangelical Theology.* Nappanee, Indiana: Francis Asbury Press, 1997.

Towns, Elmer E. ed., *A History of Religious Educator*. Grand Rapids: Baker Book House, 1975.

Tracy, Wesley. "Christian Education in the Wesleyan Mode" in *Wesleyan Theological Journal,* 17/1 (March, 1982): 31-37.

Turner, William "New Strivings in Methodism" *Christianity Today,* 3/3 (November, 1958): 15-18.

Tuttle, Robert G. *John Wesley His Life and Theology*. Michigan: Francis Asbury Press, 1978.

Tuttle, R. G. Jr., "Wesleyan Tradition" *Evangelical Dictionary of Theology,* edited by Walter A. Elwell. Michigan: Baker Academic, 2003.

Vermillion, Bill. Living Water periodical on the title of "People Who Lived for Holiness: The Life and Ministry of Ernest Albert Kilbourne", KEHC. (Seoul: Seoul Theological University.

Vick, Edward W. H. *John Wesley's Teaching Concerning Perfection.* Michigan: Berrian Spring, 1994.

Vries, George De Jr. "Phoebe Palmer and spiritual independence," *Reformed Journal,* 37/8 (August, 1987): 3-5.

Vulliamy, C. E. John Wesley. London: Geoffrey Bles, 1933.

Wallace, Charles Jr., ed., *Susanna Wesley: The Complete Writings.* New York: Oxford University Press, 1997.

Wallace, Charles Jr., "Some Stated Employment of Your Mind: Reading, Writing and Religion in the Life of Susanna Wesley," *Church History,* 58/3 (September, 1989): 355-359.

Wallace, Charles Jr., "Susanna Wesley's Spirituality: The Freedom of a Christian Woman," *Methodist History,* 22/3 (1984): 158-163.

Walson, Philip S. *The Message of Wesley*. London: The Epworth Press, 1964.

Watson, David Lowes "The Much Controverted Point of Justification by faith and the Shaping of Wesleyan's Evangelistic Message," *Wesleyan Theological Journal,* 21/1 (May-December, 1986): 10.

Wellman, Sam. *Billy Graham*. Secunderabad: OM Books, 2003.

Wesley, John. *Journal of John Wesley*. Chicago: Moody Press, 1951.

Wesley, John. *Explanatory Notes Upon the New Testament.* London: The Epworth Press, rep. 1954.

Wesley, John. "A Treatise on Baptism," *The Works of John Wesley*. Grand Rapids: Zondervan Publishing House, n.d.

Whaling, Frank, ed., *John and Charles Wesley*. London: SPCK, 1981.

Whedon, D. A. *Entire Sanctification of John Wesley's View*. London: Newby Books Noble Ind., 2015.

Whidden, Woodrow W. "Eschatology, Soteriology and Social Activism in Four Mid-Nineteenth Century Holiness Methodists," Wesleyan Theological Journal, 29/1-2 (March-December, 1994): 92-110.

White, Charles Edward. "The Beauty of Holiness: The Career of Phoebe Palmer," *Fides et historia,* 19/1 (February, 1987): 22-34.

White, Charles Edward. "Phoebe Palmer and the Development of Pentecostal Pneumatology" *Wesleyan Theological Journal,* 23/1-2 (January-December, 1988): 198-212.

White, Charles Edward. *The Beauty of Holiness: Phoebe Palmer as Theologian, Revivalist, Feminist, and Humanitarian*. Grand Rapids: Zondervan, 1986.

White, Charles Edward. "What the Holy Spirit Can and Cannot Do: The Ambiguities of Phoebe Palmer's Theology of Experience" *Wesleyan Theological Journal,* Volume 20/1 (March-June, 1985): 5-12.

Woloch, Isser. *Eighteenth Century Europe: Tradition and Progress, 1715-1789.* New York: WW Norton and Company, 1982.

Wood, A. Servington. *Count Von Zinzendorf, Introduction to the History of Christianity*, Tim Dowley, ed., Minneapolis: Fortress Press, 2002.

Wood, A. Skevington. *The Burning Heart.* USA: Bethany Publishing House, 1978.

Wood, Darren Cushman. "John Wesley Use of Atonement," *Asbury Journal,* 62/2 (2007): 57-58.

Wood, Robert D. *In these Mortal Hands: The Story of the Oriental Missionary Society: The First 50 Years.* Greenwood: OMS International, INC, 1983.

Wynkoop, Mildred Bangs. *A Theology of Love: The Dynamism of Wesleyanism.* Missouri: Kansas Hill Press, 1972.

Electronic Sources

Tim Lambert, "Daily Life in 18th Century Britain," http://www.localhistories.org/18thcent.html (accessed on 05/07/16).

Jonathan Edwards: America's greatest theologian, http://www.christianitytoday.com/history/people/theologians/jonathan-edwards.html (accessed on 12/11/16).

Brian Stableford, "Guide to Literary Masters & Their Works, of John Wesley," http://web.a.ebscohost.com/lrc/detail/detail?vid=4&sid=3d280652-becd-4260-a4dd-6db9bfbcd50e%40sessionmgr4003&hid=4204&bdata=JnNpdGU9bHJjLXBsdXM%3d#AN=103331LM78379790307789&db=lkh (accessed on 19/07/16).

Maldwyn L. Edwards, "John Wesley," httpwww.enterhisrest.orghistorybio_john_wesley.pdf (accessed on 01/08/16).

Fox's Book of Martyrs, An Account of the Life of John Wesley, http://www.umcmission.org/Find-Resources/John-Wesley-Sermons/The-Wesleys-and-Their-Times/Account-of-the-Life-of-John-Wesley#sthash.aVwDAMGg.dpuf, (accessed on 11/07/16).

G. Dan Harris, *The Early Influences of John Wesley, Concerning His Views of the Ministry to Children, The Moravians*, http://works.bepress.com/gdanharris/4/ (accessed on 21/07/16).

Inspiring Women - Susanna Wesley, http://lizparnell.com/articles/64-womanhood-and-motherhood/247-inspiring-women-susanna-wesley (accessed on 22/07/16).

http://www.raisinggodlychildren.org/2011/03/16-house-rules-by-susannah-wesley-john-wesleys-mom.html#sthash.tRjXByNj.dpuf (accessed on 22/07/16).

Maldwyn L. Edwards, John Wesley, httpwww.enterhisrest.orghistorybio_john_wesley.pdf (accessed on 01/08/16).

Ray Nothstine, "The Theology of John Wesley," http://www.acton.org/pub/religion-liberty/volume-18-number-2/theology-john-wesley (accessed on 05/09/16).

John Wesley, "On the Resurrection of The Dead," http://wesley.nnu.edu/john-wesley/the-sermons-of-john-wesley-1872-edition/sermon-137-on-the-resurrection-of-the-dead/ (accessed on 08/10/16).

William P. Farley, Francis Asbury: Spartan Apostle of Early America http://enrichmentjournal.ag.org/200603/200603_116_francis_asbury.cfm (accessed on 17/11/16).

Francis Asbury: Methodist on horseback www.christianity today.com/history/people/denomination alfounders/francis-asbury.html (accessed on 12/07/16).

Wesley.nnn.edu/other-theologian/francis-asbury (accessed on 12/07/16).

Francis Asbury Facts, http://biography.yourdictionary.com/francis-asbury (accessed on 16/11/16).

Matt Lockett, "7 Ways Circuit Rider Francis Asbury Showed Us How to Contend Against Injustice." http://bound4life.com/blog/2015/04/06/7-ways-circuit-rider-francis-asbury-modeled-how-to-contend-against-injustice/ (accessed on 16/11/16).

"Francis Asbury: Father of American Methodism," http://www.tlogical.net/bioasbury.htm (accessed on 17/11/16).

http://www.legacy.com/obituaries/indystar/obituary.aspx?pid=178004970 (accessed on 11/11/16).

William Franklin "Billy" Graham, Jr., https://en.wikipedia.org/wiki/Billy_Graham (accessed on 15/11/16).

Billy Graham Biography, http://www.biography.com/people/billy-graham-9317669#synopsis (accessed on 20/11/16).

http://www.ecionline.org/index.php?option=com_content&view=article&id=71&Itemid=517 (accessed on 17/12/16).

Charles Self, "Why John Wesley Matters for 21st Century Mission" http://www.missioalliance.org/why-john-wesley-matters-for-21st-century-mission/ (accessed on 17/01/17).

Nathan Bangs, https://en.wikipedia.org/wiki/Nathan_Bangs (accessed on 20/11/16).